The Complete Book of
Machine Quilting

ROBBIE & TONY FANNING

The Complete Book of
Machine
Quilting

CHILTON BOOK COMPANY
RADNOR, PENNSYLVANIA

To Us

Library of Congress Catalog Card No. 78-0731
ISBN 0-8019-6802-X *hardcover*
ISBN 0-8019-6803-8 *paperback*

All photos by the authors unless otherwise noted.
All drawings by Tony Fanning.
Cover photo by the Fannings.

2 3 4 5 6 7 8 9 0   9 8 7 6 5 4 3 2 1 0

Contents

Acknowledgments

Thank you—

*artists, for your freely offered advice, especially Ernest B. Haight, Caryl Rae Hancock, and Barbara Johannah;
*again, Elyse Sommer, Lydia M. Driscoll and Kathy Conover;
*Janie Warnick, Margaret Vaile, Alberta Humphreys, and Margo Wing for many years of friendship and sharing;
*Don and Rich Douglas of Douglas Fabrics (Palo Alto, CA) for your unending wealth of knowledge about machines and sewing;
*Open Chain subscribers, for all the tips over the years;
*students, for your ingenuity;
*Mother, for showing me what craftsmanship in sewing is;
*Kali Koala, for everything.

*And thanks to Jackie Dodson, Yvonne Morris, Roberta Horton, Jerry Zarbaugh, Betty Robinson, Judi Cull, Patience Corners, Bob Young of Fairfield Processing, Barbara Leonhardt of Stearns and Foster Company, the sewing machine company consumer advisors, Susan Druding of Straw Into Gold, Sylvia Moore of the American Museum of Quilts, Michael James, Wilna Lane, Marjorie Dillingham, Globe Quilting Company, and Tim Talbot of the Peninsula Library System Film Center.

—rlf

*And to Steve Sokolow.

—adjf

Preface

Quilts! The very word evokes a different pleasant sensation for each person—warmth, color, softness, texture, beginnings, safety.

Quilting! More and more people of all cultures and countries want to participate in this all-American folk art.

But as the interest in quilting in America continues to grow, the time we have for quilting continues to shrink. Many of us would rather have a quilt on our beds today than wait a year or more to finish a handmade quilt. Does this mean that you have to buy one or do without? Not at all. If you own a sewing machine, you have exactly the time-saving tool you need.

By choosing the correct materials and machine technique, you can complete a machine-made quilt in one day. A more complicated larger quilt can be done in a weekend and a very complex full-sized quilt can be done in less than two weeks.

Machine quilting fulfills both the desire to make a quilt and the need to finish it soon. Machine quilting is fast and enjoyable and satisfying. Machine-made quilts are practical, strong enough to withstand modern washing machines and dryers, and every bit as appealing to the eyes and body as hand-quilted ones. Fiber artists, always a little in advance of the rest of us, have machine quilted for years. So have the folk artists who depend on quilts for warmth for their loved ones.

However, useful instruction on machine quilting is scarce. The information in this book was collected as a response to frustration. So many times, instructions say "do this, do that, then machine quilt." But it's not quite that simple. Why does my thread break? How do I avoid skipped stitches? And what about puckers? How do I handle large amounts of fabric? Can I machine quilt on my old klunker of a machine?

This book answers those questions, integrates previously scattered information on machine quilting, and warns you about mistakes before you make them. It also shows the wide variety of machine-quilting techniques, tells how to quilt on any machine, and offers more than two dozen designs for quilts and decorative objects. Since the machine quilter can handle materials the hand quilter cannot, we tell how to deal with all kinds of modern-day fabrics—polyester blends, knits, down, silk, and more.

And finally, we hope to inspire you to develop your own designs specifically for machine-made quilts, with a full understanding of the demands, problems, and joys of that discipline. To further inspire you, the work of 19 artists who work primarily with the machine is shown throughout the book, serving as a gallery of the best in machine quilting. At the end of the book is information on developing your own designs if that is your preference.

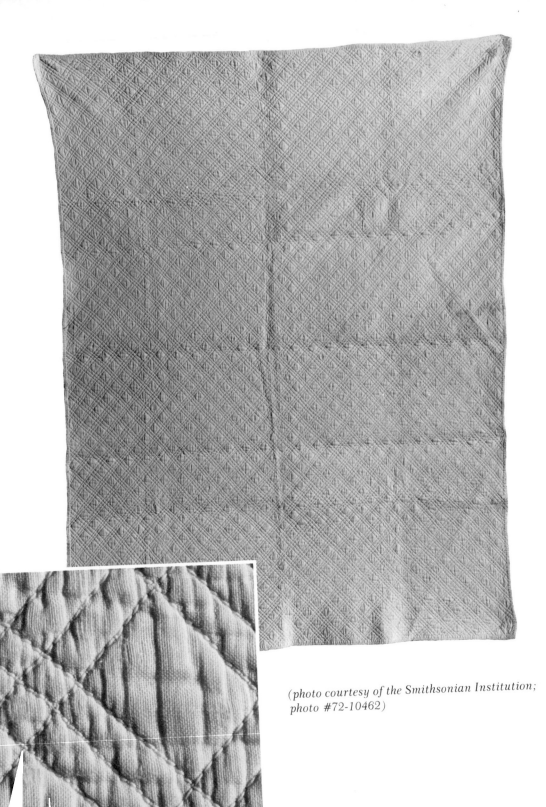

(photo courtesy of the Smithsonian Institution;
photo #72-10462)

We hope that you put this information to use in making your own quilts. We hope that these fast, easy-to-use techniques give you the ability to sleep—soon—under a quilt which you have made for yourself. That is the point of it all: to make for yourself a soft, light, warm, sensuous, useful, and enjoyable quilt.

For Working People Only. If you want something on your bed tonight, without reading through a whole book, make yourself a duvet (directions in Chapter 8). Your quilting lines will be hidden, so it doesn't matter what you do or do not know about the fine points of machine quilting.

If you used to sew, have not had time for it for years, miss working on your machine, but do not have time to read a lot of text or even make any decisions, make the Working Woman's One-Night Wonder (directions in Chapter 8). It tells you exactly what to buy and what to do and at the end of one session of sewing, you will have a lap quilt. You will have regained the lost satisfaction of completely finishing one thing. Later you can settle down each night after work under your quilt and read the rest of this book.

To All Readers. A note about this working partnership: we both shared all the work of writing the book, from conception to overall form to photography, writing, and fussing over deadlines. As artist, Tony did most of the drawings and the bulk of the designing. He was the first to question exactly how a stitch is formed on the machine (I'd never bothered to understand) and the first to notice that the feed-dogs on the machine go up and down, not back and forth. He loves the color, texture, and general sensuousness of quilts—but he doesn't machine quilt.

I, Robbie, love machine quilting, to the point of dreaming about it. I did all the machine work you see. I also did the first draft of writing and it seemed silly, in explaining how to do a technique, to say "we did this and then we did that." Therefore, the "I's" in the book are the female in the partnership.

Never have I felt more humble than in gathering the information for this book; almost every idea in it came from talking to students and other quilters. Some of these led me to yet other sources—old books, personal libraries and collections, and even experienced hand quilters.

But this funnel of knowledge makes machine quilting special. It is part of the "caring and sharing" that all needleworkers cherish. Therefore, whenever possible, I attribute where I first heard or saw a technique, either from the (alleged) originator or from the friend who first told me.

And there truly is nothing new under the sun. Every needleworker eventually begins to develop new (to them) techniques and wants to share them. I'm no different. But I soon found that what I thought were great flashes of genius and personal discovery have been done somewhere before by someone.

Another note: in this book, we concentrate on quilting with the sewing machine. There are many other decorative machine techniques besides the ones mentioned here, but lack of space kept us from including them all. For those who want to pursue these, consult our earlier book, *Decorative Machine Stitchery.*

And now a confession: I'm new to machine quilting. I've only been at it for ten years. Ernest B. Haight, whose work is shown later, has been machine quilting for 40 years. He makes and gives away 10 to 12 machine-quilted quilts a year.

But Joseph Granger of Worchester, Mass., takes the machine-quilting prize. The year after his wife had won a quilt contest with a handmade quilt which he felt had taken too long to make, he sat down at the treadle and machine quilted this 46″ × 38″ cotton crib quilt in 1879.

The Complete Book of
Machine Quilting

Introduction

Why I Machine Quilt

I love quilts. They are soft, comfortable, and warm; and they carry suggestions of home, family, protection, and practicality. I would also rather make something like that for my family than buy it.

I'd like to tell you why I machine quilt. It has more to do with the value I put on things than with anything as abstract as aesthetics, creativity, or even practicality.

Let me put it in perspective, starting with the drastic. If there were a fire in my house, I would save my husband and child before I saved a quilt. I would save the cats before a quilt. I would, if I had time, also save my typewriter, sewing machine, and camera before a quilt. Finally, I'd save the quilts.

In less drastic perspective, if my nine-year-old daughter wanders into the bedroom with a peanut-butter-and-honey sandwich, snuggles up to me on top of the quilt, and says, "Mom, it seems to me like every time I tell the truth, someone laughs at me," I'll seize the moment and talk to her, rather than scream about getting honey on the quilt.

So, you can see that there's no room for irreplaceable heirlooms on our beds. And if I am going to make a quilt, I'm reluctant to spend years making one.

Why would it take me years to make a quilt? Because I work full-time, like the majority of women today. My time for doing anything is limited to a few hours a day. If I'm both lucky and persistent, I actually get to use some of those few hours for quilting.

At the time of writing I am making a hand-worked quilt. I have been working on it sporadically for more than three years. I do love handwork and I designed it in quilt-as-you-go modules, so I can take it with me when visiting friends or traveling (something admittedly not easy with machine quilting).

But in the meantime, was our bed bare for three years?

No! In the same three years I've made several quilts by machine. With a machine-quilted quilt, I can have something durable, machine-washable, friendly, fast (as little as six hours to piece and quilt, depending on the size), and not at all so precious that I don't feel free enough to crush or desert it.

Add that to my love of the sewing machine as *the* tool to mold thread and fabric into something warm and touchable—and that's why I machine quilt.

What Is Machine Quilting?

There are so many forms of machine quilting that it is almost meaningless to say "I machine quilt." It's like saying "I'm involved in aerobic sports" and expecting the other person to understand which sport: running? soccer? bicycling? swimming? The phrase "aerobic sports" does not give us enough information. Neither does "machine quilting."

To some people it means a bed cover with all-over squiggly thread lines done by an industrial programmed machine and resembling a mattress pad. To others, machine quilting means a diamond-shaped grid over a whole quilt top, done with the presser foot and a straight stitch. Some people mean free-machine quilting when they say "I machine quilt;" others really mean "I machine piece patchwork for hand quilting." Machine quilting is all of these and more.

Other kinds of things which people think of as quiltable are outer clothing, vests, tea and coffee cosies, potholders, chair seats, bags, wall pictures, banners, pillows, stuffed toys—anything that needs either additional warmth or additional emphasis.

But before trying to explain all the possibilities of machine quilting, let's ask ourselves a more basic question.

What Is a Quilt?

Technically, a quilt is merely a sandwich of three distinct layers: a *top*, some *filler* (usually called "batting" regardless of the material used), and a *backing* (sometimes called a "lining"). The top is secured to the backing through the filler with thread to keep the three layers from shifting around.

Nowhere is it written that the connecting thread has to be worked by hand. And yet there are those who want to make a big issue of this.

There is a dying but not quite dead attitude toward machine quilting: in the subtle pecking order of the quilt world, machine quilting still suffers wicked jabs. It is not uncommon to hear people who should know better say such things as: "This is the best piece of machine quilting I've ever seen. It was sort of sewn down the seam so it still puffed out like a real quilt but you could only see the stitches on the back."

Why does this antediluvean attitude continue? Ignorance of the variety of machine quilting techniques, the misunderstanding of the nature of a quilt (it's also a "real quilt" if it's done by machine), and the assumption that machine quilting means generally low standards of workmanship explain some of it. Those who express this attitude aren't yet aware that among experienced quilters it's already a dead issue.

Good workmanship—the perfect blending of materials, design, and technique—is a result of personal standards of excellence and of experience. There are machine-made quilts in which bad workmanship is embarrassingly obvious: colors of the top design are cheap and garish, the quilting lines are sloppy and relate neither to the top design nor to the capabilities of the machine, or there are puckers on the back and the quilt hangs unevenly. But this is the fault of the quilter, not of the machine. I've also seen hand-quilted quilts with all the same characteristics (but I don't blame hand quilting).

How do you develop good workmanship? The key is experience. If you are new to machine quilting, start with easy small projects. For your first large project, practice on a simple design, such as quilting a crib sheet, or the one-night duvet in Chapter 8, where the quilting doesn't show. It won't be long before you are satisfied with the quality of your workmanship.

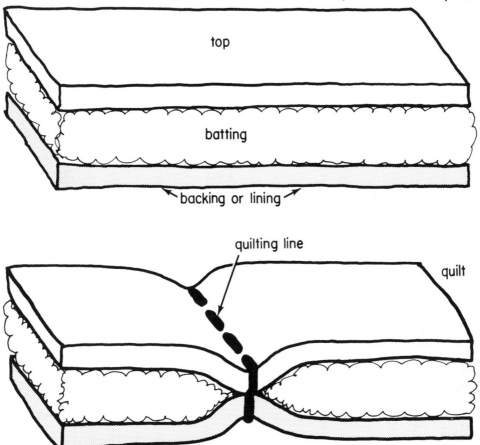

quilt sandwich (squilt)

top

batting

backing or lining

quilting line

quilt

In my years of teaching quilting, I found that saying "quilt sandwich" trips my tongue. I now call it a "squilt." Three layers in the process of being quilted make a *squilt;* once the quilting is completed, you have a *quilt.*

How To Use This Book

To get the most from this book, use it up. If it's yours, underline what strikes you. Write notes in the margins as ideas hit. Make small samples (doodle cloths) of new-to-you techniques and pin to the appropriate page. Pencil in the machine settings, threads, and fabrics you used for a project. Put ribbons, clips, or tabs on the charts you use most often. Staple an envelope (the bigger, the better) to the back page of this book, into which you put magazine clippings, sketches on scraps of paper, addresses, resources, and other odd-sized pieces of paper about quilting that tend to lose themselves otherwise. The Bibliography list contains some of the best references we've found; use it when a technique strikes your fancy and you want to know more about it. The Resource list is there for your use, too, when you can't get supplies locally. Write letters to the artists whose work moves you (addresses are at the end of the book—but please include a pre-addressed stamped envelope if you want a reply).

In short, enjoy this book—and use it up!

Chapter 1

Basic Information for Your Machine

Machine Adjustments

Must you own a fancy zigzag sewing machine to machine quilt? No, but it certainly is more fun to work on a good machine. (If you need help buying a machine, see Chapter 11.)

More important than owning the latest marvel of sewing technology is keeping your own trusty machine in good condition. If you keep your machine in smooth working order—periodically cleaning out the lint from the bobbin case, oiling it before every major project (if your machine takes oil), using new needles, avoiding sewing over pins, and singing to it regularly—you can machine quilt.

The beauty of the modern sewing machine is that it can be adjusted to suit your sewing conditions. The standard settings for your machine are for seaming together two layers of medium-weight fabric. In machine quilting, you are asking your machine to perform in an out-of-the-ordinary way. All you have to do is set your machine appropriately for these out-of-the-ordinary conditions. It's not difficult, but you must understand your sewing machine to machine quilt well.

Don't skip this information! You need to know how a stitch is formed on the machine.

1. Above the eye of the needle is a groove called a "scarf." Some needles have deeper and larger scarfs than others; use the needle sizes recommended on p.11 and always use the needles specified for your machine. When the needle pushes through the quilt, the scarf eases the friction, allowing the thread to go down through in the right way.

2. After the needle passes through the fabric and begins to draw back up, a tiny loop is formed. If all adjustments are right for the materials you're working on, the loop stays below the bottom layer of fabric.

3. The bobbin shuttle hook grabs that loop and wraps it around the bobbin case and the bobbin thread. It's something like a jump rope. At first, the loop of top thread is on one side of the bobbin thread, then it's on the other. When the needle returns to the top surface, a stitch is locked on either side of the fabrics.

Common Problems

If you understand that there is a set way in which your sewing machine works, and works properly, you will be able to understand why it may sometimes fail. And you will understand that there are simple remedies for the most common problems you'll encounter as you start to machine quilt. We'll look at each one now.

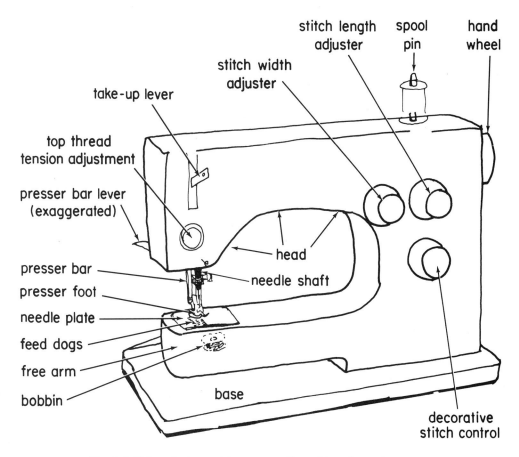

stitch length adjuster

spool pin

hand wheel

stitch width adjuster

take-up lever

top thread tension adjustment

presser bar lever (exaggerated)

presser bar

presser foot

needle plate

feed dogs

free arm

bobbin

head

needle shaft

base

decorative stitch control

Fig. 1-1 Although the positions vary, all machines have these parts.

Skipped Stitches

You can see that if the fabric *lifts* as the needle passes back up through, the top thread loop also lifts up, the bobbin shuttle hook misses the loop, and a stitch is skipped. *You must keep the fabric absolutely flat against the needle plate as the needle passes through the fabric.* This may be done in a variety of ways, depending on the technique you've chosen. Use: (1) a presser foot; (2) your fingers to press down on either side of the needle; (3) a darning foot or darning spring; (4) an embroidery hoop to keep the fabric taut.

You must also choose the correct type of needle. A sharp needle pierces the fabric fibers to make the hole for the thread. It is used on woven and most pressed (e.g., felt) fabrics.

A ballpoint needle goes between the fabric fibers. It is used on knits. If you use a sharp needle on knits, the fibers may cling to the needle as it lifts, the bobbin shuttle hook will miss the loop, and a stitch may be skipped. (Some machines are more temperamental about this than others.)

A wedge-pointed needle can pierce extremely dense fabrics like leather and imitation suede so that the material does not close up around the hole and bind the thread, thus causing skipped stitches.

Each of the first two types of needles comes in the various sizes. The wedge-pointed needles are usually 16-18(100-110).

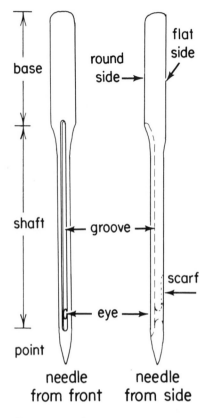

Fig. 1-2 Machine needle: front and
side views.

Incidentally, if fabric is not preshrunk before sewing, the resin finish on it may deflect the needle on some machines enough that a stitch will be skipped. Always preshrink your fabric.

Puckers

It is very important to use the correct size and type of needle and the correct thread for machine quilting—it will define your workmanship. Choose your fabrics first; then the thread; then the needle. A very general rule, broken often, is to use a thread that is as closely matched in size as possible to one thread of the fabric. To illustrate by exaggeration, examine Fig. 1-8 and 1-9.

See Chapter 2 for a further discussion of threads for machine quilting.

Because we can buy foreign threads in the United States and because different numbering systems are used around the world, it would be meaningless to give thread numbers here. Instead, divide your threads into extra-fine, ordinary, and heavy-duty (see Resources section for mail-order sources of threads).

Extra-fine are 100% cotton, rayon, and polyester machine-embroidery threads, and size A silk thread.

Ordinary are those you use for normal sewing: cotton-covered polyester, regular 100% cotton, and polyester.

Heavy-duty are buttonhole twist, invisible nylon, size D silk twist, carpet and buttonhole thread, crochet and pearl cotton.

Note: A second meaning of the word "pucker" is tucks of fabric, usually seen on the back of a quilt at cross-seams or at the edge. These are caused by improper basting of the backing fabric and by fabric creep. Continue reading this chapter for how to prevent these puckers.

Fraying

The function of the needle is to poke a hole in the fabric big enough for the thread to pass through the fabric easily. If the needle is too small for the three layers of the quilt, the hole will be too small, and the edges of the fabric around the hole will saw at the thread until it breaks. This is called fraying, and it can make your machine quilting distinctly less enjoyable. Every time the thread breaks, you have to stop and rethread the needle, pull up the bobbin thread, and reposition your quilt sandwich. *The remedy is to put in the next larger size of needle, and not necessarily to change threads.*

In choosing a needle size, don't forget that if you are quilting a pieced top, you are periodically sewing through as many as eleven layers of material (if seams are pressed to one side, this can mean three layers of top + batting + backing + 6 layers of binding). Prepare for this total thickness instead of merely the thickness

Fig. 1-3 The top thread meets the bobbin.

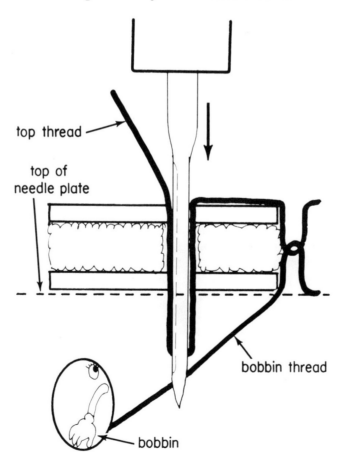

top thread

top of
needle plate

bobbin thread

bobbin

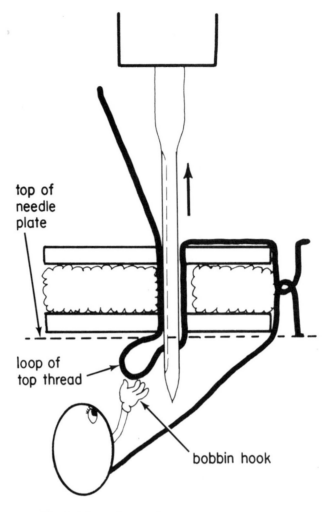

top of
needle
plate

loop of
top thread

bobbin hook

Fig. 1-4 A tiny loop is formed by the top thread.

of the top fabric. Use a larger size needle. Otherwise you may be sewing merrily along when suddenly the light cotton fabric you see on top begins to behave like heavy denim and your machine objects to the load by breaking your thread or even your needle.

Creeping

Choose fabric first, then the thread, then the needle size and type—this is the first rule for avoiding machine quilting problems. We can also avoid further problems by choosing an appropriate presser foot.

The choice of presser foot depends on the machine quilting technique selected. This will be covered more thoroughly in the following chapters.

The function of a presser foot is to help feed all three layers uniformly and to prevent skipped stitches. However, on three layers, the presser foot tends to move one layer farther than the other, and the overall effect of this is that one layer seems to creep past another. This causes misalignment of the quilt layers and/or tucks (puckers) on the backing, unless you (pick one):

1. Pin or thread-baste properly (see Chapter 2).

2. Use a walking foot.

3. Use a straight-stitch needle plate.

4. Decenter the needle to the left (and optionally, use a left-sided presser foot).

5. Choose a quilting design appropriate to the machine-quilting technique chosen, such as matching the diagonal diamond-grid (see Chapter 4) to the technique of quilting a whole top with the presser foot on.

6. Gain lots of experience and learn how to use your fingers as tools.

Fig. 1-5 The bobbin grabs the loop and locks the stitch below the fabric.

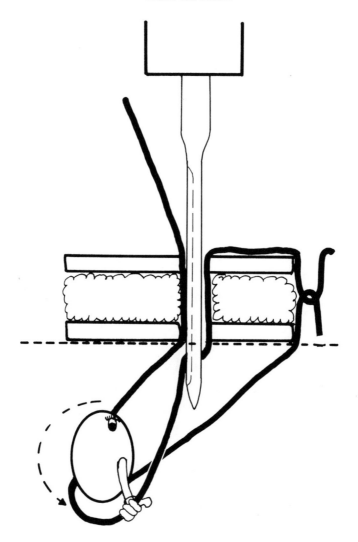

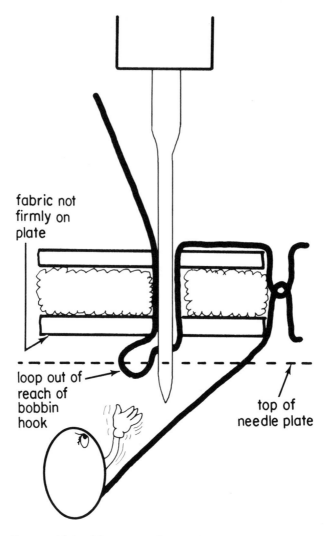

fabric not
firmly on
plate

loop out of
reach of
bobbin
hook

top of
needle plate

Fig. 1-6 If the fabric is not flat against the needle plate,
the loop lifts out of reach of the bobbin and a stitch is
skipped.

Machine Tension

For most quilting with the presser foot on, the bobbin thread and top thread
are balanced in tension. As a result, when a stitch is formed, both threads are
interlocked in the quilt. This tension setting is called universal tension.

If you are not sure whether your machine tension settings are correct, put one
color of thread in the bobbin and use a different color of the same weight as a top
thread. Stitch a line of machine quilting on a small practice quilt (called a doodle
cloth). Now examine both sides of the doodle cloth. Do tiny loops of the top thread
show on the back? Then top tension is too loose and/or bobbin tension is too tight.

To correct this, turn the top tension dial to the right, remembering Lucille
Graham's phrase, "Right is tight."

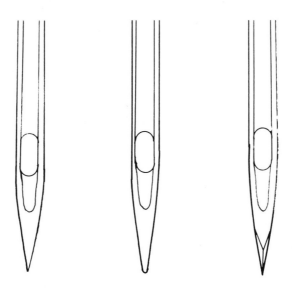

Fig. 1-7 Left to right, sharp needle, ballpoint
needle, wedge-pointed needle.

Table 1-1. FABRIC/THREAD/NEEDLE CHART FOR PIECING*

Fabrics	Threads	Needles (European sizes in parentheses)
Very sheer (lace, net, chiffon, voile, pantyhose)	Extra-fine	8/9(60)
Lightweight/transparent (organza, tricot, taffeta, Qiana, organdy)	Extra-fine cotton, rayon, polyester	10/11(70)
Lightweight cottons (gingham, calico, etc.), double-knits, silk	Ordinary cotton, Size A silk twist	12(80)
Medium-weight cottons (poplin, kettlecloth), wool, jersey, flannel, prequilted fabrics, velour, felt, fake fur, ski-weight nylon	Ordinary cotton, cotton-covered polyester, Size D silk twist, nylon (invisible thread)	14(90)
Heavy woven (denim, corduroy, sailcloth, duck)	Heavy-duty	16(100)
Leather, imitation suede, vinyl, heavy upholstery fabrics	Heavy-duty	18(110)

Adjustment for Machine Quilting
The chart shows what needle to use for piecing. Use the next larger needle for machine quilting. The higher the number, the larger the needle. The most common size used for machine quilting is 14(90).

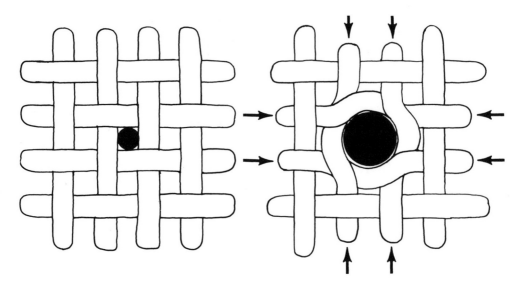

Fig. 1-8 Left: A thread the same size or smaller than the threads of your fabric slips easily through the fabric. Right: A thread too big for your material pushes the fibers apart and puckers your fabric. This shows up often in piecing quilts of lightweight cotton with too-heavy thread.

On the other hand, if loops of bobbin thread show on the top layer of the quilt, then top tension is too great. In this case, loosening top thread tension or increasing bobbin thread tension will bring the threads back into the balance of universal tension.

While you are testing tensions on your doodle cloth, it is important that you experiment. Examine the results of purposely adjusting top and bobbin thread tensions out of balance. The effect can be decorative, especially if you use contrasting colors of top and bobbin thread.

The above discussion of tension holds for top and bobbin threads of the same weight. A slightly different situation holds when the threads are of different weights.

The heavier thread will always pull slightly to its side. Sometimes in machine quilting we use extra-fine machine-embroidery thread on top and regular sewing thread on the bobbin; in this case, having tiny loops show on the back is unavoidable. Therefore for these conditions, be sure to choose a backing fabric of a color compatible to the top thread (the ageless trick to hide these loops is to use a small print on the backing).

Recommendations for Each Brand of Machine

The best information about your machine is in its instruction booklet. It will tell you how to keep your machine in good working order, how to manipulate tension settings, even how to do the simplest machine quilting.

If you've lost your sewing machine's instruction booklet, now is the right time to send away for another copy. Company addresses are given at the end of this book. When you send away, be sure to give the exact model number of your machine. You can usually find the model number on a metal plate attached to the machine, generally under it or near where the power cord plugs in. If possible, also give the year of purchase.

It is important to know whether your machine is a low-shank, high-shank, or slant-needle machine, because you can often use accessories such as a walking foot from other similar-shank brands on your machine. When the presser foot is down, measure the distance from the center of the screw that holds the foot on to the presser bar. A low-shank machine measures approximately ½″ (12 mm); a high-shank machine, approximately 1″ (2.5 cm). A slant-needle machine is obvious. Some brands, such as Bernina, have their own system. Some brands in the chart below vary according to the model you have, so you must measure to be sure.

Keeping in mind that each brand has several lines of machines, all slightly different, Table 1-2 specifies what each company generally recommends for machine quilting (usually on their top-of-the-line model).

Fig. 1-9 Top: Normal sewing, seaming two layers of fabric. Bottom: Machine quilting at its extreme. The needle must make way for the thread through eleven layers.

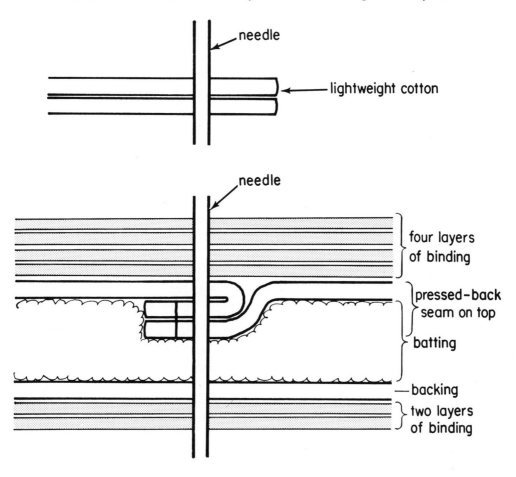

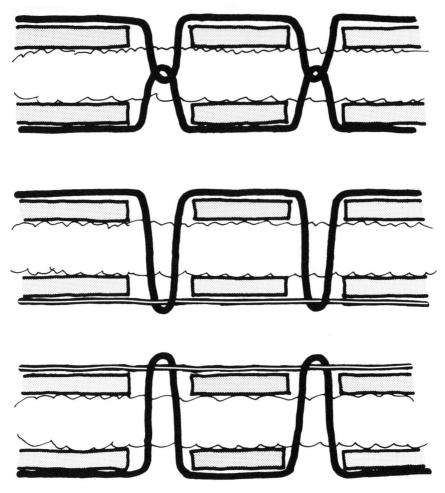

Fig. 1-10 Top: Universal tension. Middle: tight bobbin or loose top tension pulls top thread to underside. Bottom: tight top or loose bobbin tension pulls bobbin thread to topside.

Machine Accessories

Since every machine is slightly different, it is important that you keep in touch with a good sewing-machine store that sells your brand to learn how to use the newest accessories for the newest techniques.

Here are some machine accessories especially helpful for machine quilting. (These are for my machine—yours may be slightly different; see Fig. 1-12.)

1. *Open-toed quilting or applique foot:* allows you to see exactly what the needle is stitching.

2. *Applique (or satin stitch) foot:* (plastic or metal) has a wedge on the underside that allows the extra thickness of satin stitch to pass easily under the foot.

3. *Buttonhole foot:* has two parallel grooves on the underside to permit rows of satin stitches to pass easily under the foot.

4. *Walking foot (double-feed foot):* a box-like construction that helps all three layers of the quilt move evenly under the presser foot—a luxury worth owning if you plan to do a lot of machine quilting with the presser foot on (one of many methods).

5. *Zipper foot:* useful for quilt-as-you-go (see Chapter 6) so the toe of the foot doesn't catch in batting.

6. *Darning foot (or darning spring):* optional for free-machine quilting . . . but indispensable for not sewing over fingers, especially if you tend to talk while sewing—it holds the fabric down on either side of the needle as it enters the fabric, so the top loop is caught by the shuttle hook.

7. *Left-sided presser foot:* an alternative to buying the straight-stitch needle plate (and cheaper) for machines which can decenter the needle—decenter to the left and use this foot for the same reason as stated immediately above.

8. *Quilting guide:* moveable gauge that attaches to the needle shaft and is guided along the previous line of quilting—not accurate enough for numerous straight parallel lines on a whole quilt, but fine for outline quilting, clothing, placemats, and other small items.

9. *Straight-stitch (or topstitch) needle plate:* the round hole (rather than the wide slot of the zigzag plate) prevents the needle from letting the quilt dip into the hole just enough to cause puckers—standard equipment on some machines, extra on others (see Table 1-2). One reason the old treadles made such a beautiful stitch is that they had a small hole needle plate and a narrow presser foot. Don't forget to change back to a wide needle plate for zigzag.

Presser Foot and Seam Allowances

Because good machine quilting workmanship demands precise measurement of seam allowances, and a presser foot is one of the most convenient ways of measuring, it is extremely important to know exactly how wide each presser foot is. Measure from the needle hole to the right side of the presser foot (as you look at it). Put a fabric tape measure on the needle plate, perpendicular to the foot. Lower the needle to any inch or centimeter mark on the tape measure. Lower the presser foot. What is the measurement from the needle to the right side of the presser foot? If you own this book, write it next to each foot you own in the list above, and write in any not mentioned. Now when you are figuring seam allowances, you will know, for example, when you can and cannot use the edge of the foot as a ¼" (6 mm) seam allowance guide. You can decenter the needle to the right or left to

Fig. 1-11 Measure the distance from the center of the screw that holds on your presser foot to the bottom of the foot when it is in the down position. If the measurement is about ½" (12 mm), you have a low-shank machine; if it is about 1" (25 mm), you have a high-shank machine. Accessories from other similar-shank machines will sometimes fit your machine.

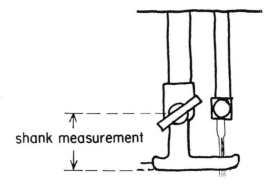

shank measurement

Table 1-2. Accessories and Adjustments for Machine Quilting

Brand	Needle	Feet Available — Darning	Walking	Roller	Embroid./applique	Open-toed	Accessories — Straight-stitch needle plate	Quilting gauge	Shank — Low(L) or high(H)	To Tighten (T)/ loosen (L) presser-foot pressure	To eliminate skipped stitches	To drop feed dogs	Comments
Bernina	Schmetz 80 sharp	S	N/A	N/A	S	S	decenter needle	S	unique/ system	Automatically adjusts	No problem	Button	Adapter allows you to use any low-shank foot. Magic Eye basting needle gives 1″(2.54cm) stitches.*
Brother	14	S	X	X	S	S	S	S	L	Leave as is	No problem	Button	*
Elna	Schmetz 130/705HJ/ 90(14)	S	X	X	S	S	X	X	L	Can't change. universal pressure	Change needle, oil race (holds bobbin case); use left-needle position	Cover with plate (optional)	No-snag foot great for one-step quilting. Biannual magazines with ideas for any machine.*
Kenmore	14	S	N	X	S	S	S	X	L	L	N/R	Button	
Morse	14 ballpoint	S	N/A	N/A	S	S	X		L	L	Add stabilizer	Use "fabric selector" lever	
Nelco	15 × 1 size 14	S	N/A	X	S	S	X	S	L	L	Decenter to left, change needle	Ratchet	*
New Home	16	N/A	N	X	S	S	S	S	L	L (light)	Close automatic sliding plate to narrow hole (ST on needle position dial)	N/R	Tricot foot prevents skipped stitches when needle-hole plate must be kept open. Spiral and flower stitchers make decorative circles.

Brand	Needle									Knob	Notes
Pencrest	14	N/A	S	S	X	S	L	L	N/R	Knob	*
Pfaff	System 130/705H/80 or 90	BI	N/N	S	X	S	N/N	H	No problem	Lever	Stop-needle feature handy for machine quilting. Built-in needle threader.*
Riccar	Schmetz 80	S	X	S	N/A	S	T, but N/N	L	Go to heavier needle	Press switch by bobbin case	Stop-needle handy for stopping quilting with needle in fabric.*
Singer	Yellow Band sharp 14	S	X	S	S	S	N/R	slant/needle/unique	Change needles; correct needle	Darning plate	Electronic model doesn't need oil; bead flashes when down to 5 yd. (4.5m) thread in bobbin.*
Viking	Husqvarna 130/705HJ/80	X (dual feeder)	S	N/A	X	S	Adjust thread tension to buttonhole symbol; adjust pressure 3 notches below normal, depending on loft of quilt	L	Must use Husqvarna needles; change often	Push button	Ankle available that screws onto any low-shank machine so you can use Viking feet. Stop-needle feature handy for machine quilting; excellent machine-embroidery hoops.*
Ward's	14	N/A	X	S	automatic sliding plate/closes	S	N/R	L	Prewash fabric; loosen top tension	Lever	*
White	Schmetz 130/705HJ size 90	X	X	S	S	S	Use normal pressure	L	Change needle, oil race; use left-needle position	Button	*

NOTE: Chart based on manufacturers' instructions for machine quilting on their top-of-the-line models. Addresses of machine manufacturers are listed in Resources and Supplies.

ABBREVIATIONS: N/N = not necessary; N/A = not available; N/R = no recommendation by manufacturer; S = standard with purchase; X = available, but extra; BI = built-in.

*Instructional material for machine quilting on specific model is available from manufacturer. Consult local sewing machine store.

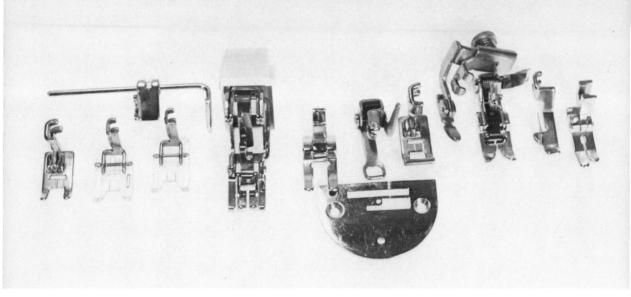

Fig. 1-12 Machine presser feet and accessories (left to right): regular, buttonhole, satin stitch, (above) quilting gauge, walking foot, open-toed, darning, no-snag, (below) straight-stitch needle plate (big slots for feed dogs, small round hole for needle), zipper, gripper foot for sheer fabrics and tailor tacking, left-needle position foot.

Fig. 1-13 Measure the exact distance from the needle to the right side of each presser foot and write the measurement next to the appropriate foot in this book. If you can decenter the needle on your machine, you can change the measurement to exactly ¼″ (6 mm) or whatever you need.

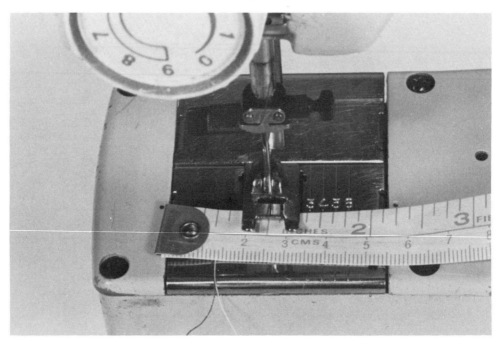

make an exact seam allowance. If you use decentering with a favorite presser foot, mark with pencil on the dial where, for example, a seam allowance of ¼″ (6 mm) is.

The seam allowance guides on your needle plate are not long enough for precision seaming. Extend them forwards and backwards with a strip of masking tape. (I remove the tape and replace it each time I sew, as I don't like to gum up my needle plate.)

Note: I have had no luck with the magnetic seam guides available in fabric stores. Pins hit them and they move. However some quilters love them.

Machine Location

A personal note about sewing-machine location: I occasionally hear the comment that machine work forces the quilter to be in isolation from her family. My response to this is, "Only by choice." When our daughter was born, I lost my tiny sewing room when we converted it to a nursery. For the next six years I complained loudly about having to move my machine around from table to table, a quilting gypsy; and about the pain of having to clean up fabric messes in order to eat or to greet guests. Finally we added a bedroom and I reclaimed my tiny sewing room . . . only to feel cramped and isolated. Soon I moved right back into the living room with the piano, the books, and the family—exactly like in the old days

Fig. 1-14 To keep the quilt from dragging off your work surface and causing problems in stitch evenness, rig a larger work area behind your machine.

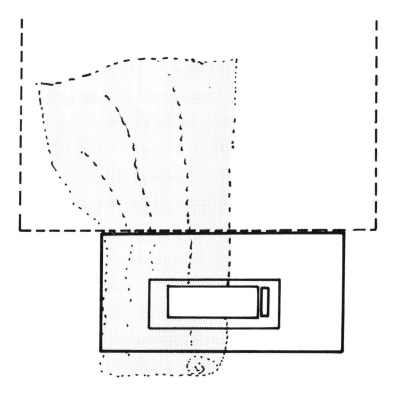

when the loom was an important fixture of every living room. I can talk as I sew, and I like incoming people to see what I'm making.

Here are some suggestions for setting up a work area for machine quilting.

Set up shop facing a large area. For ordinary sewing, a little corner is fine but for most machine quilting you need room for the quilt bulk to be supported behind the machine. Otherwise, the weight of the quilt hanging down behind the machine drags it through and distorts the quilt.

A behind-the-machine support for heavy quilts can be jury-rigged in several ways: a cardtable behind a larger table, a large piece of scrap cardboard (from appliance store or any large box opened flat) balanced on chairs in back of machine, a Ping-Pong table, a dining room table, letting the quilt spill onto a bed. In dire circumstances, I have even sat cross-legged on the floor operating the foot pedal with my knee—a method not recommended, but at least the quilt doesn't drag over the edge of a table.

Chapter 2

Planning for Machine Quilting

Undoubtedly you are eager to get on with it, to plunge into your first machine quilting project, but please take the time to read this chapter. It will save you many a headache.

Do's and Don'ts of Machine Quilting

Here are some general tips to keep in mind as you prepare to machine quilt. Many of these will be explored again in detail when the need arises.

Plan and Design

Plan as much as possible before you start, so that when you sit down at the machine, indecision will not be a stumbling block to completion of the quilt. You may find it helpful to keep notes on every project—early ideas, sketches, swatches of proposed colors, dates when you worked, and afterthoughts. The more planning and design you do beforehand, the more you'll enjoy the machine quilting, and the more you'll love the finished product afterward.

Savor Your Machine

Learn everything your machine can and cannot do—take classes, read about machine techniques, talk to other machine quilters, and most of all experiment with your machine. And don't be afraid to challenge your machine. Use feet from other brands (see Table 1-2); cut off parts of presser feet; have your needle plate slightly rounded, as Caryl Rae Hancock did, for easier free-machine quilting. Be adventurous!

Choose Strong Fabrics, Weaker Threads

If possible, choose a thread for machine quilting less strong than the material of the quilt. Ten years from now it will be easy to repair broken quilting lines; it will not be so easy to repair shredded material at seam lines.

Choose Seam Allowance and Thread Type Carefully

If you are making small items, there is very little stress on seams and on lines of quilting. But for full-sized quilts that hang over the sides of a bed, are jumped on, are shaken out and crumpled up, are tumbled in washers and dryers, use ½″ (12 mm) seam allowances. You can use ¼″ (6 mm) seam allowances in piecing and joining if your quilting lines are no more than 4″–5″ (10–13 cm) apart. Only use extra-fine machine-embroidery thread if each quilting line is stitched over

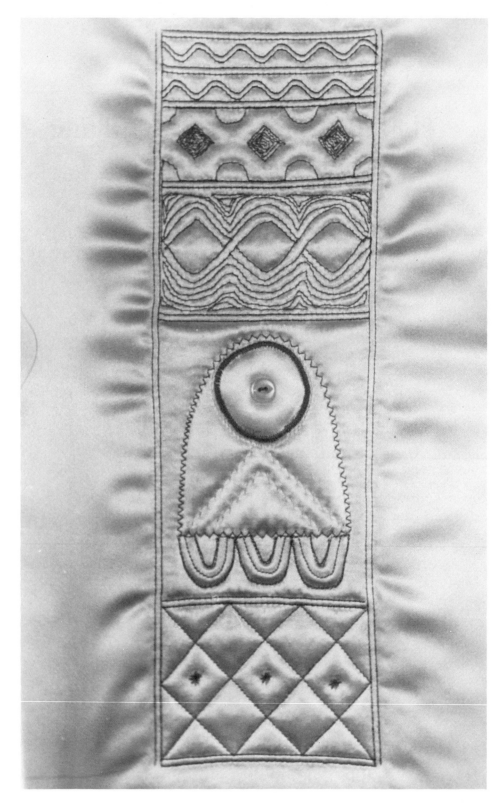

Fig. 2-1 A sampler of machine-quilting techniques: (from the top) twin-needle quilting—serpentine stitch, free-machine quilting, mock trapunto, satin stitch circle, zigzag quilting, button tying by machine, invisible thread quilting with zigzag stitch, Italian cording, straight stitch quilting with presser foot—diamond grid, decorative-stitch tying.

several times (as in some kinds of free-machine quilting) or the quilting lines are no more than 2″ (5 cm) apart.

Preshrink and Color-Test Fabrics

Preshrink and color-test all fabric as soon as you buy it. Red, especially, tends to bleed even after preshrinking. If you suspect that a color is not fast, add ½ measuring cup of salt to the rinse water, safety-pin some clean white fabric or thread to the suspected fabric, and preshrink three times. Nothing is as painful as spending hours on a quilt, only to have some fabrics run onto others in the first wash. To preshrink fabric, wet it thoroughly (it's already clean, so you don't have to wash it with detergent), spin out the excess water, and put the fabric in the dryer. (Note: some people claim that you can prevent excess wrinkles in uncut fabric by throwing a barely damp towel into the dryer with the fabric. This has never worked for me, but perhaps it will for you.)

Preventing shrinkage is not the only reason to preshrink; it removes the resinous finish on new fabrics which can deflect the needle on cantankerous machines and cause skipped stitches.

Pre-Test Marking Devices

Test your marking device to be sure it washes out. An easy time to do it is when you're preshrinking. Draw a line across the corner of the fabric and pin a safety pin next to it. Examine that corner after the fabric comes out of the dryer. If the mark didn't wash out, cut off the corner and wash it with a regular load of wash, pinning it to another garment so it won't get lost. If detergent does not remove the mark, choose another marking device. (See the Laundry/Marker Test later in this chapter.)

Practice Where It Won't Hurt

Prevent unhappy mistakes by making both a doodle cloth and a sample block before tackling a whole quilt. A doodle cloth is a small replica of the quilt sandwich, made to test tension settings and stitch lengths on. A sample is a full-size quilted block that is not used in the final quilt. Inaccurate templates, errors in design and technique, ineffective color choices, and amount of shrinkage due to quilting all show up on the sample.

Baste Properly

Take the time to baste the quilt sandwich properly. This will do more to prevent puckers than anything else (and is explained in detail later in this chapter).

Enjoy Your Work

Enjoy yourself and your machine while you work. You do not have to sit tense, hunched over your machine, sewing your nose to the fabric. Sing, praise your machine, talk to whoever walks by, listen to music. Pour love into the work. When you're done, the quilt will reflect it, and continue to reflect it for years.

Be Proud of Your Work

Sign and date all quilts you make. You can either free-machine embroider a label, machine quilt your name into the quilt, or type your name/date on interfacing (put paper behind it in typewriter) and sew onto the back of your quilt. If you plan to exhibit your quilts, put a hanging case on both the top and one side (for easier photography—see Chapter 11.) Hang quilts in your home when you don't have them on the beds. As with anything you make yourself, finish it and then flaunt it.

Don't Use Fussy Designs

Don't apply the wrong machine techniques to the wrong design. For example, small, intricate designs with sharp angles are murder to work with the presser foot on (but free-machine quilting may be perfect).

Fig. 2-2   *From "Scientific American," March 18, 1892.*

under the super-
irwell. The test
'our rockets were
id was fired with
et ; second, 1,552 ;
e of flight of the
:d, eight seconds ;

gress of German
Dr. Gilbert, of
hich were treated
itients were under
s it had become a
sence of
experi-
i habit.
er two,
Besides
roduced
patients
nd dis-
.dy, and
o right.
lthough
wn, still
iy it can
without
on, when
:oidable,
prepar-
ed on the
is cooled
t palata-
is nearly
stomach
aid to be
o twenty
eling of
experienced by the
e of sulphonal does

he price for alumi-

of such places being 22 per cent of the whole. In 1890 there were 448 such places, containing 29 per cent of the whole population.

AN IMPROVED QUILTING MACHINE.

The accompanying cut represents a new and valuable attachment for all family sewing machines, as by its use one lady can quilt comforts, quilts, coat linings, dress skirts, and any other article which it is desired to have filled with cotton or wool. The construction is simple, and any one who can run a sewing machine can operate one provided with this attachment. The top of the work to be quilted is rolled up on the inside roller, and the lining of the goods is rolled up on the outside roller, the cotton or wool is laid on the lining,

DAVIS' NEW FAMILY QUILTING MACHINE.

one layer at a time, and as the goods are quilted the quilted parts are rolled up on the inside roller. These operations are repeated until the goods are all quilted. This machine is manufactured by the inventor, Henry T. Davis, 18 to 30 W. Randolph St., Chicago, Ill., U. S. A.

passage open to t
shoe has been pa
information resj
may be obtaine
tary Woolen Sy:
York.

Th

Charles Schue
men are knock-k
pair of shoes in
with the heels wo
age of soles worn
often caused by t
About one man i
extreme
are at l
outside
shows i
Physici
dency i
courage
enough
and if
general.
usual to
or brad
some cu
driven
steel wo
thus ca
steel, b
a man
makes
wearing
Democi

WHI'
but the
are unaffected by
years in the well
Wetherill & Bro
ed good health.
McCann was an
years in the same

Don't Pass Up Unfamiliar Techniques

Don't skip techniques such as free-machine quilting because you've never done them before. Practice on items that don't matter until you feel confident enough to try larger projects.

Don't Rush Your Work

Don't hurry. Machine quilting is not really fast. It is faster than hand quilting but you are still going to put hours of work into every piece. You will enjoy the process as much as the product if you take your time.

Don't Try to Duplicate Hand Quilting

Don't expect machine quilting to look like hand quilting. Machine work has its own special qualities, which we must learn to exploit and to tout. One way to do this is to avoid machine stitching intricate traditional quilting (this doesn't mean quilt-top) designs, such as the feathered plume. You are only inviting hand quilters to examine your work closely and since it isn't hand quilting, the smaller-minded ones might sniff and say, "It doesn't look anything like hand quilting." If you use techniques and designs which look great when machine quilted, you can smile wisely and keep silent.

Glitches and Gremlins

Remember that the most common problems you will encounter are caused by the mismatching of machine settings, thread size and type, and fabric. Most of these annoying glitches fall into four categories: Creep, Pucker, Skip, and Fray. As you recall, there is a gremlin for each glitch, of the same name, and a sure method for foiling each gremlin. Let's review:

CREEP: baste well, use a hoop, use a walking foot
PUCKER: match needle size, thread, and fabric better; use fingers as tools
SKIP: hold fabric firmly against needle plate; use fingers or an appropriate presser foot; adjust tension
FRAY: match needle size and thread size to fabric

Checklist for Machine Quilting

Before each quilting session, check your machine thoroughly.

1. Clean out the bobbin case (remove the bobbin and vacuum around the case, if possible)—remove dust bunnies, lint, broken threads. Clean feed dogs, if necessary, with a toothbrush.
2. Oil your machine before each major project as specified in your instruction book (unless your machine does not require oil).
3. Check the needle size and condition—a bent or snagged needle will fray the top thread. You know how you got that snagged needle, too—from sewing over pins. Some say that sewing into fine sandpaper will smooth burred needles. Others feel that a new needle is the answer.
4. Check the needle plate—a burr on the metal surrounding the hole will break threads. If you have done a lot of free-machine embroidery, your needle plate may look like a battleground. Sand the burr smooth with fine sandpaper or ask your friendly sewing machine dealer to help.

Fig. 2-3 From upper left, clockwise: Creep, Pucker, Skip, and Fray.

5. When you choose your thread, wind a full bobbin. Better yet, treat yourself to a gift of ten extra bobbins and wind several at the beginning of each sewing session. Remember to check the bobbin before starting each long line of machine quilting. It is especially annoying to run out mid-quilt, because you usually don't notice until the end of the line.

Tools for Machine Quilting

Sewing Tools

Get the right tool for the job. Your work will be easier and more pleasureable if you take the time to assemble the tools you need and to organize them in a useable way.

Scissors

The prudent quilter keeps four closely guarded (from the family) pairs of scissors—for cutting paper, for regular fabric, for heavy fabric, and a short sharp-to-the-point pair for applique and embroidery. I am prone to hide these scissors and to growl at intruders because I have suffered the pain of trying to cut fabric accurately with fabric scissors dulled by cutting paper, string, strapping tape, and toenails. As an attempt at prevention, I also keep scissors for the family readily available in the living room, bedrooms, and bathroom.

Scissors can and should be kept sharpened. Either learn how to do it yourself, which isn't difficult (ask someone experienced in sharpening hand tools to show you how), or send them out for sharpening. Most fabric stores will sharpen scissors, but if yours doesn't, look in the Yellow Pages of the phone book under "Sharpening Services." People who sharpen saws, knives, or lawn mowers will usually sharpen scissors.

Fig. 2-4 Sewing tools. Top row, l to r: spiral-bound graph-paper sketchbook, two pincushions for extra-long and short pins; second row: two needlecases for special and ordinary needles, fabric glue in liquid and stick form, paper, applique, and fabric scissors, seam ripper; third row: sewing machine oil, brush, magnifying glass, needle threader, rolled-up tape measure, machine needles, needle-nosed tweezers; bottom row: see-through ruler, extra bobbins.

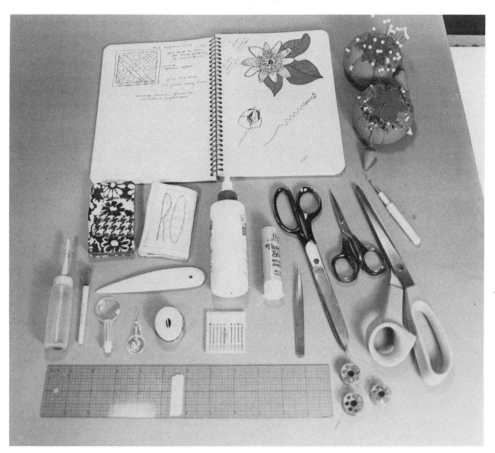

Machine Needles

Keep a full range of sizes from 8/9(60) to 16(100), ballpoint and sharp, as well as the novelty needles like twin and triple, leather, wing. Since machine quilting calls for sizes 10/11 to 14(70–90) most often, buy an extra package of those sizes. If you have trouble reading the sizes on the needle, paint the base (non-sharp end) of the needle with fingernail polish or model airplane paint and put a corresponding dot of polish or paint on the needle package or case. Then religiously return color-coded needles to their correct package. (This idea is borrowed from Roberta Losey Patterson, and is good enough that the companies which produce machine needles should follow it and save us the trouble.)

Be sure to use the needles recommended for your machine. Some needles have a deeper scarf than others (significance of scarf explained on p.4). If stitches are being skipped on an expensive machine, it's a good bet that inexpensive needles are being used.

Hand Needles and Cases

I love to sew by hand and I'm very attached to certain needles, so I keep two needlecases (both machine-made, of course). One is for tapestry, embroidery, and regular sewing needles. The other one holds my beloved short sharp betweens for hand quilting, the slightly curved one that I use for applique, and the curved needle I sometimes use for basting. (Recipes for the needlecase pattern are in Chapter 9, Quick Gifts.)

Needle Threader

Most quilters seem to go through these at an incredible rate. Use them both for hand and machine sewing. In the latter case insert the threader from the back of the needle.

Fig 2-5 Insert needle threader from back to front of machine needle.

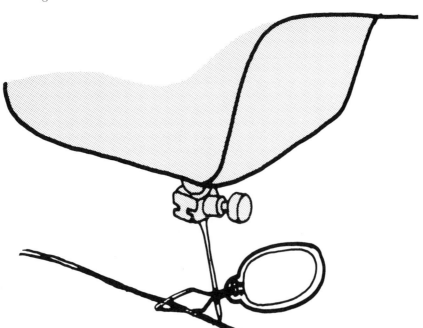

Magnifying Glass/Linen Tester

Useful for reading the needle size, helping to thread the machine needle, and counting the number of machine stitches per inch or centimeter so you know precisely how to set the machine stitch length. (Linen testers are available from photography stores as well as from fabric stores. It's worth owning one. It's also useful for designing from photographs or magazines, for examining fabrics, for enlarging details for quilts and quilt photographs, and for examining all kinds of insects, leaves, cat hairs, fingerprint whorls, etc.)

Extra Bobbins

They don't cost that much. Why not give yourself a present of ten extra bobbins? If you have wound a special thread onto a bobbin and don't want to forget which spool you used, poke a twist tie or pipe cleaner up through the center of the spool and the bobbin and twist the ends together. You can also buy bobbin holders which fit into the spool hole.

Needle-Nosed Tweezers

The uses for this handy tool are so numerous—bringing up the loop of the bobbin thread, helping to thread the needle, extracting pins at the very last moment before you sew over them, cleaning out lint from the bobbin case—that you can almost be certain that someone will walk off with them. Buy two and hide one near your sewing machine.

Oil and Brush

Follow the instructions for oiling your machine, making sure to use nothing but sewing machine oil. Because you are sewing three or more layers in a quilt and because polyester batting throws off an enormous amount of lint, you may need to oil more than once during a large project. Machines differ, but generally yours should run smoothly and quietly. If it clatters and sticks when you press the foot or knee pedal, oil it.

If it still sticks, take it in to a good sewing machine store for cleaning and possible repair. It may require more than oil. The brushes on my machine recently wore out, which made it delay and stick when I pressed the foot pedal. No amount of oil could fix this, but a simple replacement of the brushes worked miracles.

Machine-Embroidery Hoops

Keeps the quilt sandwich, top, and/or backing fabric taut, depending on what technique you're using. There are many types of embroidery hoops to choose from (Fig. 2-6).

Iron and Board

A good steam-iron is a must. If you're buying one, read *Consumer Reports* magazine (available in your public library) to find out what's the best buy for the money. An adjustable ironing board is convenient for setting up right next to your machine chair so you don't have to get up to press seams. You can also rig a temporary ironing board by using a cardtable, a board across two chair arms, or a tabletop with a towel or blanket as an ironing pad. Save used ironing board covers; they are perfect for the insides of machine-quilted oven mitts (see Chapter 9). Also use a press cloth, available in fabric stores or you can use an old sheet, to protect delicate fabrics and to keep polyester batting from scratching the iron. Always

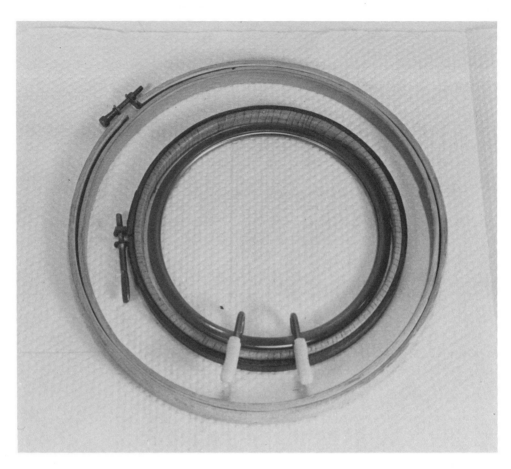

Fig. 2-6 Three embroidery hoops for machine quilting: the largest, an 8″ (20 cm) hoop. has a half-moon carved out of the outer ring to help slide the hoop under the needle; the 6″ (15 cm) hoop's inner ring is wrapped with masking tape to grip the fabric better; and the smallest hoop, made expressly for machine embroidery, is easy to move around the fabric while you're embellishing a quilt top. However, it is not thick enough to use on a quilt sandwich (top, batting and backing).

press gently, preferably from the underside, with respect for the fabric. Keep in mind that ironing, i.e., sliding the iron along the fabric and possibly stretching the seam, is not pressing.

Pins and Cushions

Use several pin cushions to keep pins separate—regular sewing pins in one, long (1¾″ or 4.5 cm) white-headed pins in one, and silk pins in another. (Also keep boxes of safety pins available for basting quilts.) If you are making your own pin cushions, don't fill them with foam rubber. The pins resist going in. Use loose polyester batting or sawdust instead (fill the toe of an old clean nylon stocking; then cover it with something nice).

Scrap Paper and Notebooks

When you machine quilt, ideas for all kinds of other quilts, realizations about subleties of workmanship, and helpful hints for next time come fast. If you write ideas down as they strike you, you clear the way for more ideas to appear. Jot them down on scrap paper kept near your work area. You can also use the scrap (typing-weight, not tissue) paper to back fabric for satin stitch. It's hard to believe that anyone wouldn't have scrap paper, but it can happen. If that's your problem, ask any office (bank, library, insurance) or recycling center to give you scrap computer print-outs, which are thrown away by the ton. Notebooks are available in art supply, stationery, and some fabric stores. A quilting favorite is a spiral-bound notebook of ¼" (6 mm) graph paper (see address in Resources).

Incidentally, don't eat or drink near your quilts-in-progress or your notebooks. As I was writing this, I spilled milk all over my notes.

Cutting Board

Available at fabric stores and marked off in inches and centimeters, this board is used to mark fabric for cutting, to cut backing squares for quilt-as-you-go, to help in blowing up designs by putting tracing paper over it, and to straighten crooked quilted edges after you're done quilting. But beware: not all cutting boards are accurate. Check yours both ways against an accurate ruler or graph paper (the length of my board is okay but the width is off ¼", or 6 mm).

Calculator

I use mine constantly—to figure yardage, to help lay out a picture of how to cut for piecing, to calculate length of bias strips, and much more. In case your memory is rusty, here's how fractions in inches or yards convert to the decimal system:

fraction of a yard	decimal	inches
⅛ =	.125	4½"
¼ =	.25	9"
⅓ =	.333	12"
⅜ =	.375	13½"
½ =	.5	18"
⅝ =	.625	22½"
⅔ =	.666	24"
¾ =	.75	27"
⅞ =	.875	31½"

When you use the calculator, all the numbers will be decimal. If you calculate that you need to buy 2.30 yards of material, round up to the next highest fraction shown in the table (in this case, .333) and buy 2⅓ yards.

You may want to type these on a pre-gummed address label, cut it to fit any empty space on the top of your calculator, and stick it there for ready reference.

Useful Miscellany

A turning bodkin for coaxing pointed corners out; tape measure and see-through ruler; a stick of gelled glue (looks like fat lipstick—available in fabric and quilt stores); a container of liquid white glue (such as Elmer's or Sobo) are all handy aids.

And, of course, a seam ripper (see end of this chapter for a fast ripping technique) should be nearby anytime you work on the machine.

Visit your fabric and quilt stores from time to time. New tools and gadgets are constantly being introduced, many of which will save you time and fuss in machine quilting.

Art Tools

Don't be afraid of the tools of precision. They are indispensable in machine quilting.

Many of us have had no art training and we are not aware of the wealth of art tools that make the design of machine quilting both exciting and easier. If you do not normally use art supply stores, I recommend that you spend an hour browsing in a well-stocked one for such useful supplies as those listed below.

Graph Paper

Have on hand large pads of transparent graph paper so you can make slopers (see p.56), try out different color schemes, copy shapes for easy enlargement. I use ¼″ (centimeter is good too) and 10-to-the-inch most often.

Tracing Paper

A roll of inexpensive tracing paper (about $1.25 for 18″ wide, 8-yard roll) is used to copy parts of designs, letters, shapes that can be moved around, rearranged, manipulated and then overlaid with more tracing paper to copy the final design (see Chapter 10).

Masking Tape

Masking tape is available in various widths from ¼″ to 2″ (6 mm to 5 cm) or wider. A 60-yard roll of 2″-wide tape costs about $2. Use it in designing to tape

Fig. 2-7 Art tools. Top row, l to r: roll of tracing paper, right angle, eraser, masking tape in two widths, flexible ruler, spray glue; bottom row: dressmaker's French curve, X-acto knife, press-on letters, graph paper pad, small see-through T-square.

down paper; use it in cutting to mark widths or strips; use it in marking for straight quilting lines; use it in basting to hold down the edges of the backing; lay it on the needle plate of your machine to elongate the inscribed sewing lines for more precision in sewing seams.

Paper Cutter

This tool is expensive, but worth it. I sometimes fold and cut four layers of fabric on mine, especially strips for string quilts, for enlarged log cabin, and for Seminole piecing. The higher the polyester content of the fabric, the less my cutter can cut sharply. And I don't try to cut widths less than 3″ (1.6 cm). When you use a paper cutter on cloth, it's important to be sure that you're always cutting on-grain.

Spray Glue

This glue is used to mount graph-paper designs onto sandpaper or acetate for templates. I've also experimented on wall hangings with spray-gluing the top fabric to the batting and the backing fabric to the batting. Use in a well-ventilated area. Don't use spray glue on any items to be washed—glue is extremely flammable and might burst into flames in the dryer.

X-acto Knife

This is the perfect tool for cutting precise templates—used with a straight-edge. Put newspaper, an old telephone book, or an artist's cutting mat underneath so you don't mar your work surface.

T-square

This is used for drawing straight lines. Tape the fabric along the edge of a table. Line up the T-square with the edge of the table and draw. I use it in place of a yardstick.

Right-angle

To check that the corners of quilting frames are at 90° angles, to construct perfect rectangles and squares, to help miter corners, this tool is invaluable.

Flexible Ruler

This bendable ruler is reinforced with metal and is useful for wavy lines and rounding edges. (See section on marking fabrics.)

Art Gum Eraser

This will erase pencil marks on some fabrics.

Press-on Letters

Art stores carry sheets of letters in any style you like (such as formal, italic, lower-case). By putting the sheet over paper and rubbing the letters, you transfer the letters from the sheet to the paper. If you rub them off onto graph paper, you can blow the message up to the size you need. Copy this onto tracing paper and use as full-size patterns for cutting out of fabric.

Fabrics for Machine Quilting

One of the many joys of machine quilting is that, unlike hand quilting, any washable fabric is fair game, from the traditional 100% cotton to closely woven polyester-blend sheets to double knits to corduroy to velour to denim. You can use nonwashable fabrics, too, if you're willing to handwash or dryclean the quilt. (I have even seen a breathtaking leather, Ultrasuede, and fur quilt.) Keep in mind that a quilt top pieced of wools, corduroys, or denims is extremely heavy when it is quilted. So if you use one of the heavier top materials, choose a lightweight batting like interfacing fleece, light flannel, or thin polyester batting.

Preparation of Fabric

Cut Off the Selvage

The selvage may shrink at a different rate than the rest of the fabric and should not be used in quiltmaking. This means the useable width of your fabric is 1″to 2″(2.5 cm to 5 cm) less than the given width. Keep this fact in mind when estimating yardage.

Preshrink Fabric

Do this as soon as you get home from the store, even if you won't use it immediately. (Directions are earlier in this chapter.)

Fig. 2-8 Know your fabric terms.

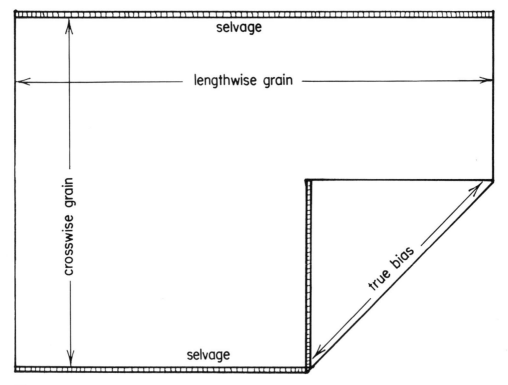

Straighten the Crosswise Edges

Do this either by tearing across an end or pulling one thread across an end.

To tear or not to tear, that is the question. The answer is yet another question: can you make accurate seams if you tear? The edges of torn fabric vary from perfectly behaved to dreadfully rippled and stretched. The only way to find out is to tear a sample from your fabric, both crosswise and along the selvage. Press it lightly and examine the results—can you sew ¼″ (6 mm) from the torn edge accurately, or are the edge fibers puckered and unhappy?

If the latter, you must cut your fabric. Straighten the grain at both ends of the fabric by pulling one thread all the way across; then use the space where the thread was as a cutting guide. Sometimes the thread breaks partway. Pull it out, cut as far as you can, pick out the broken thread end with a pin, and pull again until you're all the way across the fabric.

Straighten the Grain

Fold the fabric in half lengthwise. Pin lengthwise edge and straightened ends. If fabric doesn't lie flat, take out pins and gently pull on the bias. Some permanent press fabrics have the grain permanently locked in and you can't straighten it. If

Fig. 2-9 Straighten the crosswise edges by pulling a thread across the fabric and cutting along the line left.

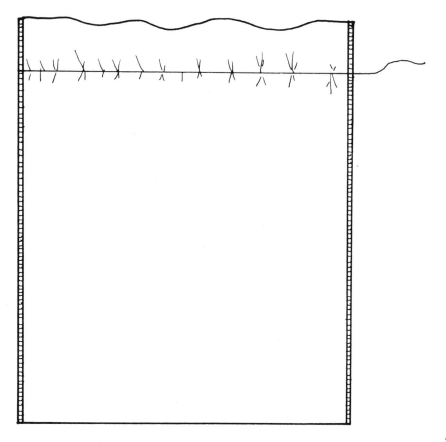

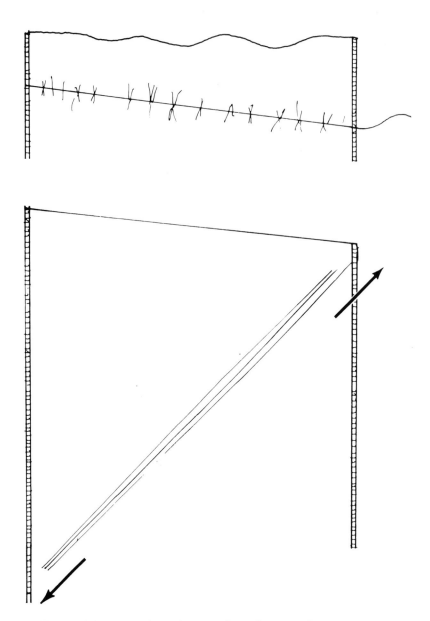

Fig. 2-10 Top: Straighten the grain by pulling one thread across
the fabric and cutting along the line left. Bottom: If the angle is
not 90°, you must pull gently on the bias of the fabric until the
grain is straightened.

you use off-grain fabric because you're too lazy to straighten the grain or because
your fabric is permanently pressed off-grain, your quilt may hang unevenly on a
wall. On a bed it usually doesn't matter, but don't try intricate pieced designs with
off-grain permanent press fabric. They'll curve funny and not lie flat.

Iron Your Fabric

Once the fabric is quilted, it's not easy to iron. Optional: Spray-starch it. It
makes lightweight fabric in top and/or backing firmer and less likely to pucker.

Fabric Selection for Quilt Tops

Four characteristics of fabrics play important roles in machine quilting: weight and texture; scale of pattern(large or small); washability; color and value.

Weight and Texture

The light to medium-weight fabrics (especially 100% cotton) have traditionally been used in quiltmaking because it is easy to push a short sharp needle through them by hand. We machine quilters do not have to so limit ourselves, as long as we realize that the heavier the material used, the more the overall weight of the quilt increases. Thus you should choose correspondingly lighter battings and backings as the top increases in weight. Also be sure the mixture of fabrics in the quilt top is compatible in weight; heavy corduroy used in one area and lightweight cotton in another will not hang, feel, or wear right unless you carefully balance the areas. With a little care in planning, you can exploit the machine's ability to handle different textures and weights. You can then use all kinds of fabrics in your quilts—furry, ribbed, satiny, bumpy.

A loose way to gauge fabric weight for quilting is by how you'd use it in general sewing:

Lightweight fabrics are those you'd make a blouse or shirt from—calicos, ginghams, most sheets, and similar weight fabrics.

Medium-weight fabrics are those suitable for skirts and pants—poplin, kettle-cloth, double knits, and such.

Heavy-weight fabrics are those used for jackets and duffle bags—denim, duck, canvas, and the like.

Beware of fabrics that are so lightweight and light-colored that seams show through the top. This is especially important in one-step quilting (see Chapter 6), where you cannot choose which way to press the seams. When you are buying fabric, make sure that you're not fooled about its weight by feeling the doubled fabric. Slip your hand over one thickness and crush it lightly. Does it wrinkle easily? If so, it won't look right tied or with quilting lines far apart. Turn the edge under with your fingers. Can you see the "seam" through the top of the fabric? Then be wary! But, if such a lightweight fabric has a special color or texture that you simply must use, you can back it with another piece of lightweight, light-colored fabric, treating the two as one.

Scale of Pattern

Large prints may catch your eye in the fabric store on the bolt, but they can look ridiculous cut up into small pieces. Carefully match the scale (large, medium, small) of the print to the kind of machine quilting you like to do. If piecing traditional blocks is a favorite with you, collect small prints such as calicos and other small florals and small polka dots. Not that large prints are unusable—you can build an entire quilt around large prints by machine quilting the designs and inserting borders, strips, or pieced blocks between the large patterns.

Don't assume that every fabric store stocks the same fabrics. They don't, and you may regret passing up a perfect small print in one store because you thought you could find it elsewhere later. Three to five yards is the minimum you need for piecing with other fabrics for a quilt top.

Fig. 2-11 Top, left: The scale of the pattern chosen depends on how you will use the fabric. If this were to be cut up for string or crazy quilting, for example, the scale of the pattern is probably too large. For a backing fabric, it is fine. Right: The small scale fabrics are most used in pieced quilt tops. Bottom: This large pattern would have to be used very carefully in a quilt top.

Be careful about buying and using prints with a definite top and bottom. You may regret having to pay close attention. (For example, the Heart Pillow in Chapter 4, I didn't notice until after I'd cut the strips that there was a direction to the print. Piecing takes longer if you must use one end of a strip and not the other.)

Washability

Once you discover that you can use almost any material for machine quilting, you may forget in your enthusiasm that one of the beauties of machine-made quilts is their easy care in modern washing machines. Think twice about using scraps of nonwashable fabrics like wool, silk, felt, or leather, if you will need to clean your quilts often. Of course, if you are machine quilting a wallhanging, then you needn't worry about washability, and you can let your imagination go wild.

For very large quilts (double bed and up), you may find it easier on you and the quilt to wash and dry them at a laundromat in the large machines. Pulling a large wet quilt out of a small home washer puts tremendous strain on the quilting thread and it may break.

Make life easier on yourself: when you buy fabric, jot down the fiber content and the care information on your sales slip, with an identifying phrase ("green polka dot"). When you get home, cut off the selvage and staple an inch of it next to the fabric description. Save the sales slip in the envelope you stapled in the back of this book.

Also see the Fabric Care Chart (Table 12-1).

Color and Value

Color is one quality of fabric in quilts that can make people gasp with pleasure. However color, like love, does not exist alone in the world; it is defined and changed by everything around it. An all-red quilt in a bedroom with black walls won't look at all like the same quilt in a white-walled bedroom. Similarly, each color you choose to put in a quilt is affected by the colors around it in the quilt.

In quilt design, it's important to organize the fabrics you're considering first into piles of darks, mediums, and lights, and then by color. If you're not sure which of these three values (light, medium, or dark) a color has, stand back from it and squint. Usually, this reduces what you see to light, medium, or dark grays. If you're still not sure, see the black-and-white photo of the color chart in "Practical Hints on Color" in Chapter 10. Compare the photo with the color-page photo. Can you see what value yellow has? red? If you own an instant camera, take black-and-white pictures of your fabrics to check the values. Another trick is to cut 2″ (5 cm) wide strips of the fabrics you're considering; paste, tape, or staple to paper; and make a photocopy of the fabrics. (The copy-machine operator may look at you as if you're insane, but just give instructions to lay the fabric side face-down on the glass plate, and smile.) See Chapter 3 for using the photocopy machine for designing your quilts.

Be sure to examine any fabric you're considering buying in natural light. The fluorescent lighting in many fabric stores changes the true color of a fabric. Also look at the underside of the fabric; sometimes it looks better than the top.

If you only have time to sew at night, think twice about working on dark fabrics—browns, navys, purples. Tired eyes have trouble following the quilting line.

Fabric Selection for Backings

Backing fabric is generally a light to medium-weight cotton or cotton-blend fabric. If you are new to machine quilting, choose a small print for the backing (glitches and gremlins are less noticeable this way). Sheets on sale or seconds/ irregulars are a good buy; but be sure to buy enough for the entire quilt. The backing fabric will shrink in quilting. If you do not have a dust ruffle on your bed, the mattress or box springs may show unless you piece two sheets together. For everything but king-sized beds, buy the next largest sheet (e.g., buy a king sheet for a queen-sized bed). To give you an idea of whether a sheet is a good buy, here's how many yards of fabric are in each size (when turnovers are opened out):

Table 2-1. FLAT SHEET YARDAGE

	Finished Size inches (cm)	yd. (m) in 36" (100 cm) wide fabric
twin	66 × 96 (167 × 243)	5 (4.55m)
full (double)	81 × 96 (205 × 243)	6½ (5.92m)
queen	90 × 102 (228 × 259)	7½ (6.83m)
king	108 × 102 (274 × 259)	9⅛ (8.3m)
standard pillowcase		1⅛ (1.02m)
king pillowcase		1⅜ (1.25m)

Divide the sale price of the sheet by the number of yards for the price per yard (use your calculator). For example, a king sheet on sale for $10 would be $1.10/yard, a good deal when 36" wide fabric is currently $2 to 3/yard.

Some fabric stores also sell a 90" (229 cm) wide fabric, which is ideal for backing quilts. Usually this wide fabric is white but it is easily dyed. If your favorite store doesn't have it, ask them to order it for you.

If you're using a thin batting and tying it, try using pre-quilted fabric as backing, to add an extra loft to the quilt.

Note: If you have light, solid colors in the quilt-top design, be careful in choosing the backing color. Dark colors may change the appearance of top fabrics. For example, with a ¼" (6 mm) batt, a navy blue backing will make top white fabric grayer and yellow fabric greenish.

Alternate Sources of Fabric

Many of the faster machine piecing techniques depend on using fresh yardage, not scraps. Sewing on and handling brand-new fabric is enjoyable, but you may not want to spend the $50 to $75 or more it may cost for new quilt materials. Consequently, it helps to have other fabric sources in addition to fabric stores. Here are a few suggestions. In each of these cases, you will not be shopping for specific colors for a specific quilt, but stockpiling for the future.

Garage and tag sales are good places to find interesting, cheap fabric, but only if you can restrain yourself. I only allow myself to buy small prints and solids in the pure rainbow colors and brown, and only if there are at least 3 yards (2.73 m) of a fabric available. Otherwise I'd be knee-dep in small scraps of pretty but unused fabric.

Thrift shops also often sell yardage and/or used sheets, which are easily dyed (see Dye Chart in Chapter 12). Don't forget to look at men's ties there. Many are part or all silk and can be combined with other fabrics for crazy-quilt and string-quilt projects.

The want ads in local and "shopper" newspapers sometimes list yardage for sale. You can also advertise free in neighborhood papers for "cotton/blend yardage and/or used sheets" with some success. Again, keep a limited color scheme in mind or you'll soon be able to open your own fabric store. (As I said, white sheets are very easy to dye. Snap them up whenever you see them.)

If you live near an industrial area, call clothing, shirt, and bridal factories to see if and when they sell off bolt ends. Check in a good bookstore or your public library for local guides to bargain hunting (also do this during any travels to metropolitan areas).

And finally, if you belong to a quilting guild, arrange a periodic fabric swap/sale. It's surprising how often someone else's discards will fill in your fabric collection.

Batting

Unlike our ancestors, who had only wool or cotton batting (or the less satisfactory newspaper, pine needles, or horsehair), we have a wide choice of fillers for our quilts today. Machine quilting gives even more latitude than hand quilting because the machine can handle such difficult materials as foam, down, and blankets.

Cotton batting is still available to quilters. It is a thin batt which makes it easy to handle (and which is why old-time hand quilters were able to get so many stitches per inch). It must be quilted no less than 2" (5 cm) apart to hold the batting securely. It is better used as one large piece than cut up for modules or quilt-as-you-go, as it tends to tear away from machine seams.

Polyester batting is made from chemicals. A machine called a card creates a web, which is an unsupported batt. At this point, four finishes can be applied to the web.

If left alone, it is *unbonded batting,* which comes in many weights and thicknesses. Loose, it is used to stuff toys, pillows, trapunto shapes. In sheet form, it is stacked to various thicknesses, which can be peeled off. Sometimes these sheets are not totally consistent in loft; pieces from the higher parts can be picked off and smoothed into the lower parts. The highest loft is about 3" (7.6 cm) thick and is chainstitched to a nonwoven backing so that it can be rolled and unrolled on and off a bolt. This high-loft unbonded batting is not meant to be quilted, but tied. The backing is easily removed by placing the fluffy side against the wrong side of the quilt backing and undoing the chain stitch on the nonwoven backing.

If resin permeates the web, coating all the fabrics, it is *bonded batting.* The loft stays high, which is nice for machine quilters, but harder on hand quilters who want small stitches. (It's actually meant for tying quilts.)

Fig. 2-12 Side view of some battings (l to r): interfacing fleece, pre-quilted fabric, cotton batting, unbonded polyester batting, bonded polyester batting.

Bonded polyester batting is the most common choice of machine quilters, because it's easy to handle, holds up well over years of use, keeps its loft, and doesn't have to be quilted as closely as cotton batting.

If resin is applied just to the top and bottom of the web, it is *glazed batting*. The center of the batt is not bonded. This batt is soft and fluffy. The resin may wash off over the years, so quilting lines should be no farther apart than 4″ (10 cm). Recently there has been talk that the glazed batts tend to migrate through quilt tops of cotton/poly blends, giving the appearance on the surface of a white mold. This is called "bearding." Some say it happens only with machine quilting, not hand quilting; others say it happens with hand quilting, too, but not with all brands of glazed batting. Actually, bearding is not a normal occurrence. It happens only occasionally, depending on the fiber content and tightness of weave of the shell fabric. Using only 100% cotton fabric is one solution. If you already have a glazed batt on hand, you can avoid the problem by covering the batt with cheesecloth or a lightweight cotton fabric before putting the quilt top on and quilting.

If the web is put in a needle loom and punched in the same way nonwoven blankets are made, it is *needle-punched batting*. This nonchemical process makes a lower loft but allows hand quilters their beloved teeny stitches.

You can buy polyester batting either pre-cut and packaged in standard bed sizes or by the yard in large bolts like fabric. The packaged batts are usually ¼″ (6 mm) thin, which makes for easier handling on the machine. They are more expensive but do not have to be pieced. They are available in these sizes: 72″ × 90″, 81″ × 96″, 90″ × 108″, 102″ × 104″, and 120″ × 120″ (180 × 228cm, 205 × 243cm, 228 × 274cm, 259 × 264cm, and 305 × 305cm). Always read the label carefully before buying a packaged batt to be sure you are getting the kind of

Fig. 2-13 When piecing batting that will not be immediately secured by quilting lines, join the two pieces with a large herringbone stitch so they won't separate.

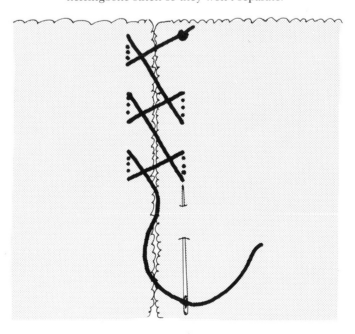

batting you want. Those on the bolt are of various thicknesses, from ¼" to as thick as 3" (6 mm to 7.6 cm) and usually 45" to 48" (115 cm) wide. While they make a puffy, delightful quilt, these extra-thick battings are recommended only for the experienced quilter or if you're making a duvet (see Chapter 8) where the quilting won't show.

If not secured immediately by seaming or a machine-quilted line, batts from a bolt should be pieced together with a large herringbone stitch (see Fig. 2-13). Otherwise, they will pull apart from each other over the years of washing.

All these battings are sold by both loft and weight. Two battings can weigh differently but have the same loft. Packaged batts are sold in pound weights. Obviously a quilt made with 2 ½ pound (1.13 Kg) batting will be warmer than 1¼ (.51 Kg) pound batting. Batting on the bolt is sold in ounce weights, meaning how many ounces a square inch weighs. For comparison, enough 3½ ounce 45" wide (98 g of 115 cm) batting to make an 81" × 96" (205 × 243 cm) quilt is roughly equivalent in weight to a 1¼ pound 81" × 96" packaged batt.

If you are making quilts for warmth as much as for decoration, choose a heavier weight batting. Choose the loft according to your experience and the technique. The thicker the loft, the more experience needed.

Also useful as batting are interfacing fleece, old blankets and quilts, flannel, mattress pads, down, pre-quilted remnants, and old clean nylons.

Threads for Machine Quilting

It is the handling of thread that sets machine quilting apart from hand quilting. (Once it was realized that the secret was using two threads, not one like hand sewing, the lockstitch sewing machine was invented in the 1830s.) We can use different colors and types of threads in top and bobbin, more than doubling the design possibilities.

This is not a new idea. In the delightful and scholarly *Quilts In America* (see Bibliography), the Orlofskys report, "To emphasize the fact that she was using a sewing machine, the [late 1800s] quilter used threads of different color to quilt and to give prominence to the quilting stitch as well as for decorative purposes. Quilts of the period frequently show white thread quilting on red, green, or brown material."

The choice of thread for machine quilting depends on what technique you're using, how large the quilted item is, whether it is whole-cloth (such as a sheet) or constructed in blocks, how close the quilting lines are, and what fabrics you've chosen. For example, when stitching with the presser foot on, any thread you use for regular sewing or hand quilting may be used. On the other hand, for free-machine quilting, use extra-fine machine-embroidery thread on top (see Resource list).

Years from now, after your machine-quilted quilt has been through the washer/dryer several dozen times, you will appreciate the subtleties of thread/fabric selection in quilts. It's better if you prepare for it now, while you are constructing the quilt. Since it's easier to repair stitches than shredded fabric at seam lines, try to choose thread less strong than your quilt-top fabric. Only use cotton-covered polyester thread for piecing and quilting if both the backing and quilt-top fabrics are polyester blends. Otherwise use sewing-weight (not extra-fine machine-embroidery) 100% cotton thread, choice of brand depending on the weight of the quilt-top fabrics.

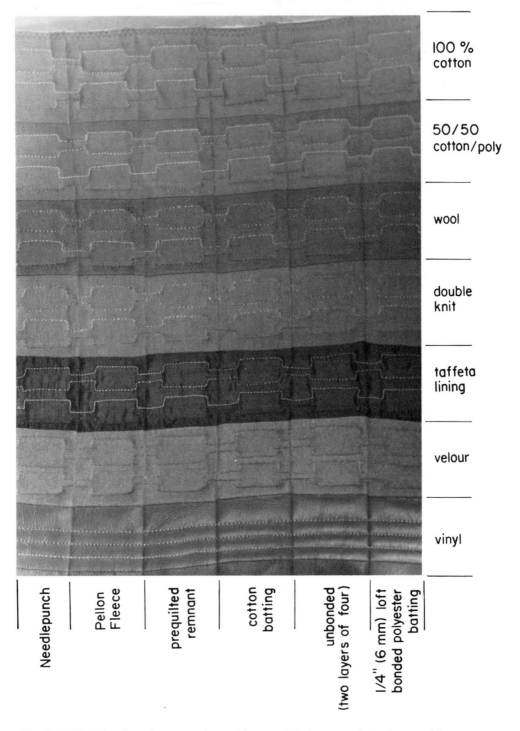

Labels at right (top to bottom): 100 % cotton; 50/50 cotton/poly; wool; double knit; taffeta lining; velour; vinyl

Labels at bottom (left to right): Needlepunch; Pellon Fleece; prequilted remnant; cotton batting; unbonded (two layers of four); 1/4" (6 mm) loft bonded polyester batting

Fig. 2-14 Test the threads, materials, and batting. Each rectangle is free-machine quilted with four threads (top to bottom): 100% cotton extra-fine machine-embroidery; 100% rayon extra-fine machine-embroidery: cotton-covered polyester; and invisible. The vinyl is straight-stitched quilted with the roller foot on.

Fig. 2-15 Some threads slip off the spool and catch on the spindle. Tape a tapestry needle to the machine to the left of the spool and run the thread through it before putting it through your first thread guide.

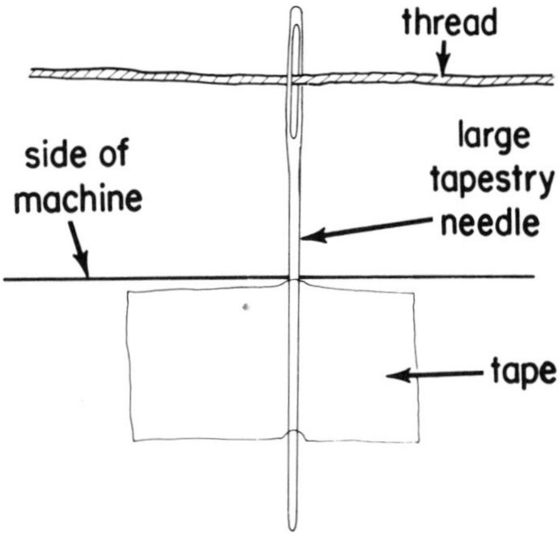

Some rayon threads have a nasty habit of slipping down off the spool and tangling themselves on the thread holder of your machine. You don't notice this until the thread mysteriously breaks. Some machines have a special gadget to prevent this, but Janie Warnick of San Mateo, CA, suggests circumventing the problem by taping a tapestry needle, eye-up, between the spool and the first thread guide on your machine.

Invisible nylon thread in the top and/or bobbin gives a machine-quilted item almost a hand-quilted look. However, it is extremely strong and doesn't give. If stress is put on your quilt, such as hanging over an edge, the fabric will rip before the invisible thread breaks. Also if you goof and have to rip out stitches, it leaves holes and may shred fabric. On smaller-than-bed quilts, there's no problem.

Silk thread is not washable.

Two matters cannot be stressed enough: (1) test threads and needle sizes on a doodle quilt sandwich before quilting; and (2) buy the best quality thread you can afford. The cheaper thread frays, breaks, shreds over the years. It's not worth saving pennies if it later causes hours of work.

(See Table 1-1, Fabric/Thread/Needle Chart.)

Transferring Designs

To transfer design lines to fabric, you will need to know about marking devices, templates, and marking methods. In general (but not always) the quilt top is marked before basting the three layers of the quilt sandwich together. The term "cartoon," which is used freely below, means a simple line drawing of a design which you can transfer.

Marking Devices

Traditionally, a soft #2 lead pencil has been used to draw directly on the quilt top—soft, so that you don't have to press hard, which would distort the fabric. However, pencil marks do not always wash out of modern-day fabrics and are hard to see on prints and medium to dark-colored fabrics. While this can be an advantage after the quilt is finished, it can be distinctly frustrating while you are sewing.

An alternative is to use colored pencils on light fabrics and a white charcoal pencil (available in quilt and art stores or see Resource list) on dark. But beware:

white charcoal rubs off with the continued rolling and unrolling of machine quilting. If you will not finish quilting in one or two sessions, use something else for marking quilting lines, or mark only as much as you can quilt in one session. White charcoal is also ideal for marking for piecing.

Recently pens that are erasable by cold water have come onto the market (see Resource list). The blue ink flows on like a felt-tipped pen, but disappears when touched with a Q-tip dipped in cold water. Be sure to test (by marking on fabric scraps) that the pen marks disappear on both the top fabric(s) *and* the backing fabric, because the marks sometimes bleed into the batting and come up in other places onto the top and backing. If you forget to wash the marks out when you finish the quilt, it is possible that the first time your quilt hits the washer, the blue lines may become set in the fabric.

Most quilters shy away from using ballpoint pens to mark fabric. Even if the ballpoint line is outside a seam line and theoretically won't show, the ink may run onto the quilt top in washing.

Also available in fabric and quilt stores are transfer pens with which the pattern is first drawn on paper and then ironed onto the fabric. The dyes in the pencil are heat-activated and sometimes bleed when wet. Be certain to test on a doodle cloth before you use such a pen.

Dressmaker's carbon paper, available in fabric stores, is used with a marking wheel or a dried-up ballpoint pen to transfer design lines to quilt tops.

For the prick-and-pounce method described below in *Marking Methods*, use light-colored pounce powder (a powdered charcoal) or any imaginative substitute, such as cornstarch, talcum or foot powder, cream of tarter, on dark fabrics and on light fabrics, use cinnamon.

Templates

Anything you trace along or around to mark pieces or quilting lines for the quilt is called a template. For straight lines, use a yardstick (make sure it's really straight by laying it on graph paper), an artists' T-square, the edge of a book, or a right angle. (These supplies are available in fabric, art supply, and hardware

Fig. 2-16 Laundry/Marker Test: refer to Table 2-2; "rows" in photo read from *right* to *left*.

Table 2-2. LAUNDRY/MARKER TEST

NG = no good
FBV = faint but visible
F/OK = faint but OK
+ = acceptable

Note: If you don't have extra fabric, do test on wrong side. Fabric tested was preshrunk 50% cotton 50% polyester.

	1	2	3	4	5	6	7	8
	#2 pencil	#3 pencil	ball-point	felt-tipped pen	water-erasable pen	blue colored pencil	trans-fer pen	Xerox transfer

first row shown at right
not treated

	1	2	3	4	5	6	7	8
1. erasers (Eberhard Faber, PlastiRace, Magic Rub, Fantastic)	NG	NG	NG	NG	NG	NG	NG	NG
2. washing soda 1 Tblsp: ½ cup warm water	F/OK	F/OK	F/OK	F/OK	+	+	+	+
3. normal detergent	NG	N	NG	NG	+	+	+	NG
4. pretreatment of hairspray + normal washing	NG	NG	NG	F/OK	+	+	+	NG
5. Grease Relief	NG	NG	NG	F/OK	+	bled	+	NG
6. E-Z-est Spot Remover (dry cleaning powder)	NG	NG	NG	NG	NG	NG	NG	NG
7. ½ cup Calgon added to normal detergent	NG	NG	NG	F/OK	+	F/OK	+	FBV
8. diluted Windex (1:1) brushed on with old toothbrush and rinsed in water only	F/OK	FBV	NG	FBV	+	+	bled	FBV

Conclusions: There are so many variables that affect whether a marking device washes out—fiber blend in fabric, type of detergent, type of water—that you really should test your own favorite marking device on each fabric you use in a quilt. A good time is when you preshrink the fabric; use the detergent you will use when washing the quilt.

stores.) Another very handy template for straight lines is masking tape in the widths you need. You can mark along both sides of it and then pick up the tape and reuse it. I am also very fond of my two see-through rulers, both available in fabric stores (see Fig. 2-17).

For wavy edges, use a scallop sewing guide, a dressmaker's French curve, or a flexible ruler (see Fig. 2-4). The latter can be bent into interesting shapes, repeated, and overlapped as shown. You can also use it to round off the floor edges of quilts. (This useful tool is inexpensive and available in art supply stores.).

For marking shapes, use household items like cookie cutters, teacups, glasses, plates, and sewing supplies like thimbles, embroidery hoops, scissors' handles; and any object that is the right shape for your design. For precise geometric shapes, draw them with a straight edge on graph paper; then spray-glue the back of the graph paper to acetate, Styrofoam meat trays, cardboard, used X-ray film, or sandpaper. Cut out the template shapes, using a straight edge (ruler)

Fig. 2-17 Anything can be used for templates: a thimble, spool of thread, scissors, cup, see-through ruler, 3″ × 5″ (7.6 × 12.7 cm) card, flexible ruler.

and an X-acto knife. Be sure to add ¼″ to ½″ (6 to 13 mm) seam allowances all around the shape if it's a template for piecing or applique. (See the Resource page for companies which sell templates for quilting.) Paper can be cut in quilting shapes, pinned to the quilt sandwich, and machine quilted around. Finally, your own stencils for marking quilting lines can be made by joining two X-acto knifes together with rubber bands or using a double-bladed knife (available in art supply stores—while you're there look at all the interesting templates that draftsmen use in their work; some are suitable for quiltmaking). If you are making a stencil for an enclosed shape, don't forget to skip cutting from time to time so the shape doesn't fall out of the stencil.

Marking Methods

The marking devices and templates mentioned above are used in two ways, direct and indirect marking methods.

Direct Marking

Trace directly onto the fabric. If it's for piecing and applique, mark on the wrong side of the fabric, including a seam allowance in the template. Be sure the marking device is kept sharp (pencil point, soap sliver, or whatever else you use) and don't push so hard you distort the fabric. If you are marking quilting lines, mark the rightside of the top fabric.

If you're brave, trace freehand or let your child, family, or class draw free-hand on the fabric. A lovely tradition is to have guests at a wedding sign their names, write messages to the couple, and/or trace their hand on pre-cut squares of fabric. These messages are later quilted and assembled into a special quilt for the newlyweds. The same idea is used in celebrity quilts where the famous sign fabric which is then quilted.

Otherwise, trace around templates, again respecting the fragile nature of woven fabric.

For large designs, trace the cartoon onto newsprint or tracing paper. During the day, you can tape the paper to a picture window and tape the fabric over it, centering the design carefully (don't center by eye—first fold the fabric into quarters, mark center with X, match centers). This works even for some dark fabrics. At night, use a lighted TV screen on a channel you don't receive. Or go outside, and use the window method by looking into a well-lit room.

Or better, use a make-shift light table. Put a sheet of clear plastic or an old window on a cardboard box (or sawhorses or two chairs) into or under which you've set a bare-bulb lamp. Cover the plastic with plain white paper so the light is diffused. Now tape down the cartoon, put the fabric over it, weight or tape it down, and trace the design.

Fig. 2-18 Trace designs by taping cartoon to window and placing fabric over it.

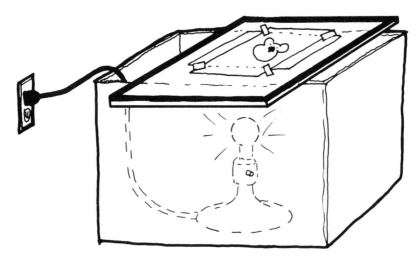

Fig. 2-19 A makeshift light table can be rigged by placing a bare light bulb in a cardboard box, placing an old window or a glass picture frame over the open top of the box, and covering the glass with plain white paper to diffuse the light. Now you can easily trace your design onto fabric.

Indirect Marking

1. Iron-on the design, either from tracings by a transfer pen or fabric crayons, or from a photocopied image. Follow the ironing directions for the pen; for the photocopied image, use the highest heat your fabric can stand, with no steam. Be sure to test on a scrap; the photocopy line does not wash out of every fabric (see Laundry/Marker Test, Fig. 2-16). Be sure to draw letters and other direction-dependent images in reverse before transferring.

2. Trace the design onto tracing paper (available at art supply stores, it's worth owning several rolls). Pin the tracing paper to the fabric, on either the quilt top or the backing, depending on the technique, and stitch through the paper and the quilt sandwich. When you are done, tear the paper away gently. Leftover paper scraps caught in the stitches can be removed with needle-nosed tweezers. The remainder will fall out and disappear the first time you wash the quilt.

When you are quilting with the presser foot on, you can stitch from the topside through the tracing paper, because the even perforations make it easy to remove the paper. However, when you are free-machine quilting, there are often several small close stitches preventing a clean break of paper, so stitch with the underside of the quilt sandwich up (meaning that the thread seen on top is the bobbin thread, so select it carefully). When working from the underside, be sure to use the wrong side of the tracing paper for nonreversible images like letters. Otherwise, you'll find that the front stitching ends up in reverse.

3. The prick-and-pounce method is ideal for machine quilting as it's done with the sewing machine (Fig. 2-21). Use a 9/10(60) unthreaded needle (so the holes won't be too big) and a piece of typing paper, acetate (available in art stores), or a manila file folder. (I like acetate because you can see what you're doing.) After copying the design, use a regular sewing stitch line, halfway between basting and fine sewing, and a presser foot. Follow the main lines of the design. Roll up a pad of felt and force pounce powder (see Marking Devices, above) through the holes of the acetate onto the fabric. Gently lift off the acetate and connect up the lines with white pencil or blue watercolor. Blow off excess powder. Save the pounced pattern

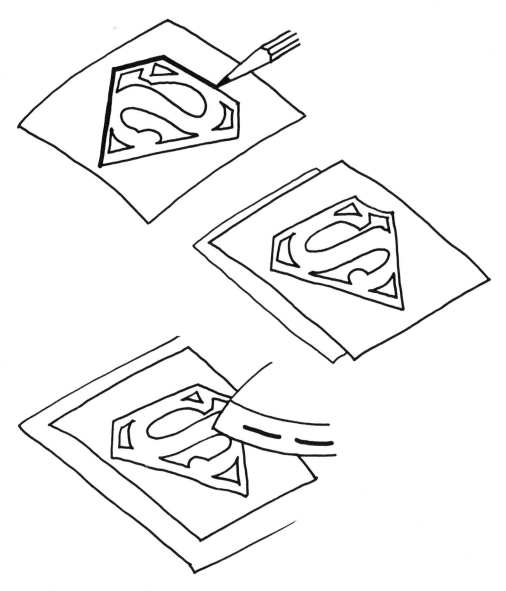

Fig. 2-20 Iron-on designs. Top: To iron-on a design, trace it with a transfer pencil (reverse letters and direction-dependent images for tracing). Middle: Place the transfer on the rightside of the fabric, pencil lines against fabric. Bottom: iron at a setting compatible with the fabric you are using.

for future use (many museums have old pounced patterns on file that women used and shared long ago). This method is especially useful for repeated quilting patterns.

Enlarging Designs

Since most books and magazines are smaller than quilts, you will often be faced with the need to enlarge a design to fit the quilt you have in mind. There are three ways appropriate to machine quilting: with an opaque projector, by the grid method, or with graph paper.

Fig. 2-21 To prick-and-pounce by machine, use a small unthreaded needle to machine stitch around your design. Middle: Tape the pricked design to your fabric and rub pounce powder (which can be anything—talcum powder, cinnamon, etc.) through the holes. Bottom: Remove the paper and connect the dots with a pencil.

1. The simplest, fastest way to enlarge a design is to use an opaque projector. You can buy a variety of models, ranging from $8 to $100 to $1000 in art supply stores (or see Resource list). The disadvantage of the smaller ones is that your design to be enlarged is often bigger than the area the projector can cover, and it is awkward to keep moving the design (or the projector) until you finish copying the cartoon.

If you belong to a guild, members can chip in to buy a cooperative opaque projector (and a light table, if you're really enthusiastic). This equipment is as useful in quiltmaking as a sewing machine. Otherwise, try to talk a quilt shop owner into buying one for customer use.

To buy a used opaque projector, call elementary or secondary schools (private and public), colleges, art schools, printers, or advertising agencies. Also try advertising in the wanted pages of local or shopper newspapers.

2. If you know the size of the quilt block you want to enlarge the design to fit, divide the fabric block into sixteen rectangles by folding it in half vertically, pressing lightly with a hot iron. Fold in half vertically again and press. Open up the fabric and fold in half horizontally, pressing carefully without destroying your previous pressed lines. Fold again horizontally and press. You have made your fabric into a 16-block *grid*.

Either copy the design (including the outside edges of the square or rectangle frame) onto tracing paper or photocopy the design. It is important for the paper your design is on to be of the same proportions as the fabric you've already gridded out. For example, if your fabric is 16″ × 20″ (40 × 50 cm), you'll get strange results if your paper is 6″ × 12″ (15 × 30 cm), but everything will work fine if your paper is 8″ × 10″ (20 × 25 cm). Fold your paper into 16 blocks as you did the fabric. Crease well with your fingers or a butter knife to get sharp folds.

Now copy onto the larger fabric grid what you see in each smaller paper grid. If a line crosses at the halfway point on one, make it cross halfway on the other.

Fig. 2-22 It's worth owning an opaque projector to enlarge designs.

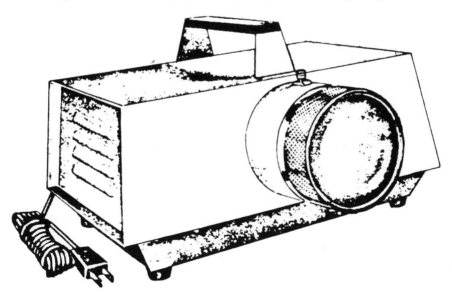

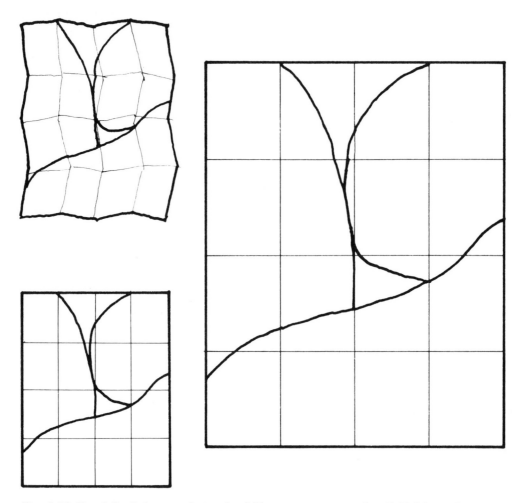

Fig. 2-23 Top, left: Enlarge a design by folding it into sixteenths. Fold fabric of proportionate size into sixteenths too. Lower left: Copy on the fabric what you see in each square of the original design. Right: If the fabric is not of proportionate size, the enlarged design will be distorted (which is sometimes intentionally done).

Duplicate one block at a time and before long, your design will be perfectly blown up to the exact size you need. If you have trouble with this, turn the original design upside down while you're working. Somehow it's easier; you get less confused.

3. The graph paper method is the same as the *grid method*, but more detailed. Lay graph paper over your design and trace it, using a light table, if necessary. (Or draw a grid of ½" or 1"—1 or 2 cm—blocks over your design.) Decide how much bigger (or smaller) you want the design. Let's say twice as big. On the same scale graph paper (you may have to tape several sheets together), rule off every second line in each direction. You now have squares twice as big as the original. As in grid method above, copy into each larger square what you see in each smaller square. If the design is complicated, number and letter each piece of graph paper as shown in the illustration to keep from becoming confused.

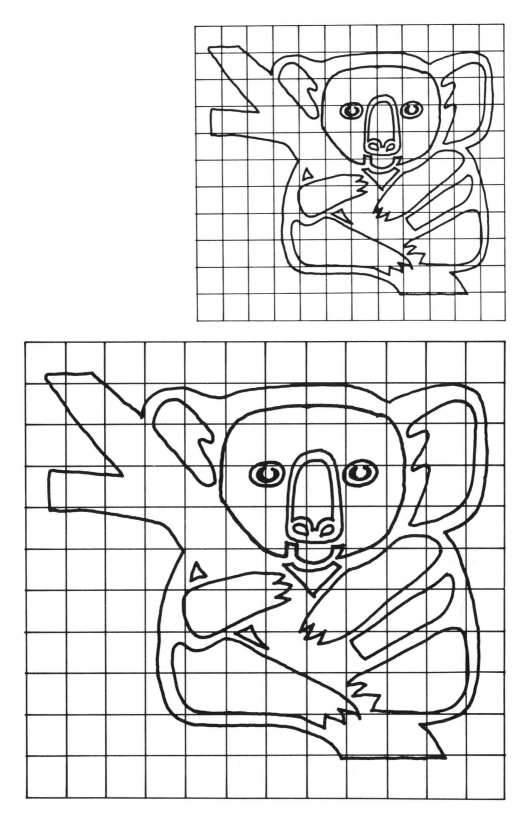

Fig. 2-24 Tracing a pattern: Lay graph paper over your design and trace it. Decide how much bigger you want the design and make a grid that large. Copy on the larger grid what you see in the smaller.

How Much Material Do You Need?

Standard Bed Sizes

These are the sizes usually given for new beds. However, you will find over the years of making quilts that there really is no "standard" and that every bed should be measured before making a quilt for it. Besides the dimensions of the mattress top, the other two important measurements are *the drop,* which is the distance from the top of the mattress (with sheets and blankets on) to the floor, and *the tuck,* which is the amount of extra fabric added to the mattress length so the quilt can be tucked under the pillows and still cover them. These two measurements vary widely, depending on whether people sleep on box springs, platforms, waterbeds, folding foam beds, or with six pillows.

Once you've decided a particular bed needs a quilt, make a sloper for the bed. (Sloper, pronounced slow-purr, is a term borrowed from sewing, meaning a master pattern.) On graph paper (¼" or centimeter), draw the dimensions of your bed, labeling all parts and whose bed it is. Now you can design for this bed by putting tracing paper over the sloper and trying out various blocks, colors, and layouts. Don't ever draw on the sloper itself; keep it flat in a file or drawer and you can use it for years. It isn't difficult to keep one sloper for each bed in your house. When the time comes to whip out a machine quilt, you can pull them out and go right to work, designing.

Estimating Yardage

How much fabric and batting you need obviously depends on the size and complexity of your quilt. Most of us rarely go out and buy fresh yardage all at once for an entire quilt. We may buy the backing and some important color, but we add bits and pieces from our overflowing stockrooms for the rest of the quilt.

Therefore it's tricky to estimate accurately. If you are browsing in a fabric store and see something you would like to combine with other fabrics, buy a minimum of

Table 2-3. Standard Bed Sizes

	Mattress (cm)	Coverlet including Standard 22" (56cm) Drop + 15" (38 cm) Tuck	Estimated Backing Yardage for Coverlet		Approximate Continuous Binding Needed*		
			36" wide(100cm)	45" wide(115cm)	inches	yards	meters
twin	39" × 75" (99 × 190)	83" × 112" (211 × 284)	9⅓ (8.49m)	5 (4.55m)	400	11⅛	(10.16)
full (double)	54" × 75" (137 × 190)	98" × 112" (249 × 284)	9⅓ (8.49m)	9¾ (8.87m)	430	12	(10.92)
queen	60" × 80" (152 × 203)	104" × 117" (264 × 297)	9¾ (8.87m)	9¾ (8.87m)	452	12½	(11.48)
king	72" × 84" (183 × 213)	116" × 121" (295 × 307)	13½ (12.28m)	10¼ (9.32m)	484	13½	(12.29)

List your beds here (include drop, number of pillows, tuck, preferred colors, misc. notes):

....

....

....

....

....

*See charts in Edge Treatment for how many yards of fabric will yield x yd. continuous binding.

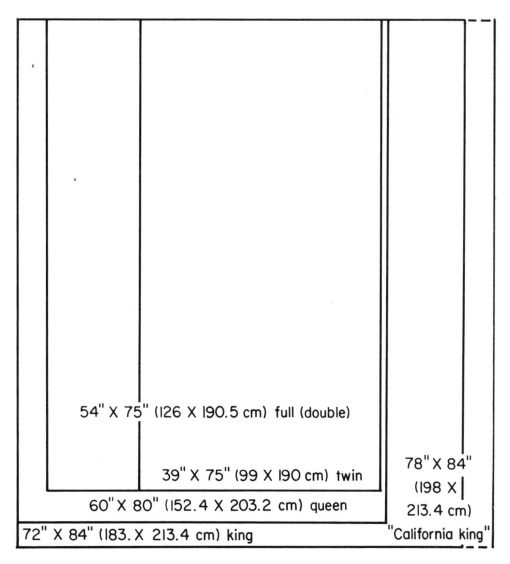

54" X 75" (126 X 190.5 cm) full (double)

39" X 75" (99 X 190 cm) twin

60" X 80" (152.4 X 203.2 cm) queen

78" X 84" (198 X 213.4 cm)

72" X 84" (183. X 213.4 cm) king

"California king"

Fig. 2-25 Standard bed size measurements for mattress tops.

3 yards (2.73 m); 5 to 6 yards (4.55 to 5.46 m) would be better. If you want to use the fabric for an entire top or backing, see the Standard Bed Size Chart above. You'll want closer to 10 yards (9.1 m) than 3.

To estimate yardage for a traditional pieced-top quilt, there is an easy way and a harder way. The easy way is to refer to *The Patchwork Quilt Design and Coloring Book* (see Bibliography), which has pages of calculations and templates for 50 traditional patterns, telling how much 36" and 45" wide (100 cm and 115 cm) fabric to buy for different block sizes.

The harder way is to draw a sample block on graph paper and measure each component of the block, including seam allowances. Multiply each component by the total number in the quilt; then use a pocket calculator to figure out how many components will fit across your fabric width. Don't forget that the useable width

Table 2-4. Yardage Conversion Chart

for every yard (meter) of material this wide that your pattern calls for:

		36" (1m)	45" (1.15m)	54" (1.37m)	60" (1.52m)
You can use this many yards (meters) this wide:	36" (1m)	1 (.91	1¼ (1.14)	1½ (1.37)	1⅔ (1.52)
	45" (1.15m)	⅞ (.80)	1 (.91)	1¼ (1.14)	1⅓ (1.22)
	54" (1.37m)	¾ (.68)	⅞ (.80)	1 (.91)	1⅛ (1.02)
	60" (1.52m)	⅝ (.57)	¾ (.68)	1 (.91)	1 (.91)

Example: The project calls for 2½ yd 45" wide fabric. Your fabric is 36" wide. What length of 36" do you need? For every yard of 45", you need 1¼ yd of 36". 2½ times 1¼ yd. = 3⅛ yd. (Use your calculator: 2.5 × 1.25 = 3.125.)

and length are each 2" to 4" (5 to 10 cm) less than store-bought, after cutting off selvages and straightening the ends. Divide that number into the total components needed; multiply *that* number by the number of inches or centimeters your template stretches along the length of the fabric.

For more modern quilt designs, the calculations are even more vague. If there are many seams in your quilt, you will need more yardage than given above (in the Standard Bed Size Chart) to line a quilt. For insurance, always buy one yard or meter more than your calculated amount; paying a few dollars extra is little compared to the pain of running out of fabric in the middle of a quilt.

For the projects in this book, we've calculated the yardage for you, mostly based on 45" (115 cm) wide fabric. If your chosen fabric is wider or narrower, use Table 2-4 to figure out how much yardage to buy.

Basting: The Secret Of Pucker-Free Machine Quilting

The single greatest problem of machine quilting comes from the very nature of a quilt—three layers of material, which can become misaligned. Here's how to overcome it.

Let's assume that you have a finished quilt top, some batting, and a backing, all ready to be quilted together—in other words, a quilt sandwich. How do you keep the components together while you pass them through the machine for quilting? How do you keep them from clumping, lumping, and puckering after you've sewn them together?

Most instructions for machine quilting blithely tell you to baste the quilt sandwich in intersecting thread X's from the center out or in a grid of thread lines. Most of those who have tried this are still wondering why they have puckers on the backing.

One secret to pucker-free machine quilting is proper basting, which depends on your *treatment of the backing,* not on the basting itself. If, as usually instructed, you lay the backing on a flat surface, smooth the batting and top in place, and pin or thread-baste, chances are you will have puckers on the back unless you are extremely experienced. The backing must be treated sternly. You have three good choices for doing this: (1) You can put the backing in a traditional quilting frame while you baste; (2) you can double-baste; or (3) you can tape all edges of the backing to a firm foundation like a tile floor or Ping Pong table before basting. But you can't be so zealous that you overstretch the backing—it will bounce back when you remove it from the frame (or take off the tape) and then cause puckers in the top.

Frame Basting

Quilting frames have been around a long time, and many hand quilters do most of their quilting on the frame. But for machine quilting, none of the actual quilting is done on the frame—only the basting is. (If you don't own a frame, skip ahead for instructions on making one.)

To baste in a traditional frame (which can often be borrowed for several hours from a friend or guild), balance the frames on saw horses or chairs or work on the floor. If you can manage to work over a table, so much the easier—but it's not necessary. The ironed backing should be placed topside down; if you pieced it, you'll be looking at the seams. Using straight pins, pin one long side of the backing to the tape on the frame, working from the center out. Repeat for the opposite long side.

Using C-clamps, fasten the short sides of the frame to the long sides. If there is canvas tape on your frames to pin into, put the short frames (tape side down) on top of the long frames (tape side up). Check where the two boards meet with a right angle to be sure the boards form a perfect 90° angle. Now pin the short sides of the backing to the short sides of the quilting frame. Remember not to over-stretch the backing. When you are done with this step, the backing is entirely attached at its edges to the quilting frame.

Spread the batting over the backing, smoothing it out. Then spread the marked quilt top over the two layers. Smooth it out by stroking it with a yardstick. Pin all around and perpendicular to the perimeter of the quilt sandwich, placing the pin heads out and the pin points in. Pin and repin until you are satisfied with the placement of the top.

Now you are ready to begin the actual basting of the components to each other. Take your choice of three methods of basting: straight pins, thread, or safety pins.

If you use straight pins, use extra-long ones with large glass heads. Always pin in one direction only, so that when you finish machine quilting, you can run your hands over the quilt to check for missed pins and not impale yourself. The extra-long pins, available in quilt or fabric stores (or see Resources List), are less likely to jump out as you sew. This method of basting is not recommended for quilts larger than crib-size. Even the long pins will come out as the larger quilt sandwich is later rolled and unrolled. If you do use pins, be sure they are steel. They may stay in your quilt for a long time, depending on how fast you work, and you don't want them rusting in the fabric.

Thread-basting is done by hand with one strand of any sewing thread, taking deliciously long and sloppy stitches. You can even let children help baste; you don't have to worry about the look of their stitches, since they'll come out. If you make parallel rows of stitching along the long side of the quilt sandwich, spacing the lines about 6″ to 8″ (15 to 20 cm) apart, you need only put in three or four rows

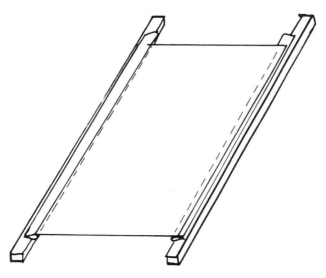

Fig. 2-27 Pin the two long sides of the backing (which is rightside down) to the two long frames.

of thread-basting the other way, across the quilt. Some experienced quilters recommend the tailor basting stitch. Others like to use a curved needle to baste; since both hands work on top, you can reach in farther before needing to roll the quilt. To roll up the quilt as you baste, undo the C-clamps on one long side. Unpin the backing only, and roll the quilt onto the long side. Replace the C-clamps. For large quilts, it's much easier to have someone help you roll.

Safety pins are the simplest way to baste. Use 1½" (3.8 cm) steel safety pins, again so they won't rust in the fabric. Ernest B. Haight, whose book is worth owning (see Bibliography; also see Chapter 4), uses about 200 safety pins for an 80" × 96" (203 × 243 cm) quilt, placing them about 6" to 7" (15 to 18 cm) apart. Look in resale stores, Army-Navy surplus stores, and at garage sales for used safety pins.

Whichever method of basting you use, when you are done, remove the rest of the straight pins that hold the backing to the frames (but don't remove those that hold the quilt sandwich together). Take the basted quilt to the machine and machine-baste ¼" from the edge all the way around, removing the perpendicular straight pins holding the top to the backing as you work. Sewing over pins dulls the needle; don't do it. You are now ready to machine quilt (see Chapter 4).

If you don't own a quilting frame, you can make one easily. It's well worth it to take advantage of this satisfying method of basting. At a hardware/lumber store, ask for two straight-grained fir 1 × 2s (2.5 × 5 cm), each a foot (30 cm) longer than the long side of your quilt (see standard measurements, p.56); and two more

Fig. 2-26 Upper left: If you don't have a quilting frame, a trip to the lumberyard is the first step in making one. Upper right: Stapling tape around frame. Middle: Straight pins are used to attach backing to frame. Bottom: In machine quilting, basting is the only thing done on a frame.

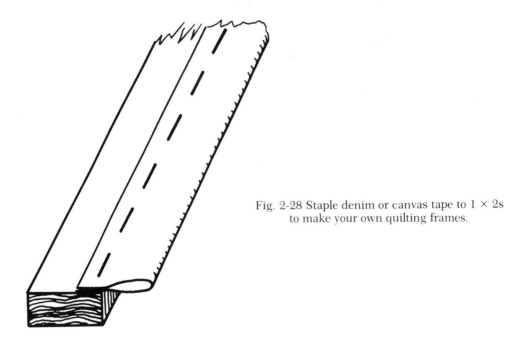

Fig. 2-28 Staple denim or canvas tape to 1 × 2s
to make your own quilting frames.

lengths of straight-grained fir 1 × 2s a foot longer than the short side of your quilt;
and four 2½″ (6.35 cm) C-clamps. (This would cost about $20 for a king-sized
quilt.)

Staple denim, pillow ticking, or canvas tape to each wide edge of the four
frame pieces (see Fig. 2-26, where I used a doubled layer of canvas material 4″ or
10 cm wide, doubled over like belting). If you're really a perfectionist, you will

Fig. 2-29 Making sure the edges of the frames are at right
angles to each other, pin the remaining two sides of the
backing to the short frames.

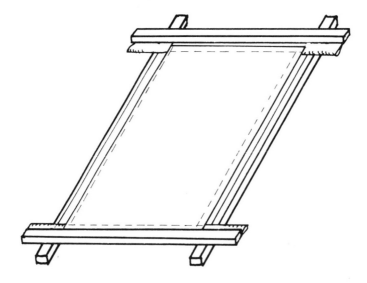

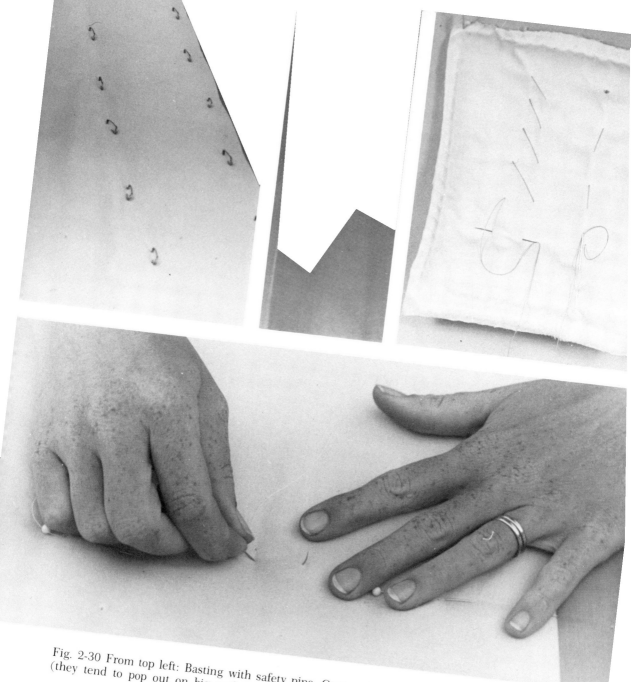

Fig. 2-30 From top left: Basting with safety pins. Center: Basting with long straight pins (they tend to pop out on big quilts). Right: Tailor basting and straight thread basting. Bottom: Basting with a curved needle.

mark the center of each board on the tape. When you clamp the pieces together, always make sure the pinning fabrics face each other (Fig. 2-31).

Double-Basting

Another method to ensure pucker-free machine-quilted quilts is to double-baste. This means basting the backing to the batting, then the top to this double layer. For this method try to have the backing 2″ (5 cm) wider than the batting or

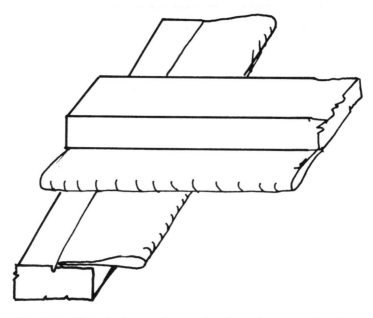

Fig. 2-31 With C-clamps, fasten the short frames to the long frames, tape edges meeting.

Fig. 2-32 Top: To double-baste, lay the backing *over* the batting, tape or weight the fabric down, and baste. Bottom: Turn the basted material over. Lay the top on and baste again.

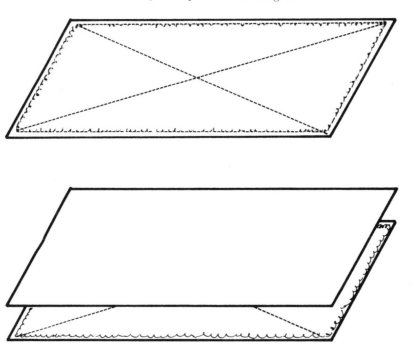

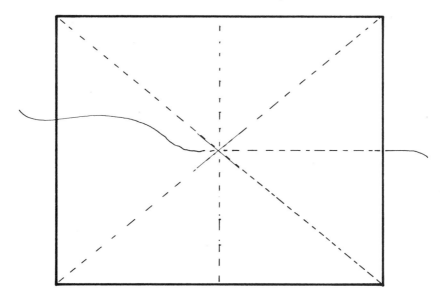

Fig. 2-33 Baste in intersecting Xs. A trick: Cut your thread twice as long as you normally would. Start in the center and pull the thread halfway through, leaving half the thread at center. Baste out in one direction to the edge. Then thread the needle with the long tail left in the center and baste out in the other direction.

top (not always possible if, for example, you're using sheets). Spread the batting on a flat hard surface. Smooth the backing *over* the batting, underside of the backing against the batting. Tape or weight the edges down. Do not overstretch the backing. Straight-pin or thread-baste the two layers together. Release the edges and turn over so the backing is underneath. Tape the edges again. Smooth the top in place and pin or thread-baste. You have now double-basted. If you pin-basted the backing, remove the pins from the lining side.

Taping the Backing For Basting

Tape the backing all the way around, securing it to a firm surface without overstretching it. Smooth on the batting and top. Pin or baste all three layers of the quilt sandwich. Since you can't get your fingers underneath to help push pins through and up, thread basting is easier, especially if you can learn to use a curved needle.

A Method of Basting *Not* Recommended

The only way heartily *not* recommended for machine quilting is to smooth the backing, lay the other two layers on, and baste. When you do it this way, if your fingers can easily get in under the backing to baste, so can Pucker's.

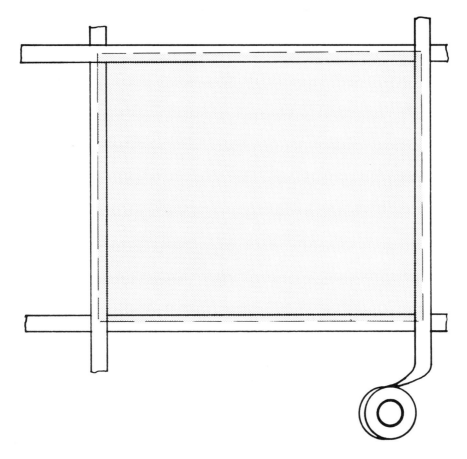

Fig. 2-34 Tape the backing to a hard surface before basting.

Finishing Your Quilt by Machine

Edge Treatments

There are at least five ways to finish the edges of a quilt.

1. Continuous binding—sew one long piece of binding around the four edges of the quilt.
2. Lapped binding—sew a piece of binding on each quilt edge and lap the bindings at the corners.
3. Inserted edge—edge material is placed between the backing and the top and sewn into place.
4. Mitered corners.
5. A machine curiosity.

However, with the wide range of materials and techniques available to machine quilters, you can expect to see an increasing number of nontraditional finishes to machine-quilted quilts—fringes, loops, scallops, tucks, Ultrasuede binding, and more. For example, the side drops on quilts do not necessarily have to be quilted, as long as they are balanced in weight against the quilted part. Why not take giant tucks or stitch rows of flappets (Fig. 2-35) instead of quilting that part?

Fig. 2-35 (Left to right from top) Continuous binding. Lapped binding. Mitered corners. Inserted edge.

Continuous Binding

The simplest of all bindings is sewing one long piece of material around all the quilt edges, without mitering. To do so, round off the corners of your quilt, using the edge of a teacup, plate, or French curve to make a smooth line. Zigzag or straight stitch the edge of your quilt before applying the binding. This makes it easier to fold the binding over the edge. At the four curves, clip the quilt and binding almost to the seam before turning the binding over the edge (Fig. 2-36).

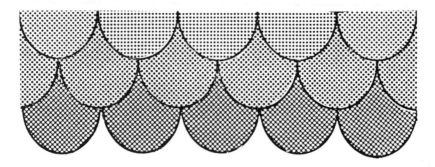

Fig. 2-35 (continued) Rows of flappets.

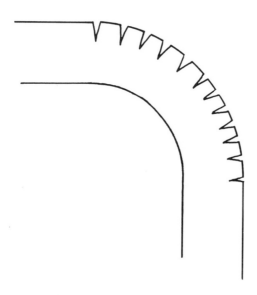

Fig. 2-36 When you don't want to miter corners, round the edges of your quilt and apply the binding continuously. Clip the binding and the quilt to the stitching line. (Note: This method looks best with bias binding, not straight-grain binding.)

You can buy binding, but your quilts will look better if you make the long strips from material which matches the rest of the quilt. How much binding will you need to make? Add the width of your quilt to its length, multiply this sum by two, and add 10″ (25 cm) for safety. This edging can be made from either the bias or the straight-grain of the fabric. (Ernest B. Haight prefers the latter.)

First we'll show how to put the binding on; then we'll show how to join ends, how to make your own bias binding, and how to calculate how much yardage you need for binding.

In order to do it all by machine, work from the back of the quilt to the front, in either of two ways:

Single fold continuous binding. Start binding on the underside of the quilt halfway down one side. Don't start bindings at a quilt corner. Leave 2″ (5 cm) of unstitched binding to be joined at the end. With right side of binding against right side of backing, seam all around the quilt, allowing at least a ½″ (13 mm) seam. (A

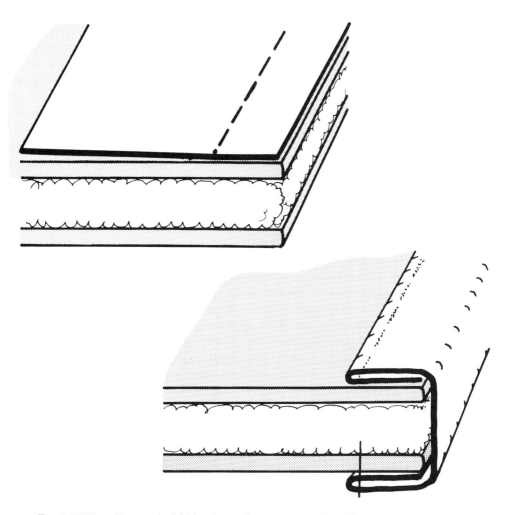

Fig. 2-37 Top: For single-fold binding, place one raw edge of the binding against the raw edges of the quilt. Stitch. Bottom: Fold the binding over the edge, turn under the seam allowance, and hand or machine-stitch the edge down.

smaller seam is tricky—if you are inaccurate in seaming, the quilt may pull away from the binding.)

Fold in the raw edge of the binding to the raw edge of the quilt. Then fold the binding up to and a little beyond the seamline on the topside. Pin in place and sew down near the edge. (Optional: Use a walking foot to keep the fabric from shifting and invisible thread in the bobbin if you fear your stitching line will wobble back and forth over the binding seam line on the back.)

Note: It is faster, initially, to use purchased bias tape, but there are several reasons why you should think twice about it. For one, the colors do not always match your fabrics exactly. Secondly, the turn-under is usually only ¼" (6 mm), which makes for a weak edge. You could always buy wider bias tape, iron it flat, and use a wider seam allowance. And finally, with light-colored binding, the fabric of your quilt often shows through, which looks awful.

The binding is usually the first part of your quilt to show wear. If you have to replace a purchased bias-tape edge with home-made bias binding sooner than

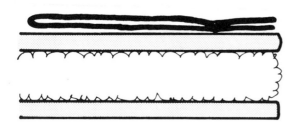

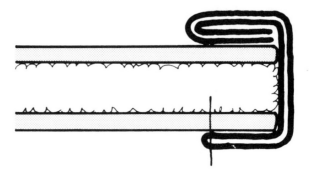

Fig. 2-38 Top: For French fold binding, fold the binding in half the long way, wrongsides together. Place the raw edges of the binding against the raw edges of the quilt and stitch. Bottom: Fold the binding over the edge and hand or machine-stitch the edge down. If you work from the underside of quilt first, you can do it all by machine.

normal, how much time have you really saved? If you do use purchased binding, be sure to preshrink it.

French fold continuous binding. Cut the bias strip six times as wide as what you want to show on the front and add two times the loft (at least ¼" or 6 mm) to allow for quilt thickness. Fold the strip in half lengthwise, wrong sides together, and press lightly. Leave a 2" (5 cm) end on the binding for joining to the other end. On the underside of the quilt, stitch the binding to backing, right sides and raw edges together. Fold the binding up over the quilt edge, as in the single-fold method, and pin a little beyond the seam on the topside. Sitch as in single-fold method.

How to join ends. To join edges of bias binding, leave 2" (5 cm) unstitched when you begin and end the binding. Fold the quilt and match the two binding edges. Sew across the binding, joining ends (See Fig. 2-39 top). Unfold quilt and fill in missing stitches.

On thin quilts and small items (such as placemats and potholders) fold the beginning end to the wrongside ½" (12 mm). When you reach the starting point after stitching all around the item, lap the end over the beginning 1" (See Fig. 2-39 bottom).

How to make your own continuous binding. To make *continuous straight grain binding*, mark along the length of your fabric on the rightside as wide as binding (Fig. 2-40). You will probably have to discard the last section marked, if it is less wide than the width of binding you need. Fold the fabric in half and match A to A, B to B, and so forth. The first width of binding will extend above the folded fabric.

70

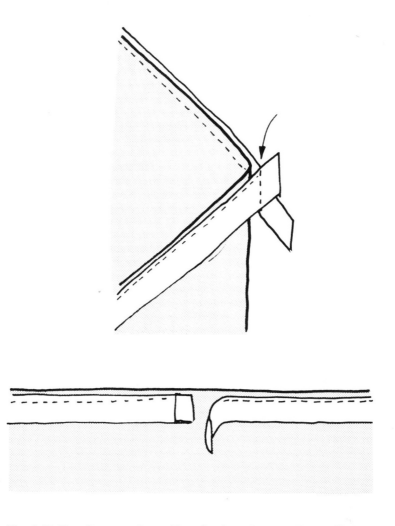

Fig. 2-39 Top: Joining edges of bias binding. Bottom: On small items, overlap edges of bias binding.

Sew a ¼″ (6 mm) seam. Press open. Turn rightside out, Cut along the marked lines and your binding will be continuous.

To make *continuous bias binding*, fold the upper left corner down to meet the lower edge, forming a square. Mark the diagonal line this fold makes (which is true bias). Cut along the diagonal line and move the triangle formed to the right crosswise edge of the fabric (Fig. 2-41). Sew a ¼″ (6 mm) seam.

On the rightside of the fabric, mark diagonal lines across the parallelogram you just made as wide as your binding requires. Be careful: the bias width is "a", not "b", as shown in Fig. 2-41. The bias width "a" is perpendicular to the diagonal lines; "b" is larger than the width you need.

Fold the parallelogram in half, matching A with A at the seam lines, B with B, etc. (Fig. 2-41). Sew a ¼″ (6 mm) seam. Press open. Turn rightside out. The first strip will extend to the left of the seam. Cut along the marked lines for a continuous bias strip (Fig. 2-41).

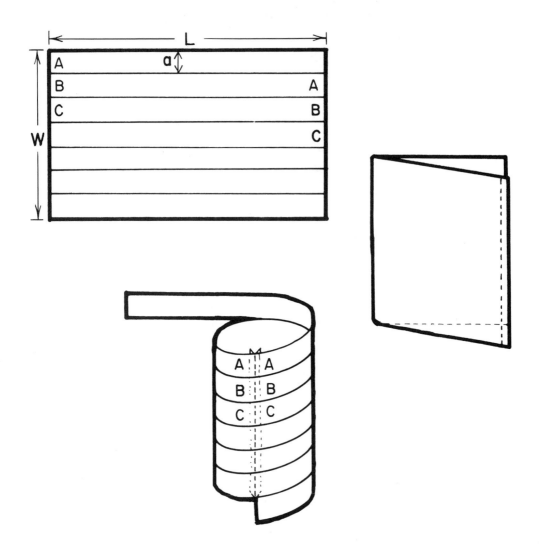

Fig. 2-40 Continuous straight grain binding. Top, left: Marking your fabric to width of binding. Right: Fold fabric, matching marks, and stitch a ¼″ (6 mm) seam. Bottom: Cut along marked lines for continuous binding.

How to calculate yardage

Calculate what length of continuous binding you need:

	quilt length	_____
+	quilt width	_____
=		_____
		× 2
		_____
		+ 10″ (25 cm) overlap
=	inches (cm) needed	_____

(divide by 36 to get number of yards needed; divide by 100 to get number of meters needed)

Now ask yourself four questions:

1. What method of binding, single or French fold?
2. Straight-grain or bias binding?
3. How wide a finished edge on the front?
4. How wide is the fabric you're buying/using?

Fig. 2-41 Continuous bias binding. Top, left: Finding the true bias. Middle: Mark diagonals the width of the bias you want. Bottom: Matching diagonals and sewing seam before cutting. Right: When you are finished cutting, your continuous bias strip will look like this.

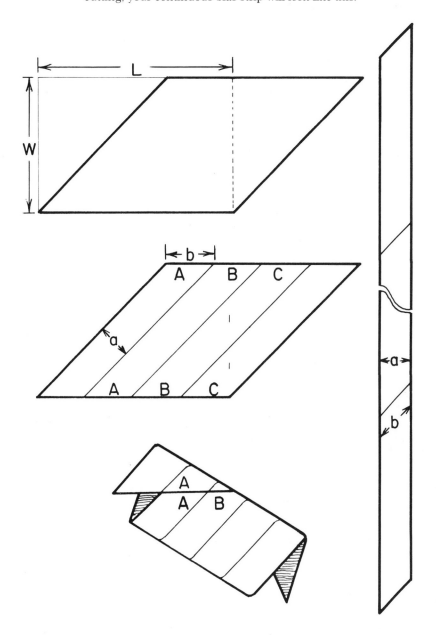

To find out how many yards of fabric to buy to get the number of inches(yd) of continuous binding you need, consult the appropriate table:

Table 2–5   Straight-grain Single Fold
Table 2–6   Straight-grain French Fold
Table 2–7   Bias Single Fold, for widths of 36″, 45″, 54″, 60″ (91.6, 114.3, 137.2, 152.4 cm)
Table 2–8   Bias French Fold, for widths of 36″, 45″, 54″, 60″ (91.6, 114.3, 137.2, 152.4 cm)

Note: All calculations based on useable fabric width—e.g., after trimming 36″ or 1 m wide fabric, useable width is approximately 34″ or 95 cm.

How to use the tables:

Example 1. For a king-size coverlet, the Standard Bed Size Chart says we need 484″ of continuous binding. We choose to make a single-fold bias binding 1″ wide. Our chosen fabric is 45″ wide fabric. We look at Table 2-7 for 45″ wide fabric. For a finished 1″ edge, one yard of fabric will yield 300″ of bias strips cut 4¼″ wide. We need 184″ more. Each bias strip is 60″ long across the fabric, so we need four more strips (three strips would only yield 180″).

$$4 \text{ strips} \times 6'' \text{ each strip} = 24'' = 2 \text{ feet} = \tfrac{2}{3} \text{ yd.}$$

We need one yard + ⅔ yard = 1⅔ yd to cover the edge of the king-sized coverlet in continuous binding.

Table 2-5. CONTINUOUS STRAIGHT-GRAIN BINDING, SINGLE FOLD

Finished Front Width in (cm)	Cut Strip This Wide*	Number of Inches (Yards)/Meters of Binding You Can Get from Each Yard of Material if it is This Wide			
		36″ (1m) in(yd)/m	45″ (1.15m) in(yd)/m	54″ (1.35m) in(yd)/m	60″ (1.50m) in(yd)/m
½ (1.3)	2¼ (8.2)	510(15)/12.95	817(19)/20.80	1196(23)/30.38	1450(25)/36.83
¾ (2.0)	3¼ (8.2)	340(10)/8.63	559(13)/14.20	832(16)/21.13	986(17)/25.04
1 (2.5)	4¼ (10.8)	272(8)/6.91	430(10)/10.92	624(12)/15.85	754(13)/19.15
1½ (3.8)	6¼ (15.8)	170(5)/4.32	258(6)/6.55	416(8)/10.57	522(9)/13.26
2 (5.1)	8¼ (21.0)	136(4)/3.45	215(5)/5.46	312(6)/7.92	406(7)/10.31

*4 times finished edge + loft, calculated for ¼″ or 6 mm loft

Table 2-6. CONTINUOUS STRAIGHT-GRAIN BINDING, FRENCH FOLD

Finished Front Width in (cm)	Cut Strip This Wide*	Number of Inches (Yards)/Meters of Binding You Can Get from Each Yard of Material if it is This Wide			
		36″ (1m) in(yd)/m	45″ (1.15m) in(yd)/m	54″ (1.35m) in(yd)/m	60″ (1.50m) in(yd)/m
½ (1.3)	3¼″ (8.2)	340(10)/8.63	559(13)/14.20	832(16)/21.13	986(17)/25.04
¾ (2.0)	4¾″ (12.1)	238(7)/6.05	387(9)/9.83	520(10)/13.21	696(12)/17.68
1 (2.5)	6¼″ (15.8)	170(5)/4.32	258(6)/6.55	416(8)/10.57	522(9)/13.26
1½ (3.8)	7¾″ (19.7)	136(4)/3.45	215(5)/5.46	312(6)/7.92	406(7)/10.31
2 (5.1)	12¼″ (13.1)	68(2)/1.73	129(3)/3.28	216(4)/5.49	232(4)/5.89

*(6 times finished edge + 2 times loft—calculated for ¼″ or 6 mm loft)

Example 2. You have a double-bed coverlet and only one yard of gorgeous 36″ wide fabric for binding. What is the best width and method of binding to use and not run out of fabric? The Standard Bed Size Chart (Table 2-3) says you need 430″ (12 yd) binding. Looking at each table under 36″ wide fabric, you see that you have enough fabric to make a ½″ straight-grain or bias single-fold binding, but not enough for any wider edge or for a French fold edge.

Table 2-7. CONTINUOUS BIAS BINDING, SINGLE FOLD

	Finished Front Width		Cut Strip This Wide		Length of Bias Strip		Number Strips Per Yard	in(yd)/m Continuous Binding/yd	Additional Yardage Per Strip
	in	*cm*	*in*	*cm*	*in*	*cm*			*yd(m)*
36″ (1m) wide fabric	½	1.3	2¼	5.7	47	119	11	517(14⅜)/13.13	⅛ (.11)
	¾	2.0	3¼	8.2	47	119	7	329(9⅛)/8.36	⅛ (.11)
	1	2.5	4¼	10.8	47	119	5	235(6½)/5.97	⅙ (.15)
	1½	3.8	6¼	15.8	47	119	4	188(5¼)/4.76	¼ (.23)
	2	5.1	8¼	21.0	47	119	3	141(4)/3.58	⅓ (.30)
45″ (1.15m) wide fabric	½	1.3	2¼	5.7	60	152	11	660(18⅓)/16.76	⅛ (.11)
	¾	2.0	3¼	8.2	60	152	7	420(11⅔)/10.67	⅛ (.11)
	1	2.5	4¼	10.8	60	152	5	300(8⅓)/7.62	⅙ (.15)
	1½	3.8	6¼	15.8	60	152	4	240(6⅓)/6.10	¼ (.23)
	2	5.1	8¼	21.0	60	152	3	180(5)/4.57	⅓ (.30)
54″ (1.35m) wide fabric	½	1.3	2¼	5.7	73	185	11	803(22⅓)/20.39	⅛ (.11)
	¾	2.0	3¼	8.2	73	185	7	511(14⅛)/12.98	⅛ (.11)
	1	2.5	4¼	10.8	73	185	5	365(10⅛)/9.27	⅙ (.15)
	1½	3.8	6¼	15.8	73	185	4	292(8⅛)/7.42	¼ (.23)
	2	5.1	8¼	21.0	73	185	3	219(6)/5.56	⅓ (.30)
60″ (1.50m) wide fabric	½	1.3	2¼	5.7	81	206	11	891(24¾)/22.63	⅛ (.11)
	¾	2.0	3¼	8.2	81	206	7	567(15¾)/14.40	⅛ (.11)
	1	2.5	4¼	10.8	81	206	5	405(11¼)/10.28	⅙ (.15)
	1½	3.8	6¼	15.8	81	206	4	324(9)/8.23	¼ (.23)
	2	5.1	8¼	21.0	81	206	3	243(6¾)/6.17	⅓ (.30)

Table 2-8. CONTINUOUS BIAS BINDING, FRENCH FOLD

	Finished Front Width		Cut Strip This Wide		Length of Bias Strip		Number Strips per Yard	in(yd)/m Continuous Binding/yd	Additional Yardage per strip
	in	*cm*	*in*	*cm*	*in*	*cm*			*yd(m)*
36" (1m) wide fabric	½	1.3	3¼	8.2	47	119	7	329(9⅛)/8.36	⅛ (.11)
	¾	2.0	4¾	12.1	47	119	5	235(6½)/5.97	⅙ (.15)
	1	2.5	6¼	15.8	47	119	4	188(5¼)/4.76	¼ (.23)
	1½	3.8	7¾	19.7	47	119	3	141(4)/3.58	⅜ (.34)
	2	5.1	12¼	31.1	47	119	2	94(2½)/2.38	½ (.46)
45" (1.15m) wide fabric	½	1.3	3¼	8.2	60	152	7	420(11⅔)/10.67	⅛ (.11)
	¾	2.0	4¾	12.1	60	152	5	300(8⅓)/7.62	⅙ (.15)
	1	2.5	6¼	15.8	60	152	4	240(6⅔)/6.10	¼ (.23)
	1½	3.8	7¾	19.7	60	152	3	180(5)/4.57	⅜ (.34)
	2	5.1	12¼	31.1	60	152	2	120(3⅓)/30.48	½ (.46)
54" (1.35m) wide fabric	½	1.3	3¼	8.2	73	185	7	511(14⅛)/12.98	⅛ (.11)
	¾	2.0	4¾	12.1	73	185	5	365(10⅛)/9.27	⅙ (.15)
	1	2.5	6¼	15.8	73	185	4	292(8⅛)/7.42	¼ (.23)
	1½	3.8	7¾	19.7	73	185	3	219(6)/5.56	⅜ (.34)
	2	5.1	12¼	31.1	73	185	2	146(4)/37.08	½ (.46)
60" (1.50m) wide fabric	½	1.3	3¼	8.2	81	206	7	567(15¾)/14.40	⅛ (.11)
	¾	2.0	4¾	12.1	81	206	5	405(11¼)/10.28	⅙ (.15)
	1	2.5	6¼	15.8	81	206	4	324(9)/8.23	¼ (.23)
	1½	3.8	7¾	19.7	81	206	3	243(6¾)/6.17	⅜ (.34)
	2	5.1	12¼	31.1	81	206	2	162(4½)/41.14	½ (.46)

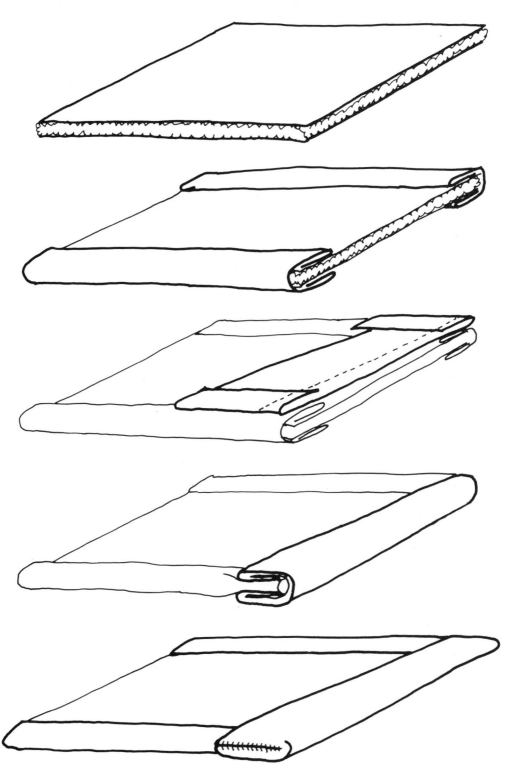

Fig. 2-42 From top down: Quilt is ready for lapped binding. Sew single fold binding to opposite ends of the quilt. Turn under the ends ½″ (12 mm). Sew single fold binding to the remaining two sides. Fold binding around quilt, turning under the ends ½″ (12 mm). Close the ends with the toymaker's ladder stitch.

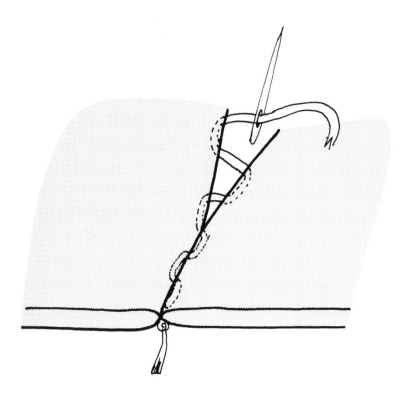

Fig. 2-43 The toymaker's ladder stitch alternates between the two edges being joined, always running inside the fold.

Lapped Binding

Bind two opposite edges of the quilt, using single-fold or French-fold continuous binding. Be sure to turn under the top and bottom edges ½″. Then bind the other two edges, including the binding you just finished (Fig. 2-42). Handstitch the ends closed, using a ladder stitch (Fig. 2-43).

Inserted Edge

Any number of decorative treatments can be inserted at the edge—for example, large rickrack, ruffles, cording, or triangles. Fold back the backing and batting. Sew the pre-shrunk trim to the top only, right sides together. The part of the trim that extends to the left of the seam line will stick out of the finished quilt edge. Trim the batting close to the stitching line. Fold the top over the batting on the stitched line. Press. Fold the backing and pin it in place. Stitch close to edge (Fig. 2-44).

Another way is to lay the decorative insertion (rightsides together) against the quilt top. Lay a ribbon or piece of bias binding on top (with seam closest to quilt edge opened out), rightside to the insertion's wrong side. Stitch; grade seam. Then fold bias to underside and hand stitch in place (stitches exaggerated for photo).

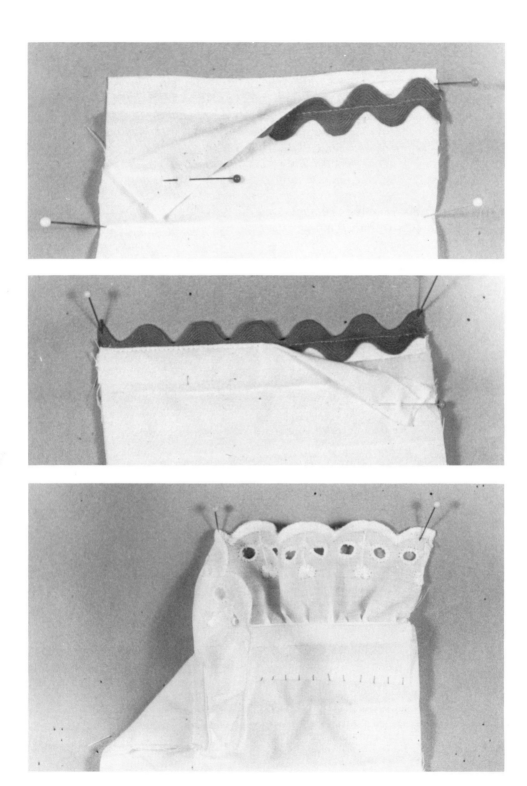

Fig. 2-44 Top: For an inserted edge, rickrack is sewn to the top edge only. Middle: The batting is trimmed to the top edge, which has been turned in. The backing is turned under and stitched close to the edge. Bottom: Bias binding is stitched to the lace insert.

Mitered Edges

I have always had trouble visualizing and remembering how to miter corners. Every time I make a quilt, it's like starting at zero again. Surely I'm not alone. Here, then, is an illustrated guide to machine mitering: First, you will learn how to make a miter guide and then you will learn the various ways to miter. There are three methods (A,B,C) for mitering a self-binding and three methods (D,E,F) for mitering a continuous binding. (All drawn lines and stitches in photos exaggerated for illustrations. You use pencil and the ladder stitch.)

Note: While I usually put on bindings completely by machine, I almost always baste the folded edge down in place by hand in preparation for machine stitching (using a walking foot). It doesn't take that long to hand-baste and it ensures that Creep will not play with the binding fabric.

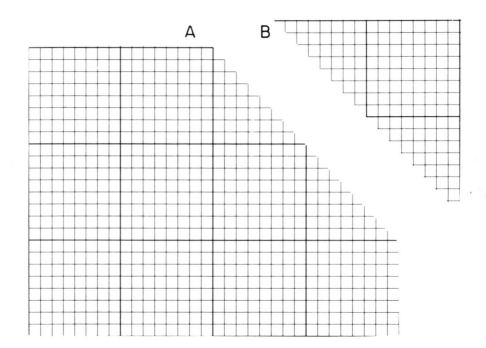

Making a Miter Guide

Make a miter guide by gluing a sheet of ¼″ (6 mm) graph paper to a piece of acetate (available in art supply stores or cut one from the top of a stationery or candy box). With an X-acto knife and a straight edge, cut diagonally across a line of 1″ (2.5 cm) squares so that the piece cut away is a triangle (see figure). Save both parts you cut. I call the larger piece with the 135° angle the miter guide and the smaller, triangular piece with the 45° angle the little miter guide. *Warning:* If you iron over the edge of the acetate, it may melt or bubble (but I do it anyway). You might try gluing the graph paper to sandpaper.

Mitering a Self Binding

When mitering a self binding the back is brought to front or vice versa for ½″ (12 mm) edge. (Don't forget to allow for ¼″ + (6 mm +) loft in calculating turnover; the ¼″ (6 mm) sits next to quilt and is ignored while mitering.) Here are Methods A to C.

Fig. 2-45a Working from the backside, allow 1¼″ (3.2 cm) for seam allowance but only press in 1″ (2.5 cm). If seam line is not sharp, draw on wrong side with pencil. Be precise.

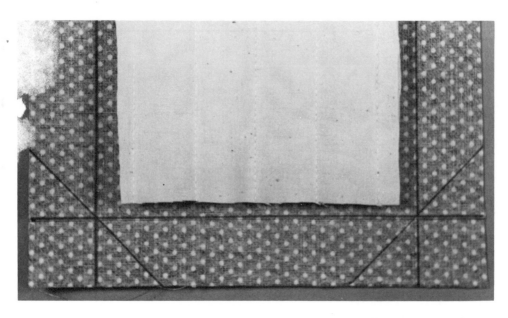

Fig. 2-45b Open out seam allowance again. Put miter guide at corners and press over, matching one straight edge to side or bottom and having diagonal line cross exact corner of quilt. Trim ¼″ (6 mm) outside pressed diagonal edge.

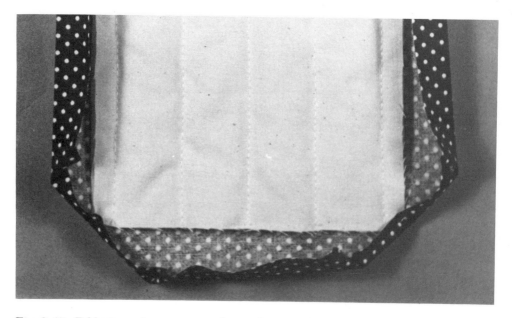

Fig. 2-45c Fold trimmed corner up on diagonal crease. Turn under seam allowance ½″ (12 mm) on pressed lines.

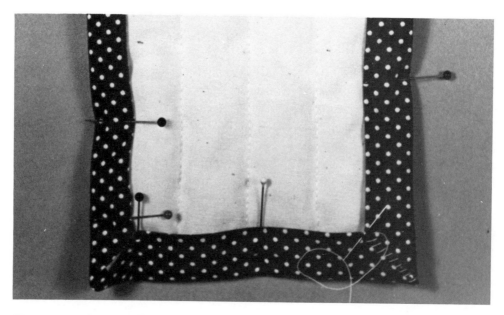

Fig. 2-45d Fold seam allowances over quilt and pin from corners out. Hand stitch mitered corner. Machine stitch edge in place.

Fig. 2-46a Mark 1″ (2.5 cm) from edge on wrongside. Turn in ½″ (12 mm) on raw edges and press. Open out again. Cut out corner square where two pressed lines intersect.

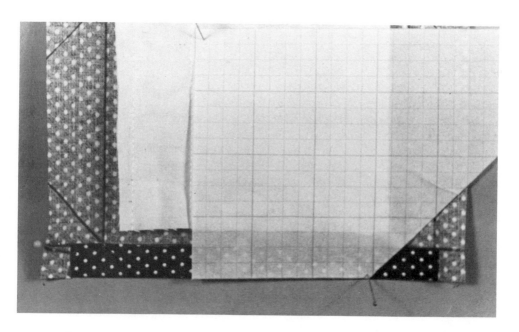

Fig. 2-46b Turn in only one ½″ (12 mm) edge. Use miter guide to mark 45° angle, crossing the point where the 1″ (2.5 cm) seam lines cross. Part of this diagonal line is on the wrongside and part on the rightside of the ½″ (12 mm) turned in.

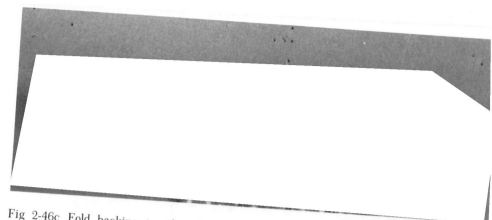

Fig 2-46c Fold backing together diagonally from clipped corner through the intersection of the 1″ (2.5 cm) seam allowance lines (quilt removed from sample for photo purposes—your quilt is connected to its backing). Turn up pressed ½″ (12 mm) edges. Make sure folded edges match exactly. Machine stitch on the diagonal line you just drew in b, backstitching both ends (open-toed foot lets you see what you're doing). Trim ⅛″ (3 mm) from stitched line. Clip off tiny triangle of extra seam allowance fabric to point. Finger press seam open.

Fig. 2-46d Turn mitered edges rightside out. Poke out corners with little miter guide. Press lightly. Pin up over quilt from corners out. If corners are not perfect, hand baste them in place across corner area only. Machine stitch near edge with straight stitch or narrow zigzag.

In this method, the trim is applied on top of the quilt to hide all the raw edges. The binding is actually some sort of trim, such as ribbon, embroidered trim, pieced strip with seam allowances pressed under, string quilt strip, etc.

Method C (A Sneaky Fast Edge)

To use this method, you must plan from the beginning for the backing to extend ½″ plus ¼″ (18 mm) for loft beyond quilt. The backing is folded up over the edge of the quilt and the ribbon is applied over it, hiding all the raw edges.

Fold backing out of way. Zigzag or straight stitch edge of top and batting. Be sure you have planned backing to extend ½″ + ¼″ + (18 mm) for loft beyond quilt. Press edge of backing in ½″ (12 mm). Open up and press 45° angle at corners, using miter guide. Trim ¼″ (6 mm) away from pressed diagonal line. (See Method A, Fig. 2-45b.)

Fig. 2-47 Turn edges up over quilt and pin perpendicular to edge. Align ribbon along edge of quilt and topstitch both sides of trim to corner. Fold ribbon in half on itself, matching long edges. Use miter guide to mark 45° angle on ribbon from lower right corner upward to the left. Stitch along marked line. Corner of ribbon is now mitered and the trim falls in place along the next edge. Topstitch both sides to next corner. Repeat for all corners.

**Method D
Mitering a
Continuous
Binding**

This method illustrates front and back miter for purchased, self-made, or French fold binding (bias or straight-grain).

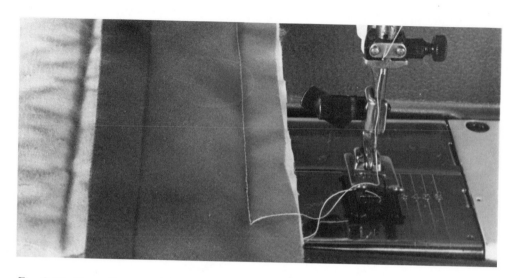

Fig. 2-48a Raw edges together, sew binding to front or back of quilt. Stop sewing exactly ½″ (12 mm) (or your seam allowance) from corner. Lift needle and presser bar lever and pull fabric to left of machine without cutting threads.

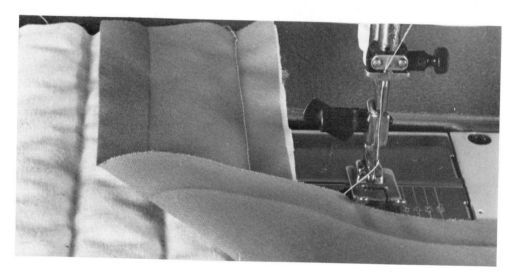

Fig. 2-48b Fold binding to right side, forming a diagonal fold running from upper left to lower right corner of quilt past the last stitch you took.

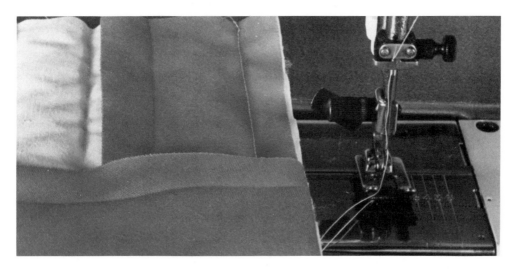

Fig. 2-48c Again fold binding back on itself to the left. The fold in the binding that runs parallel to the stitched seam should be even with the raw edges of the quilt.

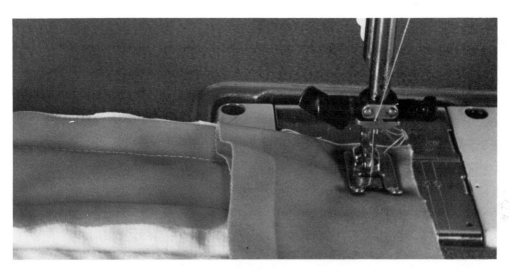

Fig. 2-48d Pivot material 90°. Lower needle into fabric where two seam allowances cross without catching the binding pleat you just made. Hold loop of thread behind needle; lower presser bar lever. Stitch along seam allowance to ½" (12 mm) from next corner and repeat the steps in Fig. 2-48a to d.

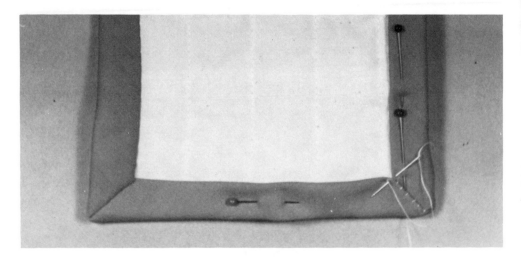

Fig. 2-48e Press binding lightly toward edges. Turn it to other side of quilt, forming a miter on both sides. Handstitch the miters closed. Then hand or machine stitch the remaining binding edge to the quilt.

**Method E
(By Machine)**   In this method, the binding is mitered first and then applied in one step. Note: For lightweight fabrics, make turned-under seam allowance as big as final width of binding on one side (that is, to have ½″ binding showing, use ½″ (12 mm) seam allowance) so there will be a double layer of binding; for medium to heavy-weight fabrics, binding width can be wider than turned-under seam allowance.

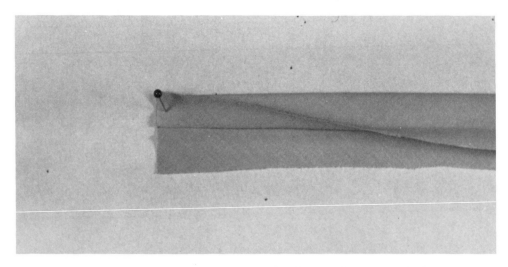

Fig. 2-49a Start working the first corner about 6″ (15.3 cm) from the end of your binding strip. Turn in seam allowances on both long sides of binding and press. Rightsides together, fold binding in half lengthwise and press.

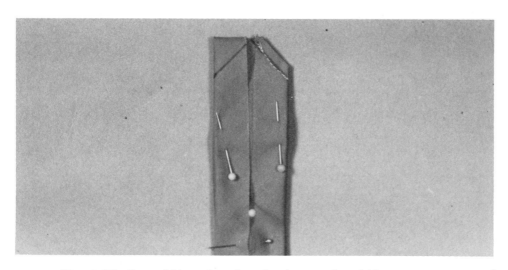

Fig. 2-49b Open fold, and with rightsides together fold again crosswise and perpendicular to first fold (use miter guide) exactly at point where corner will be. (You don't have to worry about first corner but you have to measure exactly for other three.) Keep seam allowances turned in. Use your miter guide to mark two 45° lines going out from the center fold line. Making sure folded edges are exactly matched, stitch on those lines (seam allowances are turned in). Trim ⅛" (3 mm) from stitched line. Don't clip into point area because it will fray in turning. Finger press seams open. *(continued on next page)*

A Machine Curiosity

If you have a blind hemming stitch on your machine, you can use this technique to turn the front edge to the back, invisibly (see Fig. 2-51).

Miter the four corners, using any method shown above. Press under the turn under allowance. Fold edge over quilt to back. Pin close to edge. Rightside of quilt against needle plate, fold quilt back on itself as shown. Load invisible thread in bobbin. Using the blind-hemming stitch, start stitching as close to one mitered corner as you can, along the turn-under. The needle will swing over and catch the backing every few stitches, but it doesn't go all the way through the quilt so it doesn't show on the front.

How to Start, End, and Remove Threads

Your choice of how to start and end threads depends on how much of a stickler you are for craftsmanship. Always remember to hold the threads behind the presser foot as you start stitching, so they won't be drawn into the bobbin case. Here are five tried-and-true methods.

1. To start, set your stitch length dial close to 0 (or "fine" on some machines). Take 3 to 4 stitches. Then reset the dial for the stitch length you want. Also end with small stitches. Threads are locked; clip ends.

2. Holding the threads, machine quilt. Later, pull the threads to the back, tie a square knot (so it won't pull out), and cut off the ends. Some quilters put a spot of glue on the knot for extra insurance.

3. On your stitching line, begin stitching ⅛" in (3 mm); stitch backwards to the beginning of the line; then stitch forwards as usual. Threads are locked; clip ends.

Fig. 2-49c Zigzag or straight stitch the edge of your quilt; it's easier to fit the binding over it. Turn rightside of binding out. With the binding strip flat, the corners look like two little ears. Fold binding in half, wrongsides together, which miters both sides of the corner. Fit binding corner over quilt corner so that you can measure accurately for the next corner. Pin binding in place. Mark exact corner with pencil dot on wrongside. Remove pins and binding. Repeat Steps 1–3 to stitch other three corners.

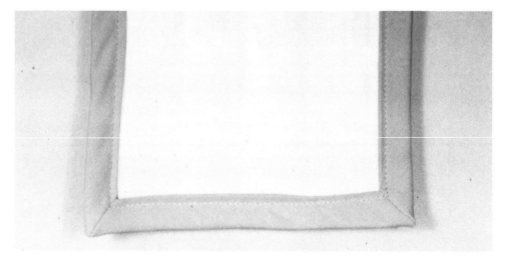

Fig. 2-49d Fit binding over quilt edge. Join beginning and ending of binding in a handmade seam. Pin liberally. Stitch ⅛″ to ¼″ (3 to 6 mm) from edge to make sure you catch both front and back. (Invisible thread used in sample shown.)

4. Holding threads, machine quilt. Later thread each end through a hand needle. Tie a knot near the surface of the fabric and lead the thread through the top and batting only (or backing and batting only) about 1″ (2.5 cm) away. Gently pop the knot through the fabric into the batting. Clip end. (If you are using extra-fine thread and a fabric not too closely woven, you can pull ends to the back, knot them together, thread them into one needle, and pull them through the backing fabric and batting together.)

5. Design your quilt so most, if not all, quilting lines end in a seam allowance, to be covered by binding, other blocks, or lattice strips.

An easy way to remove stitches from an entire seam is to cut threads with a seam ripper every three or four threads. Place a strip of masking tape over the seam. Turn the quilt over and pull the other thread, which will be long and uncut. Separate the fabric. Then pull off the masking tape and all the cut stitches will come off on the tape (Fig. 2-53).

How Much Quilting?

Before machine quilting be sure to experiment on a doodle cloth to see what stitch length you prefer; generally the shorter the stitch, the puffier the effect.

This method is good for nonfrayable fabrics (like double knits and velours); for narrow edges (less than ½″); and for quick small items that are not for show (like placemats). Note: Cut binding width three times your seam allowance plus ¼″ loft plus ⅛″ (9 mm). Here we're using a ½″ (12 mm) seam allowance with velour. **Method F Mock Miter**

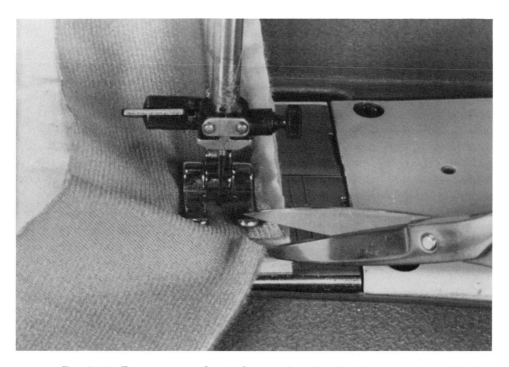

Fig. 2-50a Zigzag or straight stitch raw edge of quilt. Place raw edge of binding next to raw edge of quilt. Sew to within 1″ (2.5 cm) of corner. Stop, leaving needle in fabric. Clip diagonally on binding only, from corner of quilt to within a few threads of seam allowance.

Fig. 2-50b Continue sewing, stopping exactly ½″ (or your seam allowance) from corner. Leave needle in fabric. Lift presser bar lever and pivot material 90°. Fold tuck in binding to left. Lower presser bar lever and continue sewing, taking care not to stitch through the tuck. Repeat steps in Fig. 2-50a and b at all corners.

Clip corners of quilt diagonally in seam allowances. Fold binding over edge, making a quasi-miter on the back—more like a deliberate pucker. Pin in place. Edge of binding will overlap seam line ⅛″ (3 mm) and is not turned under.

Turn over, rightside of quilt up. Stitch-in-the-ditch to catch the back binding (invisible thread used here).

In this book "regular stitch length" means 10 to 12 stitches per inch (4 to 5 per cm). If you own a European or Japanese machine with 0 to 5 settings, set your machine at 1, 2, 3, 4, and 5 and machine quilt a line on a doodle cloth. Measure at each of those settings how many stitches per inch and write it directly on the doodle cloth. Pin that cloth to this page or near your machine.

However, stitch length is not absolute. There is no one stitch length that is right for all machine quilting. Stitch length also depends on the type of fabric used. Lighterweight fabrics may pucker with too long stitch lengths. You must experiment on a doodle quilt sandwich for each new situation.

The amount of quilting to put in a quilt depends on the thread, seam allowance, and type of batting used. (For smaller-than-full-quilts, you have much more latitude.)

If the quilt hangs over the side of a bed, tremendous stress is put on the thread every day when you pull up the quilt, fluff it up, and smooth it on the bed. If you use extra-fine thread (as for free-machine quilting), plan to break up the quilt top into modules. The joining strips do relieve some of the stress.

If your quilting lines are more than 2″ to 3″ (5 to 8 cm) apart, you should probably use ½″ (12 mm) or wider seam allowances, again to relieve stress and pulling on the fabric.

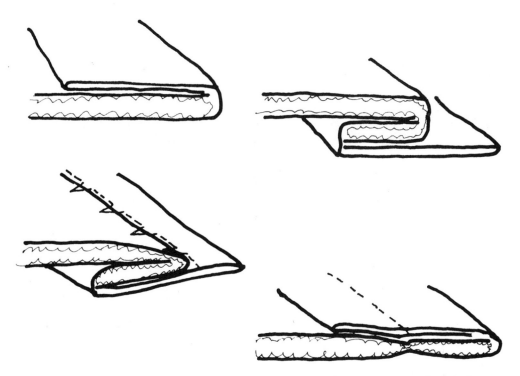

Fig. 2-51 If you have a blind hem stitch on your machine, you can make a hidden edge on the binding.

Fig. 2-52 Left: To make a square knot that won't pull loose, lap *right* thread over left. Pull tight. Then lap *left* over right and pull tight, as at right.

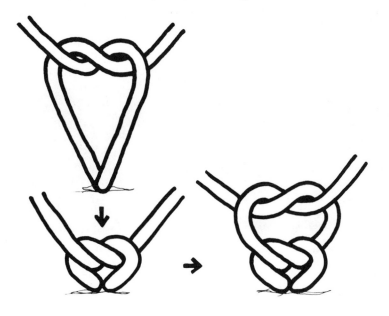

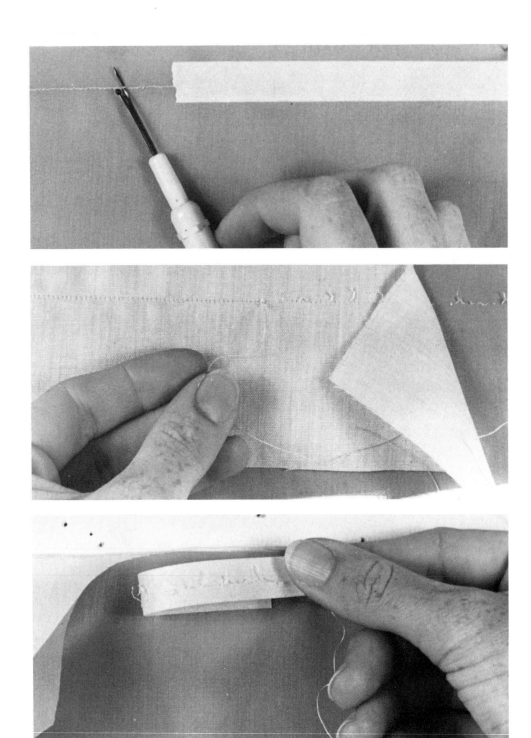

Fig. 2-53 Top: Removing a seam is easy with masking tape. On one side cut about every third stitch with a seam ripper; put masking tape over this side. Middle: Turn over the fabric and remove the long thread on that side. Separate the fabric. Bottom: When you remove the masking tape, all the loose ends pull out with it.

94

Fig. 2-54 The Closed Fist Test.

A cotton batting needs lines of quilting no farther apart than 2½″ or 6.4 cm (2″ or 5 cm is better). But a bonded polyester batting needs quilting only every 4″ to 6″ (10 to 15 cm) and here's where standards of craftsmanship start to slip.

The current trend in both hand and machine quilting is to put in fewer and fewer lines of quilting. This is not always pleasing, depending on the quilt-top design.

My own standard for whole quilts (but not necessarily for smaller items), which I am flexible in meeting, is the "closed fist test." I put my closed fist on the quilt and if there are not quilting lines nearby and all around my fist, I add them. One of the joys of machine quilting is that we *can* put in the extensive quilting so attractive in the quilts of our forebears.

Chapter 3

Construction of Quilt Tops

Perhaps the most common idea of the traditional way to make a quilt is to (1) construct the top of the quilt by piecing, patching, or some other way of making a large piece of fabric out of small pieces; then (2) quilt, joining the constructed top, batting, and backing together with lines of stitching.

Machine quilting frees you of slavish dependence on this technique. Such modern techniques as one-step quilting and quilt-as-you-go (covered in later chapters) give you alternatives; but some of the most attractive quilts are still best made by constructing the top first and then quilting.

We will not spend much time discussing construction of quilt tops in the traditional way. Among the many books devoted to that, there are some which are extremely useful for reference, even for machine quilting (see Bibliography).

However, there are several new and faster methods of piecing, as well as machine embellishing techniques, with which you should be familiar before you consider actually making a quilt. They will turn what used to be the work of years into the work of days—at the most.

Piecing and Patching

Most traditional quilt designs can be adapted for machine piecing. As with hand piecing, the beauty of the final quilt depends on your craftsmanship, and the key to craftsmanship is precision. Precision is extremely simple to obtain. It's all in measurement and cutting. As the carpenters say, "Measure twice, cut once."

Your accuracy in measuring affects the actual size of each block vs. the planned size, and the precision of your seaming.

Precision and Finished Size

To illustrate the effect of measurement on final size, the two nine-patch blocks in Fig. 3-2 were intended to be 6″ (15.3 cm) square, finished size. And they would have been, except for one slight error. A new presser foot was used on this sample block. Like most people who use their sewing machine often, I use the presser foot to measure seam allowances, and my favorite one is ¼″ (6 mm) wide from center to right side. Observe how the new presser foot tricked me.

In making the nine-patch, I cut 2½″ (6.4 cm) squares of light and dark fabric and sewed them (I thought) with ¼″ (6 mm) seams, using the edge of my presser foot as guide. This would have made each little square 2″ (5 cm) to the side and the finished block 6″ (15.3 cm) square. Surprise! The finished block size was only 5⅝″ (14.28 cm) square. I then measured my presser foot: it is ¹/₁₆″ (1.6 mm) wider than

Fig. 3-1 Top row, from left: Whole-cloth quilt. Strip quilt. Blocks separated by lattice strips. Bottom: Adjoining blocks. Blocks set on diagonal separated by lattice strips. Medallion quilt.

¼" (6 mm). That sounds negligible, doesn't it? But it adds up. Each little square becomes ⅛" (3.2 mm) smaller than it should be; each completed block ends up ⅜" (9.5 mm) shorter on each side. For a king-sized bed top 13 blocks wide, the top would be 13 × ⅜" (9.5 mm) short or only 73⅛" (185.7 cm) wide, instead of 78" (198.1 cm). That 4⅞" (12.4 cm) difference is definitely not negligible!

So, for accurate quilting: (1) measure your presser foot; (2) mark a ¼" (6 mm) line on your needle plate with masking tape or consider using ½" (12 mm) seams (also mark them with masking tape, for greatest precision); (3) make a sample block and measure it; (4) be precise—fractions count in quiltmaking!

Precision and Seam Joins

The second way your accuracy shows up is in the quality of seam joins. In that same nine-patch sample one of the yellow strips was cut narrower than 2½" (6.4 cm) and not double-checked before sewing. Therefore some of the cross-seam joins are off-kilter. When this happens, you either live with it, or rip out the seam and do it right, or cut a new strip and start over.

Better yet, train yourself to double-check before sewing. Double-check by comparing each cut strip or shape to an original template before piecing. If the shape is larger, carefully trim it. If it is smaller, discard it and cut a new one—and don't forget to double-check the new one, too.

Fig. 3-2 The seams of one nine-patch are pressed open and the seams of the other pressed to one side. Can you tell which is which? Answer: right = pressed open. The joins of cross-seams are not good enough to use in a quilt. Not enough precision was followed in cutting and seaming.

Even if your pieces are cut accurately, you can still make a botch of the seam joins unless you take care. The secret is to pin-baste and to press the seams intelligently.

The usual advice on pressing seams in pieced work is to press them toward the lighter-weight fabric (the direction in which they naturally tend to fall); or if that means the seams would show through on the top, to press them toward the darker side.

I suspect this advice has been handed down from early quilting when seams were handpieced and could not stand up to the strain of having the seams pressed open. But we now use modern threads so strong they are apt to last longer than the fabric. Our machine stitches can be as even and as close as we wish. So why not press open machine-pieced seams?

Nobody knows the answer to that one. This just may be one of those places where tradition makes no sense at all.

Most seams pressed open look better and make it easier to match cross-seams. You can do this by sticking a thin pin straight into the pressed-open seam allowance on the underside ¼" (6 mm) or whatever your seam allowance is—from the raw edge. Push the fabric to be joined (rightsides together) onto the pin. Insert the sharp end of the pin back through both seam allowances. Pin all cross-seams this way; then pin the rest of the raw edges together so nothing will shift as you sew. (If you're really a perfectionist, use the walking foot to keep the fabrics from creeping.) As you sew, be sure to remove the pin across each seam before you sew over it. Examine each finished seam. If it's not right, rip it out and do it again. That's what craftsmanship is all about.

The reasonable exception to pressing open seams is a lot of ¼″ (6 mm) seams close together, where it's more trouble than it's worth to slide an iron over one seam without messing up the others.

With a light fabric, pressing open seams sometimes means a seam allowance will show through to the top. In this case, press both seams toward the darker fabric. In joining such cross-seams try to arrange it so when rightsides are together, the cross-seam you see on top points *toward* the presser foot and the cross-seam underneath points toward your belly (see Fig. 3-4). (Stick a pin through both seam lines, as for pressed-open seam allowances, and don't stitch over it.) The presser foot nudges the top seam into the ridge of the bottom seam for a perfect join. (If you forget and need a mnemonic reminder, say to yourself "Tp"; it doesn't mean toilet paper—it means Top toward Presser.)

Always match seam lines, not raw edges, in joining pieces, particularly with shapes that do not have 90° edges like some triangles (Fig. 3-5).

To piece curves or angles, stay-stitch both pieces of fabric slightly inside the seam allowance (Fig. 3-6). Clip to the stitching. Now you can coax the two seam lines for machine piecing (Fig. 3-6).

You can cut down on piecing problems by using a 10/11(70) needle and extra-fine machine-embroidery thread and by using the straight stitch needle plate or left-needle position.

In extremely difficult cases, after stay-stitching and clipping, lower the needle into the corner and stitch in place to lock thread. Stitch away from the corner in one direction. Then go back to the corner, lower the needle again, lock threads, and stitch away from the corner in the other direction (Fig. 3-7).

Fig. 3-3 When seams are pressed open, pin right through the seam to match seams.

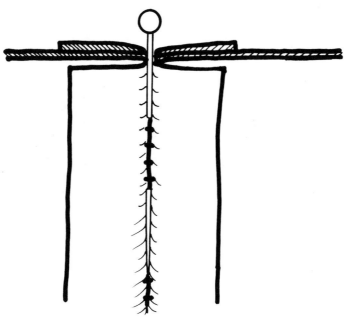

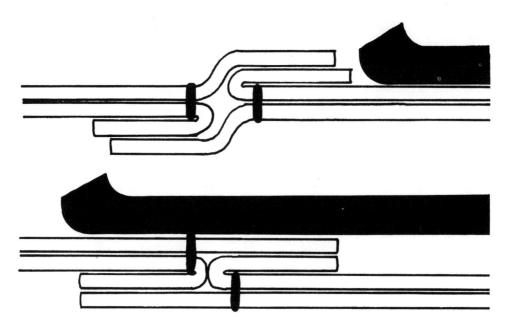

Fig. 3-4 Above: When you have a choice, place the cross-seam on top *toward* the presser foot. As shown below, after the presser foot passes over the seam, it will be nudged into place and your cross-seams will match exactly. Otherwise the presser foot may move the cross-seams apart and you will have a bad join.

If many identical units are being joined, you can sew one after the other without cutting the thread. There is no need to backstitch starts and ends when the threads will be locked later by cross-seams. This process is called *chaining,* and is a well-known dressmaking technique (Fig. 3-8).

If you have enough *identical* units (same fabrics, same shapes) to chain, there may be a faster way. Read about the faster piecing methods below and be sure that you are not using outmoded piecing techniques appropriate to hand quilting rather than machine quilting. Chances are you can sew long seams and then cut them apart into shapes, rather than cutting shapes first for seaming.

Seminole Piecing

The Seminole Indians of Florida developed an ingenious method of piecing that has sparked the imagination of many quilters. If you want to see what excites these quilters, look at Fig. 3-9. Until you understand how it was actually constructed, you might hesitate to try piecing something that looks so complicated.

Here's how it is done.

First, 2″ (5.08 cm) wide strips are cut or torn from solid-colored fabric and sewn together down the long seam. The new fabric is sliced across at regular intervals. These pieces are sewn together again at a slant and the pointed edges lopped off.

And that's just about the simplest application of Seminole work imaginable.

By varying colors and widths of original strips and by combining patterns, the Seminoles come up with colorful bands of many different patterns in one design.

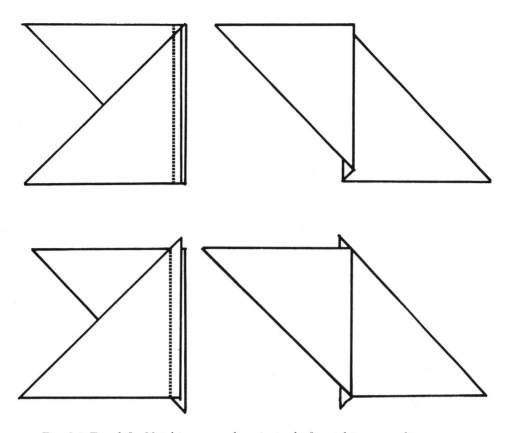

Fig. 3-5 Top, left: Matching raw edges instead of matching seam lines, your joins (right) will be off. Lower left: Match seam lines, and your joins (right) will be perfect when you press open the pieces.

Fig. 3-6 Left: To match curves or angles, stay-stitch slightly inside the seam allowance and clip to stitching. Right: Now you will have no trouble matching difficult pieces.

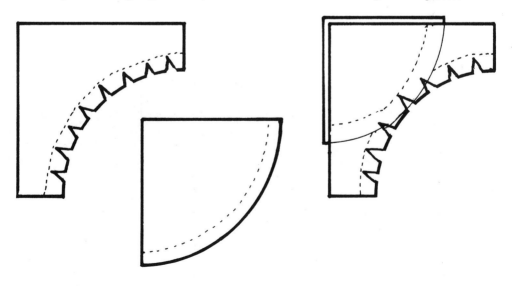

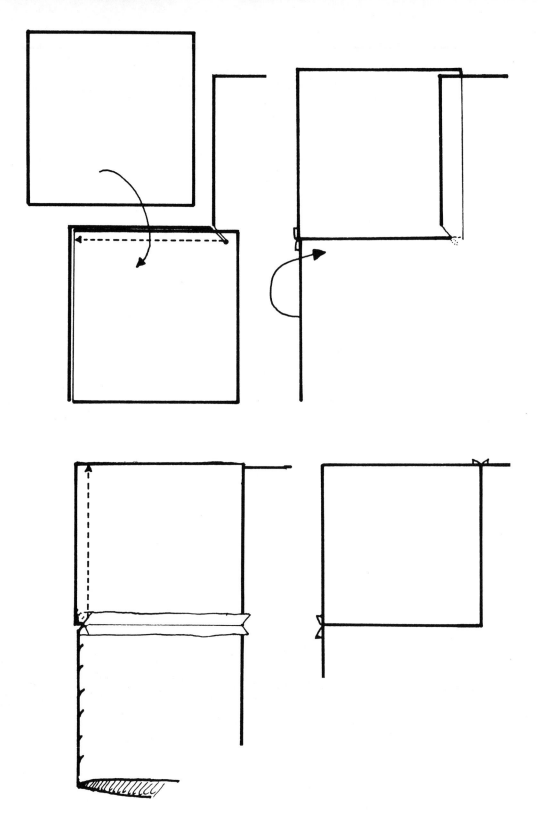

Fig. 3-7 Top, left: In extremely difficult situations, stitch from the corner exactly at the seam line out to one edge. Clip at inside corner to the stitching. Right: Flip piece up and press open seam gently. Bottom, left: Fold the fabric back and match remaining raw edges. Lower the needle exactly into the corner on the seam line and stitch out to the opposite edge. It helps to use a small needle and extra-fine thread and to put on your straight-stitch needle plate or use the left-needle position. This cuts down on puckering and having the material jam into the needle plate hole. Right: A perfectly joined corner.

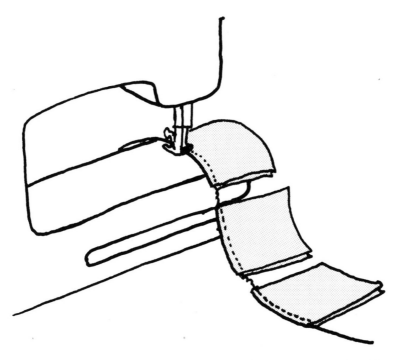

Fig. 3-8 Chaining is handy in certain cases but it may be outdated by
faster piecing methods.

The skirt pictured shows one such application, but there are endless variations. (See the Bibliography for books on Seminole patterns.)

It is the concept of strip piecing that is so exciting to modern quilters. If you apply the idea on a larger scale, all sorts of interesting possibilities arise (see sleeping bag in Chapter 6). No longer, for example, do we have to laboriously trace around templates to make squares, rectangles, or triangles. Read on.

Barbara Johannah's Clever Nine-Patch

All of us use ideas and methods which have been handed down to us. In quiltmaking, this means we are still using methods of piecing based on dressmaking and on the use of scraps. Even though we often buy fresh yardage to make our quilts, we continue to use these old ways. Sometimes there are dramatically better ways, and here is one of them.

Barbara Johannah (pronounced Yo-hannah) has developed three major revolutionary ways to piece, each inspired by Seminole piecing. (See Bibliography for her book, which is strongly recommended for machine quilters.) One of them is the nine-patch shown here.

Barbara's clever nine-patch is constructed as shown in Fig. 3-11.

Decide on the overall width of the finished block and thus of each square within the block. Add ¼″ (6 mm) seam allowances to each side of each small square. For a 6″ (15.3 cm) nine-patch block, the small squares are 2″ (5 cm), so each square is cut 2½″ (6.4 cm) wide. Choose and prepare a light fabric and a dark fabric. Cut or tear the fabric into 2½″ (6.4 cm) wide strips across the grain. (If cutting, mark lines on underside of fabric using a cutting board for complete accuracy.) You will need three strips of each color.

Fig. 3-9 Top, left: Child's skirt, made by Seminole Indians of Florida. (Collection of Kali Fanning, gift of Doris Losey). Right: Inside of child's skirt. Seams are pressed to one side. Bottom: The simplest Seminole piecing: 2″ (5 cm) wide strips are sewn together in long strips. Then the new fabric is sliced across at regular intervals. These slices are staggered diagonally, seamed, and the points lopped off.

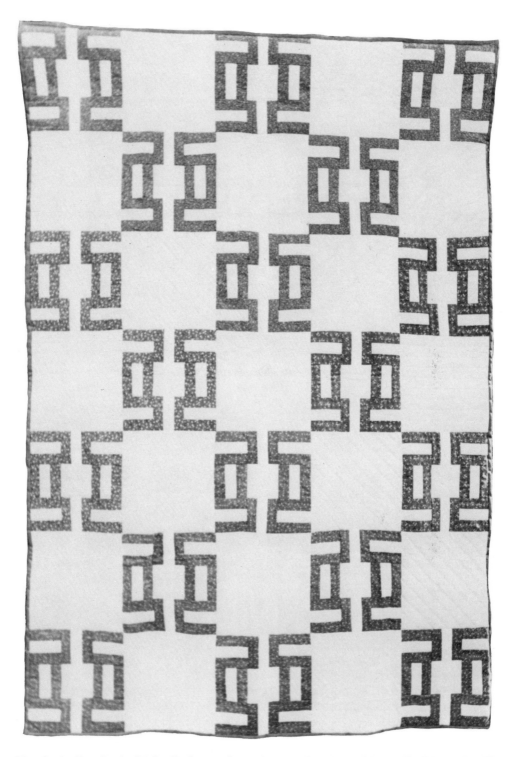

Fig. 3-10 "Family Quilt" by Barbara Johannah, pieced and machine quilted in under 10 hours, using her extraordinary methods. Names of family members are written in ink on the white centers of the pieced blocks.

Fig. 3-11 Barbara Johannah's streamlined nine-patch. Cut long strips of two colors and seam them together in two sets of triplets: dark-light-dark and light-dark-light. Slice across at regular intervals; then sew the slices into a nine-patch.

Fig. 3-12 Ernest B. Haight's assembly-line nine-patch. This shows the first two steps in making enough nine-patches for a whole quilt.

Arrange the strips into two groups, dark-light-dark and light-dark-light. Sew the long seams together. Now cut across the seams at 2½" (6.4 cm) intervals. Combine into a nine-patch as shown and sew the seams, matching cross-seams carefully. For a 6" (15.3 cm) block, 36" (100 cm) wide fabric yields two nine-patches for every three strips of both colors; 45" (115 cm) wide fabric yields three blocks.

Ernest B. Haight's Assembly-Line Nine-Patch

Another modern quilting innovator is Ernest B. Haight, who has been machine quilting for 40 years. His book is also strongly recommended (see Bibliography). Using the same principles as Barbara Johannah, Ernest B. Haight has streamlined the process even further. His method gives you as many nine-patches as you need for an entire quilt. Again, the key is to use yardage, not scraps. You do not tear the fabric in this method.

Mark the back of the light-colored fabric across the grain with parallel lines 2½" (6.4 cm) apart. Mark another line ¼" (6 mm) to the left of each marked line. The left line is the seam line and the right line is the cutting line—but don't cut yet. Slide the dark fabric under the light fabric, rightsides together.

Pin the fabrics together perpendicular to each marked seam line. Take the whole thing to the sewing machine and sew each marked seam. Then cut through both layers of fabric along the marked cutting line (Fig. 3-12). When you open them up for pressing, you have long narrow pairs of light-dark fabric. To complete the nine-patch, you must cut two long dark-colored strips and one long light-colored strip for every seamed pair. Add the strips this way. Now slice across as you did before and seam the nine-patch.

If you have trouble visualizing this method, try it on fabric. You are probably being blinded by thinking in terms of traditional piecing. This method is entirely different—and definitely worth understanding.

This strip method of piecing is extremely useful in many traditional patterns, such as Sunshine and Shadow, Trip Around the World, Rail Fence (see project in Chapter 4), and Roman Stripe. You can also cut across the pieced strips at angles instead of straight across, giving you diamonds and triangles. This can be used for fast piecing of Star of Bethlehem, Spider Web, and variations of string quilting.

Any time you see parallel seam lines in a traditional pattern, try to figure out how to construct the pattern using strip piecing (see Fig. 3-13). Imagine the lines extended out and then chopped up into parts. If you have trouble doing this in your head, doodle with a pencil or cut strips of dark/medium/light paper to manipulate. The advantage in doing this extra brain work is that you can keep a library of patterns appropriate to fast piecing. An entire complicated-looking quilt top can be pieced in a few hours using strip piecing.

Barbara Johannah's Extraordinary Half-of-a-Square Triangles

Another shortcut in piecing developed by Barbara Johannah is based on the same principle as Ernest B. Haight's assembly-line nine-patch. A length of light-colored fabric is marked on the back into a square grid. A shortcut here is to use a 3″ (7.62 cm) square gingham print. Diagonal lines are marked across the squares and ¼″ (6 mm) seam lines on either side of the diagonal line. Slide a dark-colored fabric under the light-colored fabric, rightsides together, and carefully pin the two layers together. Take to the sewing machine and sew along the diagonal seam lines. However, do not sew through the points of any triangles (Fig. 3-14). Stop at all vertical and horizontal lines, lift the presser-bar lever, carefully push the fabric forward past the triangle point, lower the presser bar lever, and sew again. When all the seam lines are sewn, cut the fabrics apart on the vertical, horizontal, and diagonal marked lines. Magic! Half-of-a-square triangles! These can now be combined and pieced into larger patterns.

Many traditional blocks, such as Eight-Pointed Star, Pin Wheel, and Spool, are based on half-of-a-square triangles (sometimes combined with solid squares).

No longer do you have to sit marking around a template for hours and then cutting out triangle after triangle for piecing. If you have trouble understanding this fast procedure, try it on a scrap length of fabric. It is worth understanding and using.

Then when you comprehend the brilliance of this approach, try analyzing more and more complex patterns, perhaps combining both strip piecing and triangle piecing. Then you can recombine them in your own original patterns. For more specific instructions on precise measurements and for quilt patterns, see the Johannah book (Bibliography).

Log Cabin

A long-time favorite pattern of quilters, log cabin can be worked in several ways and combined to produce striking overall patterns of light and dark. The secret is to sort your fabric into light-colored and dark-colored piles and not to use middle-range colors (unless you intentionally want to). If you are not sure whether your fabrics are dark, medium, or light, there are several simple ways to check:

1. Look at them in a dimly lit room or with squinted eyes—color usually disappears and you can judge the lightness and darkness of the fabrics.

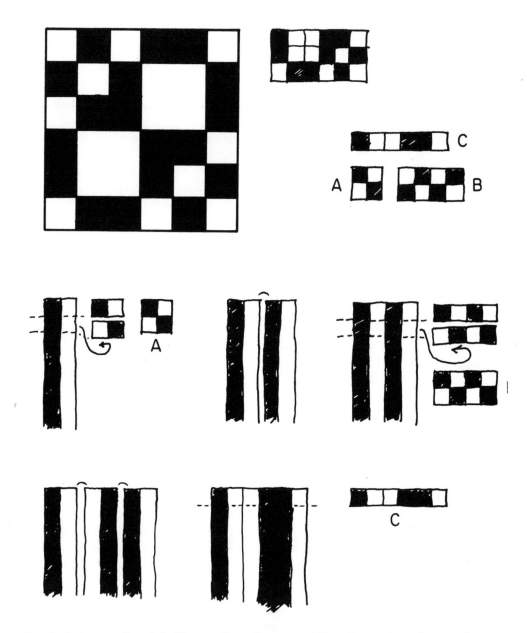

Fig. 3-13 Top row from left: Many traditional patterns (this is Domino) can be pieced in fast ways, once you analyze the elements of the block. Here Domino is seen to consist of a reverse mirror image (divide the large block in half horizontally and you'll see it). Separating the pattern even more, a small checkerboard is seen in the lower left corner (A), a larger checkerboard in the lower right (B), and a repeat pattern on the top line (C). Middle row: Long strips are sewn for each element (A) of the pattern and sliced across to give the pattern for each block. Enough blocks for the whole quilt are made this way. Strips sewn to form next element, then cut for element B. Bottom row: Strips planned for element C. Strips for element C joined, then cut for element C.

Fig. 3-14 Half-of-a-square triangles. Continuing Ernest B. Haight's assembly-line concepts, the Johannah half-of-a-square triangles can be made fast, without tracing around a single template. (Note: Do not sew through the corners of the squares. See how the thread has been lightly pulled over these corners.)

2. Take a black-and-white Polaroid shot of the fabrics.

3. Pin strips of the fabric you're considering onto a piece of typing paper and photocopy it. This reduces the colors to dark, medium, and light values. If you're happy with the results, make as many copies as blocks in the coverlet. Trim extra paper away and you can play around with overall light/dark variations until you find the one you like best.

Log cabin is usually worked from the center, spiralling out. Traditionally, the logs were pieced to squares of newspaper, which was later torn away. Sometimes people piece it to muslin or an old sheet. Log cabin one-step quilting (see Chapter 6), which combines the piecing and the quilting into one operation, is one of the most popular forms of modern quilting.

Barbara Johannah has also developed an ingenious method for strip piecing log cabin. Again it depends on using yardage and making nearly all the blocks for a top at once.

Choose your light and dark fabrics. To keep from being confused, make a reference block by gluing or pinning small strips of each fabric in position. Write the numbers on top of the reference fabrics in ballpoint.

In this example, all fabrics are cut 1½" (3.8 cm) wide across the grain. Using a ¼" (6 mm) seam, sew color 1 to color 2 down the long right seam. Don't press them. Mark and cut across this long strip every 1½" (3.8 cm), through both fabrics. Press open seam allowances. Place each of these little rectangles rightsides together down the strip of color 3, with color 2 always on top and edges of rectangles abutting each other. Sew down the long right edge. Cut across at the raw edges of the color 2/color 1 rectangles. Open up and press seam open. Place the new rectangles down the color 4 strip, rightsides together and color 3 on top. Sew the long right seam, cut across raw edges, and press open seams. Continue until you've used all the colors and until you've made enough blocks for the entire quilt top.

Fig. 3-15 Log cabin, traditionally made and contemporary: In the upper right is a log-cabin block made in the traditional way, by spiralling around and out from the central square (this is the one-step quilted block shown being made in Chapter 6); below is Barbara Johannah's amazing method for making enough blocks for an entire bed at once. The reference block is at lower right.

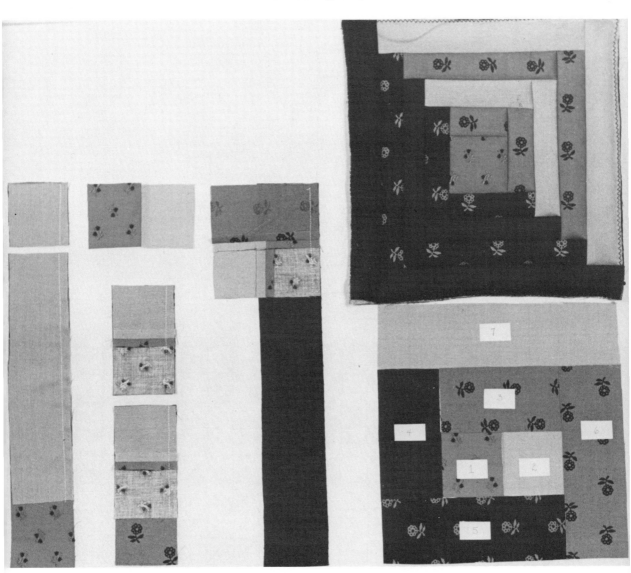

Figure 3-16 shows traditional ways to set the log cabin squares together.

Strips for log cabin (and string quilts) can be easily marked for cutting by laying down masking tape in the correct widths. Or you can use the log cabin technique with narrow pre-finished "fabrics" like ribbons, trim, braid, and lace. Edges should abut and be sewn down with a zigzag or straight stitch. As insurance against gaps in the adjoining edges, put glue (preferably from a stick) on the underside edges of the "fabrics." (Or you can overlap the "fabrics" slightly before sewing.)

Log Cabin Gone Wrong

Traditionally log cabin has depended on an orderly stairstep of light and dark fabrics, but interesting effects can be had by tossing precision and color value out the window. This method is almost the link between log cabin and crazy quilt, and

Fig. 3-16 Top: The traditional log cabin block. Bottom left: Straight Furrow variation. Bottom right: Barn Raising variation.

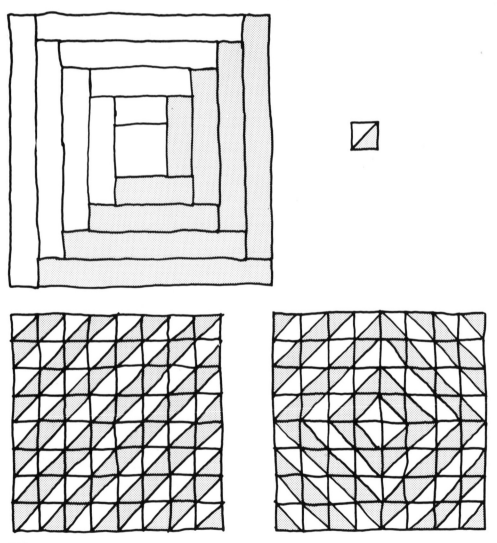

Fig. 3-17 Close-up, "Chicken Quilt" by Doris Hoover, showing a controlled log-cabin-gone wrong technique. See color section.

while it cannot be carefully planned and controlled, it is pleasing to work because of the surprises.

Start with a backing fabric or square of paper in any size. Choose a pile of fabrics in a narrow color range—all reds, for example; you'll have so many eye-catching seam lines that you won't want to confuse the viewer with an abundance of color. Fabric with a sheen or nap (such as corduroy or velveteen) looks particularly exciting in this technique, as it snakes its way around the edges.

Cut a center square or rectangle free-hand and pin it in place in the center of the backing. For once you don't have to worry about precision. Rightsides together sew a strip to it. The strip should not have parallel sides, but one straight edge is lined up with the edge of the center square. Sew a ¼" seam and flip out the second strip, topside up. Trim it off even with the ends. Continue sewing odd-sized strips around and around until you cover the base. You can always trim the blocks to any size later.

If you tire of working around a rectangle, use any odd-sized center or sew additional strips across corners. As long as you always spiral in the same direction, you will cover raw edges.

String Quilts

Originally intended to use up all left-over strips (or "strings") of fabric, the string quilt links together strips of fabric along their long edges in order to construct a new fabric.

If the color has been carefully selected, the overall effect is stunning. The easiest way to control the color, especially if you're using prints, is to choose one hue and use only dark, medium, and light values of it. If you chose red, for example, you'd assemble strings in wine-red, red-red, and faded red. Don't overlook using both the front and back of some fabrics.

The strings are usually pieced to a foundation of fabric or of paper (which is later torn away) so that any strings sewn off grain are not stretched or distorted. Be sure to select a scale of pattern that matches the width of your string; a large design, for example, does not complement a ½" (12 mm) wide string.

Figure 3-18 shows the most elementary string piecing.

Applique Using Pieced Strings

Any shape can be cut out of pieced strings and used in traditional quilt patterns, either pieced to other shapes or appliqued to quilt tops. You can use string appliques as borders or frames for family photos or in toy patterns or in clothing shapes (such as yokes or cuffs). Try replacing one dominant line in your favorite pieced pattern, such as Mexican cross, with a line of strings. (For one-step quilted string quilts, see Chapter 6.)

For precision in piecing string quilts, use masking tape laid on fabric as a cutting guide.

Appliques can be cut from pieced strings and applied in any of the straight-stitch or zigzag motion ways shown later in this chapter.

If you want to emphasize the seams of a string quilt, lap the raw edge of the left fabric ¼" (6 mm) over the raw edge of the right fabric and satin stitch. Although no short-cut in time, this method of seaming helps bring unity to the overall piece by the repeated color and line of the stitching.

Fig. 3-18 String piecing has many possibilities: (left) poncho made of string-pieced blocks (made by Margaret Vaile, collection of Kali Fanning); (upper right) string-piecing that changes direction, having been pieced across half the block, and then raw edges covered by piecing perpendicular to the first pass; (right middle) string-piecing is being herringboned, alternating sides off a central triangle of fabric—two strips have been pieced and on the right, one is pinned in place, rightside against the previous piece, ready for sewing; (lower right) the upper half of the block has been string-pieced while the lower half of solid fabric covers the raw ends of the middle string.

To give the eye a rest and to best show off the variety, set off areas of printed string piecing with areas of plain fabric (or vice versa), either in borders, binding, frames, or inserts.

Crazy Quilt

When left-over fabric scraps are too small and irregular to use in string quilts, the thrifty quilter will make crazy quilts. Like string piecing, crazy-quilt piecing is usually sewn onto fabric or paper (which is later torn away). Traditionally the seams are decorated with hand embroidery stitches. Again, careful control of the color and of the scale of the patterns makes the difference between chaos and design. In choosing scraps, try to relate them to each other by color or by pattern—limit yourself to a variety of floral fabrics in navy and white, for example, with small touches of red.

To piece by machine, cut a foundation of paper or fabric. Begin in any corner by putting a scrap of fabric down and pinning it in place. Right sides together, pin another scrap to the first, sewing a ¼" (6 mm) seam (Fig. 3-22). Flip the second

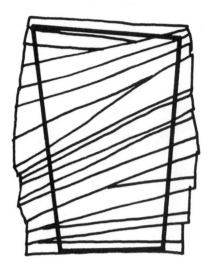

Fig. 3-19 Any shape can be cut
from string-quilt yardage.

fabric over and pin down. Continue to build, scrap by scrap. Whenever you feel like it, change direction. You may cover up parts of previous scraps in order to use a new scrap.

On curves, clip the curves before flipping the fabric. You may have to fudge sometimes by finger-pressing under a curved edge and topstitching it in place over a raw edge.

Emphasize some or all of the seams with the decorative stitches on your machine.

Fig. 3-20 String quilts come in many forms and can be used for clothing, for toys or anything you dream up.

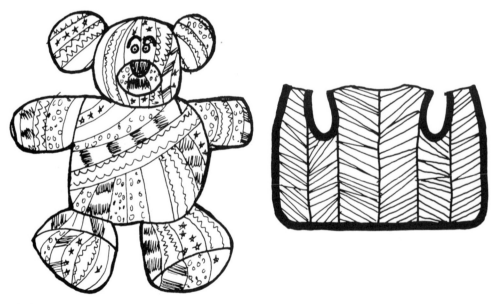

Fig. 3-21 "Gold Family Ties" by Fay Quanstrom. Disassembled neckties were stitched to a base fabric in long strips. The strips were joined to make a quilt top, velour used for backing, and the whole thing quilted stitch-in-the-ditch. (Collection of Sharon and Keith Tice)

117

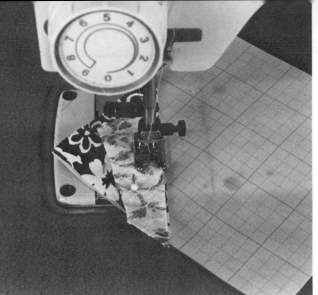
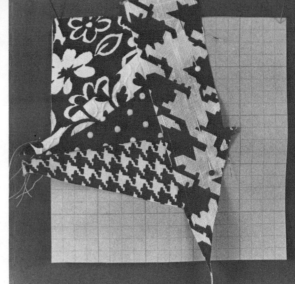
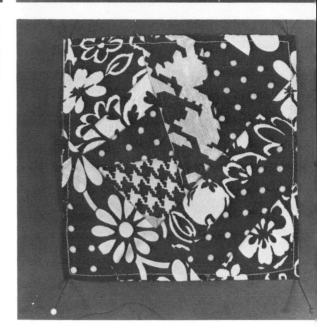

Fig. 3-22 Top: A crazy-quilt block in progress: a scrap of fabric has been cut to fit a corner of a square of paper. A second scrap of fabric is being sewn rightsides together to the first. Middle: Scraps are freely added in any direction. Bottom: The completed block.

Like string quilts, crazy quilts look best set off against areas of plain fabric. If, for example, you are piecing onto a clothing pattern, bind the edges with solid-colored braid or insert narrow panels of plain fabric.

For one-step crazy quilting, see Chapter 6.

Machine Embellishing

Before actually beginning the quilting, your design may include decorative touches to the quilt top: appliques, free-machine embroidery, decorative stitches. Here's how to do each.

Applique

One fabric can be applied to another by machine in many ways, depending on whether you use a straight stitch, an open zigzag, or a satin stitch.

Straight Stitch

There are four ways to apply fabric by a straight stitch (Fig. 3-23).

1. A ¼″ (6 mm) edge can be turned under by hand or pressed under over a paper template. Remove the paper and topstitch near the edge.

2. The applique shape is cut with a ¼″ (6 mm) seam allowance. The same shape is cut from lightweight fabric. Seam the two shapes rightsides together all around the edges. Clip curves. Cut a slash in the middle of the lightweight fabric. Pull the applique fabric rightsides out through the slash. Press edges. Sew applique shape to foundation fabric (i.e., quilt top) with straight stitch (or zigzag or blind hem stitch). This handy method is called Hidden Applique. (Note: for nonreversible images like letters, do not trace them backwards on the self-lining.)

3. The edge is deliberately left frayed as part of the design. Cut applique shape with no seam allowance. Topstitch ¼″ (6 mm) in from edge. Fray edges.

4. This is a method I learned from Peggy Moulton, who is clever at using ordinary scraps in innovative ways: lay small scraps of fabric on a foundation (old sheet, muslin, etc.). Sew back and forth with close rows of straight stitch.

Open Zigzag

Here are five ways to use zigzag for applique (Fig. 3-24).

1. Nonfrayable fabrics like double-knits, felts, leathers, imitation suedes, vinyls, and ribbons can be appliqued with a zigzag on the edge, without turning it under. If you can decenter the needle on your machine, do so to the right so that the zigzag stitches fall exactly on the edge. To keep applique fabrics from creeping, bond them with glue in stick form, fabric glue, or fusible interfacing. The open-toed applique foot is best to use so you can see what you're doing.

2. Edges can be turned under as shown in straight-stitch applique and attached to the foundation with a zigzag stitch.

3. Cording, pearl cotton, or trim can be zigzagged around the edge after the first go-around has attached the applique to the backing. Use the buttonhole foot so the cord will pass through one of the channels. Thread the ends of the cord into a tapestry needle and pull to the back. Tie off or glue ends together.

4. The blind hemstitch can be made to look like hand buttonhole embroidery. For best results use two threads on top, both threaded through the same needle. If your machine doesn't have two thread spindles on top, put a plastic drinking straw over the one you have, to elongate it so that it can handle one spool on top of another. Keep the stitch length short. (Practice on a doodle cloth first to find the best setting for your machine.)

5. Another method, slightly more complicated, is to attach the appliques to the foundation with a straight stitch as explained above. Load dark pearl cotton into the bobbin (see Chapter 5). Tighten top tension slightly. Practice on a doodle cloth to get the tensions right. Underside up, stitch around the applique. Pull dark thread to underside and tie off or glue together.

Fig. 3-23 Straight-stitch applique four ways. See corresponding numbers on p. 119.

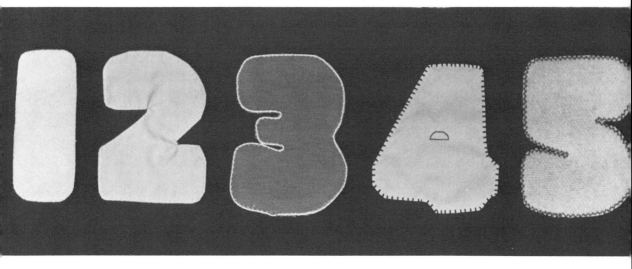

Fig 3-24 Zigzag applique five ways. See corresponding numbers on p. 119.

How to Handle Strange Shapes in Applique

Turning under the seam allowance for applique is harder on some shapes than others. For a square corner, see Fig. 3-25; for a sharp angle, see Fig. 3-26.

The Perfect Satin Stitch

For years I was unhappy with the sloppiness of my satin stitches. When I saw hangings and banners at shows, I always waited till no one was looking and then snuck up within inches to see if their satin stitch was any better than mine. Usually it wasn't. Then I discovered the secret of the perfect satin stitch: using extra-fine machine-embroidery thread. (If your favorite store doesn't stock it, see the Resource list at the end of the book.)

If you've ever done a hand satin stitch with all six strands of embroidery floss, you know how coarse and sloppy it looks. The same principle applies here: the finer the thread, the better-looking the satin stitch.

However, all those stitches pulling on the threads of the backing fabric cause a terrific strain, which is why you often get puckers and tunneling if you don't take precautions. Always strengthen the foundation fabric, either by backing it with typing-weight scrap paper (it tears off easily afterwards) or stabilizer (interfacing) or by putting the foundation fabric in an embroidery hoop (take the applique or embroidery presser foot off to get the hoop under the needle; then put the presser foot back on).

Use a size 10/11(70) needle. Loosen top tension slightly. Be sure to practice satin stitch on your doodle cloth. For most machines you can use any thread in the bobbin (I usually use cotton-covered polyester), but some machines object if the same threads are not used in top and bobbin. If the fabric puckers, loosen top tension even more. An open-toed embroidery or applique foot makes it easier to see what you're stitching.

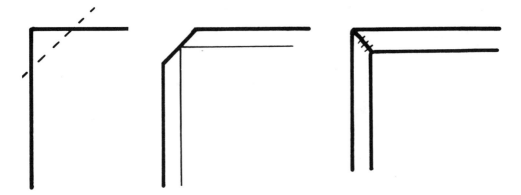

Fig. 3-25 To turn under a square corner, cut off the corner at a 45° angle just a few threads outside the intersection of the seam lines. Fold in the seam allowances and take a few hand stitches through the seam allowances to hold them in place for applique.

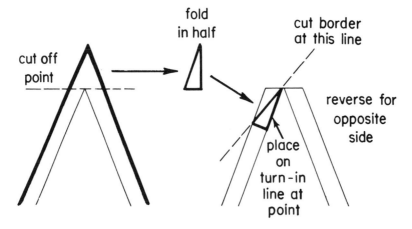

Fig. 3-26 A sharp angle must be trimmed as shown before edges are turned in for applique.

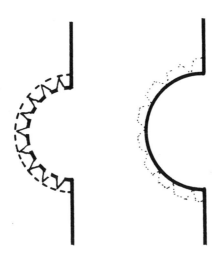

Fig. 3-27 To turn in a curve, stitch along the seam line. Clip to stitching. Press under along stitching.

To start and end threads when satin stitching, use one of the following methods:

1. Overlap several satin stitches, pulling the top thread to the back, and tying a knot or dropping a spot of glue onto the threads.

2. Pull the threads to the back, threading them into a sewing needle and hiding them under the satin stitches on the underside.

3. Set both the stitch width and stitch length controls to 0, taking 3 to 5 stitches in the same place, cutting off the top thread close to the fabric, leaving a small tail on the bobbin thread (yank it to bring the top thread end to the back), which will be hidden when you construct the quilt sandwich.

Satin Stitch for Applique. Machine quilters are very vehement about their preferred method of satin-stitch applique. One person insists on stabilizing the background fabric with such-and-such a product and abhors using scrap paper. Another person abhors the feeling of the background stabilizer and insists that straight stitching first is the secret. Try the following five methods on a doodle cloth to see which you prefer; your way is the best way.

1. Cut out the shape to be appliqued with no seam allowance. Run the stick-type glue around the under edge and place the applique on the foundation.

Fig. 3-28 Satin stitch four ways. See corresponding numbers on pp. 123-26; method 5 not shown.

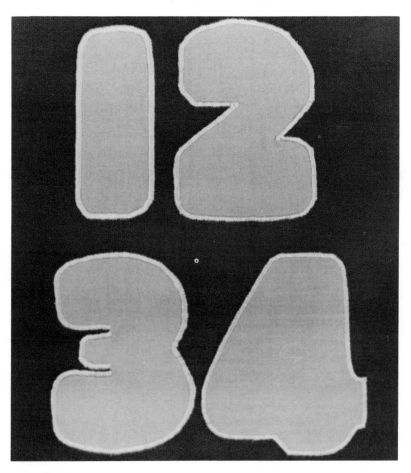

Strengthen the foundation fabric by pinning typing-weight scrap paper underneath, to be torn off after stitching. Or if the applique is small, place the background fabric in an embroidery hoop (see p.130 for directions on how to put on an embroidery hoop for machine work). Satin stitch around the edges. Be sure the bulk of the satin stitches are on the applique fabric. Otherwise frayed edges of the applique will peek out or will escape from the stitching and possibly pull out. If you can decenter your needle to the right, you can more accurately place the needle at the exact edge of the applique. Using an open-toed applique or embroidery foot also helps.

Advantages: easy, long-lasting.

Disadvantages: difficult fabrics may fray and creep, small points and shapes move under the presser foot.

2. Karen Bray's method (see Bibliography): Trace the shape of the design onto the applique fabric. Cut a large square or rectangle around the applique design so that 1″ to 2″ (2.54 to 5.08 cm) remains all around the design. Pin the applique fabric to the background fabric. Straight stitch around the lines of the design, using 10 to 12 stitches per inch, and trim the applique fabric close to the stitching. Now satin stitch around the applique shape. Karen does not use any stabilizer or paper beneath her applique work, and yet it is pucker-free.

Advantages: it works and is pucker-free.

Disadvantages: extra fabric is required for each applique which is wasteful and expensive for some fabrics and not useable on small scraps; straight stitch is an extra step that takes more time.

3. Barbara Lee's method (see Bibliography): First stabilize a square of the applique fabric by fusing an iron-on interfacing to the back of it. Remember to use a damp press cloth for the strongest bond. You can dampen with a plant mister. Transfer the design to the applique fabric via heat transfer pencil, light table, or whichever method you prefer. Cut out the applique shape and pin it to the background fabric. Pin a piece of stabilizer (interfacing) underneath everything (stabilizer, because Barbara believes paper dulls the machine needle). Satin stitch. Optional: Cut away extra stabilizer on back.

Advantages: The fused applique will not fray or pucker, nor will the stabilized background. Small bits of fabric can be used in this way without fear of movement.

Disadvantages: Fusing tends to erase the very tactile quality we love in fabrics, making everything flat and even. For quilts, the fusing method can make the appliques too stiff.

4. European instructions for satin-stitch applique start with marking the pattern on the back of the foundation fabric. Pin a square of applique fabric bigger than the applique shape to the topside of the foundation fabric, matching grains. Underside up, stitch the applique shape with a narrow zigzag (not satin stitch). Turn it over and trim applique fabric close to the stitching. Now satin stitch the applique shape from the topside. For extra insurance against puckering, put a piece of typing-weight scrap paper under the foundation fabric, to be torn away after stitching.

Advantages: All pattern transfers go on the underside of the foundation fabric, so you don't have to worry about transfer marks being seen. The method is neat and pucker-free.

Disadvantages: Some people are uneasy about not being able to see what's happening to the applique fabric until after the preliminary step. When the applique is complicated, with many layers, you may become confused about which fabric to stitch first.

5. Layered satin stitch, sometimes called reverse applique, is worked by stacking three or more layers of the same-sized fabric together and machine or pin-basting the edges. The design is satin-stitched from the topside and then layers of fabric are carefully cut away to expose the other colors underneath. Small swatches of fabric can be inserted by straight-stitching a shape, cutting away the top layer(s), and pinning a square of the special fabric in place on top. Turn the

Fig. 3-29 One block of "Marriage Quilt" by Fay Quanstrom for Tim and MaryBeth Person. The words of the marriage vows were designed by manipulating paper strips within a frame. This block says "in sickness and in health." For the top of the quilt, denim blocks were cut in the designed phrases, colorful fabric inserted behind each cut-out, a quilt-as-you-go quilt sandwich made, and edges satin-stitched. Cross, interlocking rings, and other symbols were incorporated when the blocks were assembled into a whole quilt. "I love quilts and quilting, the heritage, warmth and tactile qualities they represent. Quilts combine the new and old in my favorite medium of expression. I prefer to explore what hasn't been done before, to innovate. I find this process grows most easily from a combination of fabrics on hand, found materials, and a self-imposed or commissioned assignment, although some ideas simply pop into my mind and have to be done! From each idea, more seem to grow, making the list of future projects longer than that of past accomplishments." [Worked on a Singer 500A, recently purchased a Bernina, has made 56 quilts in five years.]

fabric over and straight-stitch or zigzag (with a narrow stitch) the design shape again. From the topside, trim away excess applique fabric close to the stitching. Satin stitch, making sure you cover the two previous rows of straight stitches. Depending on what fabrics you use, this method can be made to look like Cuna Indian molas, Persian Resht applique (an insertion technique), lace or transparent insertion, or stained glass. For the latter, on a small scale, as long as the proportion of the width of the satin stitch to the size of the design shapes is the same as full-sized stained glass, you can use dark thread (black, brown, gray) to achieve a stained-glass look to layered satin-stitch applique. In other words, you must scale down the colored glass shapes and work small. But if you wish to work larger, you must either combine rows of satin stitching, use black ribbon or bias tape, or layer black fabric on top, to be satin-stitched and cut away, exposing the colors underneath.

Advantages: The satin stitch is strong and faster than turning under the edge and handstitching. It adds interest and texture to the design.

Disadvantages: If the fabrics used are slippery or have a nap (velvet, corduroy), they will move around unless you take precautions. Straight stitch the design line before cutting away fabrics for satin stitching.

Figure 3-29 is a terrific example of layered satin stitch.

No matter which method of satin-stitch applique you choose, some angles and shapes will need special handling. See Fig. 3-30, 3-31, 3-32, 3-33.

For precise circles, tape a thumbtack, head down, onto the bed of your machine either to the left or to the right. The distance from the point of the thumbtack to the needle (in a straight stitch position) is the radius of the circle. Push the centers of both the background fabric and the applique fabric onto the tack point. With a straight stitch or narrow zigzag stitch, stitch once around the circle. Remove the fabric, making certain you know where the center hole is (mark it with a pencil circle or pin if you're not sure you can find it again). Trim the applique fabric close to the stitching, put fabrics back onto the thumbtack, and satin stitch around the circle. (Note: This method has many possibilities; see Chapter 7 for machine quilting this way.) Try using decorative stitches around the

Fig. 3-30 To turn a corner with zigzag or satin stitch, end a line with the needle in the outside corner (at left). Pivot the material 90° and continue stitching.

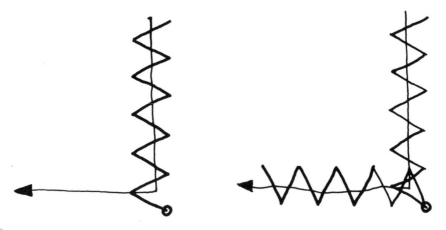

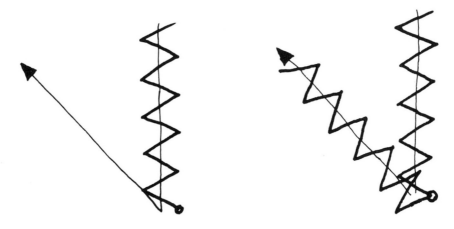

Fig. 3-31 To get around a point if you can't taper your satin stitch, end with the needle outside the turning point (at left). Pivot, being sure the first stitch you take falls within the line of stitching you've already made.

edges instead of satin stitch. Don't be afraid to use the circle method on single layers of fabric (Fig. 7-12), cutting the circle into slices, and then applying the wedges to a foundation fabric.

Any of these shapes can be further emphasized by pushing a little batting under the applique before finishing the satin stitch (Fig. 3-34).

Free-Machine Embroidery

Setting the stitch length control on your machine determines how much the feed dogs bob up/down and back/forth; the longest stitch setting (baste) activates the greatest movement in the feed dogs. The presser foot works with the feed dogs to move the fabric straight through in a smooth line.

When you take off the presser foot and set the stitch length to 0, you are freeing the fabric to be moved sideways, backwards, diagonally, in fact in any direction you want. This is called free-machine embroidery and it is especially useful to the machine quilter struggling to handle large amounts of fabric.

Fig. 3-32 To round a curve, pivot from the outside in.

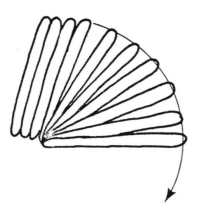

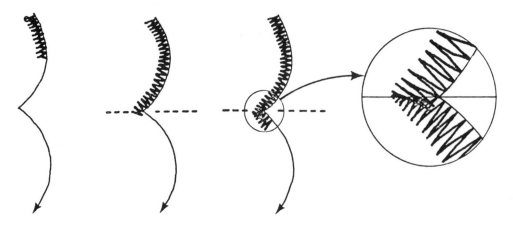

Fig. 3-33 How to handle a scallop.

Here we'll explain how to do basic free-machine embroidery with a straight stitch and a zigzag. In Chapter 5 we'll explore free-machine quilting. We will practice on a solid-colored medium-weight cotton or cotton-blend scrap big enough to fit in your hoop. If you work on a portable machine, put on the flat-bed extension; otherwise the hoop will tip over the edge.

Free-Machine Straight Stitch

Since there is no presser foot to hold the fabric taut against the needle plate, you must take precautions against skipped stitches. The easiest way is to put the fabric in a screw-type embroidery hoop. This is done backwards from hand embroidery. The outer ring is set on a flat surface (with the carved half-moon

Fig. 3-34 Appliques can be further stuffed with loose batting.

Fig. 3-35 "Bus Stop" by Cindy Hickok, machine-quilted muslin mounted on brown background (photo by Joel Draut, courtesy of *The Houston Post*). Compare with Cindy's piece on the color pages where she used the same woman. "The greatest amount of time involved in each piece comes at the beginning, before I get out any materials . . . and that is observing. The subjects for my pieces go before me each day in a constant parade of life and I pick up more ideas daily than I could use in a lifetime." [Works on a twenty-year-old Singer 403A, loosens pressure on presser foot.]

up—see Introduction). The fabric is spread topside-up over the ring and the inner ring is carefully pressed into place.

To adjust your machine, take off the presser foot, lower the feed dogs (optional), loosen top tension slightly, set both stitch width and stitch length on 0. (On some machines 0 is the place between "fine" and reverse.) For best results in the beginning, use 100% cotton or rayon extra-fine machine-embroidery thread and a size 10/11(70) needle. Choose a color that contrasts with the fabric. Any color and type of thread can be used in the bobbin.

For an extra precaution against skipped stitches and against running a needle through your finger, use a darning foot or darning spring—but this is optional. The foot comes down with the needle as it enters the fabric and holds the fabric flat against the needle plate as a stitch is formed. When the needle goes up, so does the foot, which allows you to move the fabric in any direction.

Slide the fabric and hoop under the needle. (The underside of the fabric is now flat against the needle plate.) For thick hoops and on some machines, you may have trouble fitting the hoop under the needle. Try sliding the hoop on its side and tipping it under. In drastic cases, you may have to take the needle off to fit the hoop under. (A slender machine-embroidery hoop is worth owning.)

Hold the top thread securely in your left hand. Turn the handwheel toward you one revolution so that the needle enters the fabric to the left of center hoop.

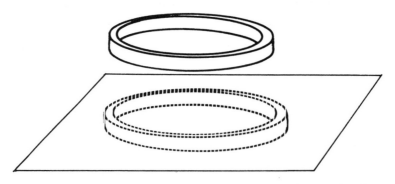

Fig. 3-36 To put fabric in an embroidery hoop for machine embroidery,
put the outer ring (with the screw) flat on a table. Place the fabric over
it and press in the inner ring.

Bring up the bobbin loop. Use a pin or tweezers to pull the bobbin thread to the
surface of the fabric. *Lower the presser bar lever*. This is easy to forget but
important! You have no top tension at all unless the presser bar lever is down. Now
take about three stitches in one place to lock the threads. You could theoretically
cut off the threads now because they are locked, but to keep from cutting the
actual sewing thread, wait to trim thread ends until you've stitched away from the
area.

Fig. 3-37 Bringing up the bobbin loop for free-machine embroidery. See the text
for further details.

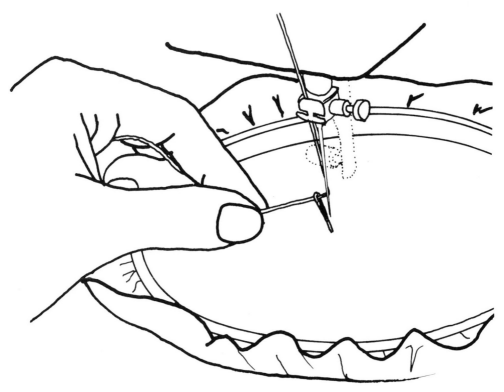

Now place your pinkies and thumbs on the outside of the hoop and your index and pointer fingers on either side of the needle, pressing down lightly. Pretend that your name is written in script on the fabric and that you are tracing it with the needle. Slowly and carefully stitch your name. Take your time; there's no need to hurry or to stitch your nose to the fabric. To dot i's or cross t's, either (1) lock threads at the end of your name, raise the presser bar lever, and gently draw the hoop into the new position, lower the presser bar lever, lock the threads again, and stitch (cut off excess threads when you're all done); or (2) stitch around and over to the needy letter in a continuous line.

The worst thing that can happen: you'll break a needle. Big deal, who cares? If you pull or jerk the hoop, the thread will pull the needle which will bend, hit the needle plate, and break. Stitch more slowly. You have lots of time.

If you run the machine too fast without moving the hoop, the needle will pierce the thread and it will then fray and break. Using extra-fine machine-embroidery thread is a precaution here. Slow down; there's no need to rush.

If you allow the hoop to lift up as the needle leaves the fabric, the bobbin hook cannot catch the top thread loop and a stitch is skipped. Keep your fingers on each side of the needle, pressing the fabric against the needle plate.

Free-machine embroidering is fun, easy, and exciting. It can be done by anyone of any age (past about four years old) on any machine. Although your first attempts may be laughable, keep practicing. It's especially worth learning for machine quilters. One expert has said it takes about 10 hours (cumulative, not in a row) of practice to be proficient. Practice the maneuvers in Fig. 3-38 on your doodle cloth (don't bother to transfer the designs—just eyeball it).

When you feel more confident, practice on small items that are not terribly important, like making a nametag or filling in a third color on a two-color printed fabric.

Free-Machine Zigzag

The same maneuvers you practiced with the straight stitch can be done with a zigzag stitch. The only difference in setting is the stitch width control which is set between 1 and your widest zigzag. By running the machine fast and moving the

Fig. 3-38 Try these maneuvers on your doodle cloth.

hoop slowly, you can pack in stitches as close as you did for satin stitch with the presser foot on—and yet still have the freedom of stitching off in any direction. If you think the stitches are skimpy in some places, back up and fill them in.

Again, you are using this technique to embellish the quilt top, not actually to quilt. One good use for free-machine zigzag is to sign your name and date your quilt, as Caryl Rae Hancock does. She also stitched into the quilt shown in the color section, "For Heidi with love from Mommy" and the date.

The tops of letters are usually stitched without rotating the hoop, so that all the stitches are roughly parallel (Fig. 3-39). (For ways to develop and transfer letters for your needs, see Chapter 9.)

Decorative Stitches

Not many people have explored the use of decorative stitches in quiltmaking, other than to enhance seam edges, as in crazy quilting. Part of the reason is the scale of the machine stitches to the whole quilt. The stitches are dwarfed by the rest of the quilt.

Yet the decorative stitches are useful in many ways: to change the value of a color you're not satisfied with (light stitching on a dark fabric, for example, makes it appear more midgray); to perk up dull or ordinary materials; to create centers of interest; and to actually quilt or tie the quilt sandwich (see Chapter 4).

Choose the background color you stitch on very carefully, so that it will contrast with and show off the stitching, not swallow it. White backgrounds, for example, are difficult unless you're using strong colors—black, brown, purple, charcoal. I once stitched a rainbow of decorative stitches on white and for all the hours of work, compared to how little the stitches showed up, I might just as well have drawn the rainbow with felt-tipped pens on the fabric. In *How to Attract Attention With Your Art* (see Bibliography), Ivan Tubau lists these color combinations as the most striking (in order of most impact): black on white, black on yellow, red on white, green on white, white on red.

For decorative stitching, use extra-fine machine-embroidery thread in the top. Rayon is a good choice because it catches the light like silk yet is long-wearing and washable. Use any thread in the bobbin and loosen top tension slightly. Test on a doodle cloth to be sure the stitches are not pulling in the fibers of the background material. If so, back the fabric with interfacing or typing-weight scrap paper (to be torn away later).

Make your work easier by stitching long rows of decorative stitches on a strip of background fabric and then cutting it up and reassembling it like you did for Seminole piecework (Fig. 3-40). Use small pieces as appliques, in which case you may want to bond iron-on interfacing to the back of the decorated fabric before

Fig. 3-39 The hoop is not rotated for free-machine zigzag letters.

Table 3-1. Figuring Block Sizes and Borders

Finished Block	Twin, 39" × 75" (99 × 191 cm)			Full, 54" × 75" (137 × 191 cm)			Queen, 60" × 80" (152 × 203cm)			King, 72" × 84" (185 × 213cm)		
	Number of Blocks	Border Around Each Block	Gives a Pillow Tuck of;*	#	B	PT	#	B	PT	#	B	PT
6"(15.3cm)	6×12	¼"(6mm)	3"(7.6cm)	9×13	0	3"(7.6cm)	10×14	0	4"(10cm)	12×14	0	0
8"(20.3cm)	4×3	1"(2.54cm)	5"(12.7cm)	6×9	½"(12mm)	6"(15.3cm)	6×9	1"(2.5cm)	10"(25.4cm)	9×11	0	4"(10cm)
10"(25.4cm)	4×8	0	5"(12.7cm)	5×7	¼"(6mm)	0	6×8	0	0	6×7	1"(2.5cm)	0
12"(30.5cm)	3×6	½"(12mm)	0	4×6	¾"(18mm)	6"(15.3cm)	5×7	0	4"(10cm)	6×7	0	0
14"(35.6cm)	not recommended			3×5	2"(5.1cm)	15"(38cm)	4×6	½"(12mm)	10"(25.4cm)	5×6	¼"(6mm)	3"(7.6cm)

*Add on one or two blocks to length for a deeper pillow tuck

Note: This chart does not include side or end drop measurements, only mattress top measurement.

133

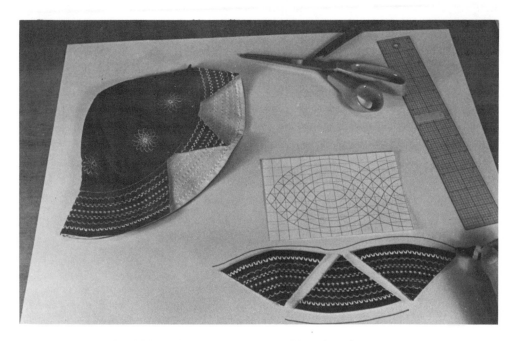

Fig. 3-40 Don't be afraid to cut up old work to design new.

applying it to another. This prevents the stitches from pulling out, which would be difficult to repair, and the edges of the applique fabric from fraying.

Traditionally, needleworkers have saved extensive embroidery, cutting up earlier work to insert it in later, removing bands from worn clothing and adding them to borders of new clothing. Often such needlework will be passed down through the family for hundreds of years, changing a little each generation. Since many people today do not take the time to hand embroider extensively, perhaps we machine-embroidery enthusiasts should step into this gap. By machine, we can embroider as much and more than our ancestors, thus saving what some fear is a dying art. The only danger is in making our machine-embroidery look too mechanical, with rows of unbroken parallel lines like trims bought in a fabric store. Make yours outstanding by changing colors, direction, and scale. Don't be afraid to cut up and manipulate what you've stitched.

Another way to bring interest to decorative stitches is to use a heavier thread in the bobbin—anything from cotton-covered polyester to buttonhole twist to pearl cotton. (Make sure all threads chosen are washable.) Stitch with the underside up, laying the bobbin thread on the topside. For sure, practice on a doodle cloth to check thread tensions for each thread used. Write the settings with pen on the doodle cloth so you can duplicate them again if you need to.

Now that you know how to piece, patch, and machine embellish your quilt top, you can think about how to set the blocks together in an attractive way. The traditional quilt arrangements are shown at the beginning of this chapter. For the quilts in this book we've tried to use as many different settings and patterns as possible.

However if the directions are for a double-sized bed mattress top and yours is queen-sized, you will need to know what changes to make. For the projects herein, don't change the basic block size; change the total number of blocks and add or subtract borders around the blocks to make adjustments.

To adapt a given block size to your size mattress top (not coverlet size), add or subtract borders all around each block as specified in Table 3-1. Example: Project gives directions for queen-sized mattress top with 6″ (15.3 cm) block. You have a twin bed. Use the 6″ (15.3 cm) block, but change the number of blocks and use a ¼″ (6 mm) border around each block.

You can also set blocks directly together without borders and make up the difference between finished quilt size and mattress size with a border or borders all around the outside of the quilt.

Chapter 4

Quilting with a Presser Foot

There are many ways to quilt with the presser foot on. In this chapter we will explore them, with accompanying projects so you can learn by doing. It is crucial that you understand proper basting if you want to quilt with the presser foot on. Review Chapter 2 if you need to, for the three best basting methods.

Stitch-in-the-Ditch

The most straightforward machine-quilting technique with the presser foot on is stitch-in-the-ditch. The term is borrowed from sewing on knits. After a quilt top has been pieced and the quilt sandwich basted, stitch along selected major seam lines, using a regular stitch length. If you have a walking foot, use it. Sometimes it's difficult to remember whether you've quilted a seam or not; when you're not sure, turn it over and examine the back.

Since the quilting does not always show on the top with this method, either you must use a very interesting design, such as log cabin or a traditional pieced design, or you must add additional quilting. The simplest addition is to machine quilt ½″ (12 mm) in from all major seams, using the quilting guide or masking tape as a gauge. Continue to add quilting lines until your personal standards of craftmanship are met; mine is the Closed Fist Test (see Chapter 2).

Game Plan for Half-of-a-Square Block Quilt

For those who are frustrated by very little time to quilt, here is a game plan for satisfaction. This is not a fast method, but it is designed to give a feeling of accomplishment as you progress. The secret is to make and to quilt thin pillows, finishing edges as you go. (This is not a new idea, having been around since at least the Civil War.) When you are done making all the pillows, you handstitch them together—that's the slow part! But the advantage is that as you complete each pillow, you have a project you can display. Once the initial piecing is done, one pillow can be done an evening.

Even if you do not intend to make this quilt, read the directions to understand the concept and to learn how to make sharp corners.

Our design fits a double mattress (including a 9″ pillow tuck) bed. If your bed is smaller or larger, make the changes in the borders around the blocks, not in the block sizes. We have used Barbara Johannah's methods to speed things up. You can preshrink and mark the fabric one night, sew some of the half-of-a-square triangles the second night, and construct and quilt one "pillow" the third night.

Fig. 4-1 Close-up, "Sampler Quilt" by Caryl Rae Hancock (see color section for full quilt). "My work is really in the elementary stages. There are so many things I want to try and areas in which I feel I need to grow. Teaching is also part of my 'work', and I feel that if I can help my students derive more use, enjoyment and creativity through their investment in a sewing machine, then I am satisfied. Also, I try hard to encourage them to have more confidence in their designing decisions—we all seem to be so hung up on only professional artists being able to design." [Works on a three-year-old Elna SU; favorite accessories: clear plastic Singer darning foot, Viking walking foot, had needle plate bent slightly to cover feed dogs for free-machine embroidery. Writing a how-to book on her sampler quilt—see Resources.]

Fig. 4-2 Stitch-in-the-ditch.

After that, you'll be so exhilarated, there'll be no stopping you. If you don't understand the Johannah half-of-a-square method, go back and review it in Chapter 3.

Finished size (mattress top): 56″ × 84″ (142 × 223 cm)
Finished block size: 12″ (30.5 cm) with 1″ (2.54 cm) borders = 14″ (34.6 cm)
Technique: stitch-in-the-ditch
Thread: 100% cotton
Needle size: 10/11(70) for piecing, 12(80) for quilting
Machine setting: straight stitch, regular length
Machine accessories: zipper or roller foot, walking foot (optional)
Seam allowance: ½″ (12 mm)

You Will Need

3 yd. of 45″-wide (2.73 m of 115-cm-wide) dark fabric
3 yd. of 45″-wide (2.73 m of 115-cm-wide) light fabric
6 yd. of 45″-wide (5.5 m of 115-cm-wide) border and backing fabric (dark or mid-gray, solid if you use prints in the half-of-a-square triangles)
additional fabric for the sides of the quilt (see "Estimating Yardage" in Chapter 2)
thread
3½ yd. 48″-wide (3.18 m of 127-cm-wide) batting (double that amount if you use a double batt as we did)

(Note: You could use scraps instead of fresh yardage, but you'd have to make templates and sew individual blocks, which is much slower, and not recommended.)

Construction

1. Make a sloper for your bed (see Chapter 2, p.56). Indicate the top mattress area. If your bed is larger than double mattress size, add 12″ (30.5 cm) blocks to the width and the length to fit. Adjust the border width around each block to fit your mattress (see Table 3-1 at end of Chapter 3).

2. Preshrink all fabric. Cut off and mark one yard (0.91 m) at a time. More than this is difficult to handle. Mark the back of the light fabric, as shown in Fig. 3-14. The grid lines should be 4¾″ (12 cm) apart. The diagonal seam lines should

Fig. 4-3 Sections from a half-of-a-square quilt *(Collection of Pat and Roberta Losey Patterson)*

be ½″ (12 mm) from the center diagonal lines. Use ½″ (12 mm) seams; be precise. For the top, you will need 384 half-of-a-square triangles. Mark 192; when you cut them open, you'll have the full number. You will also need twenty-four 15″ (38 cm) squares, including ½″ (12 mm) seams all around, of dark backing fabric and ninety-six 15″ × 2″ (38 × 5 cm) strips for the block borders. Cut open the squares and carefully press the seams open.

3. It's easy to figure out the block in its positive and negative form by studying the cartoon (Fig. 4-4). But you do not have to use the blocks pictured—in fact, you have four quadrillion choices for each block. Some of the possibilities are shown without borders in Fig. 4-6. It is far more fun to discover your own as you work, playing with the 16 squares of each block until you find something you like. If you are feeling adventurous, make each block different on your own quilt.

The finished pieced block with borders is 15″ (38 cm) square, including ½″ (12 mm) seam allowances. Sew the vertical seams between half-of-a-square triangles first and press open. Then sew the three horizontal seams and press open. Match cross-seams carefully. Add border strips to the top and bottom edges of the blocks. Then add border strips to the sides.

4. To construct the pillow, change to a size 12(80) needle and a zipper foot. Cut one or two 15″ (38 cm) square pieces of batting. If you use a double batt for extra loft, remember this will cause the actual finished block size to be 13½″ (34.3 cm) rather than 14″ (35.6 cm). Place the batting on the wrong side of the pieced top and sew together along the ½″ (12 mm) seam. Trim batting close to stitching. Place the pieced square on the 15″ (38 cm) square backing, rightsides together. Sew again on the seam line, but leave a 7″ (17.8 cm) opening in the middle of one side for turning.

To make corners sharp, stop stitching one stitch from the corner. Reduce stitch length to tiny and handwalk the needle across the corner at a 45° angle for

Fig. 4-4 Half-of-a-square cartoon, showing two versions with borders.

Fig. 4-5 Layout of quilt, using two variations of the same half-of-a-square blocks.

Fig. 4-6 Some of the many possibilities for designs from light/dark half-of-a-square blocks.

two or three stitches. When you reach the seam line again, reset stitch length and continue until you reach the next corner. Clip corners; turn pillow rightside out; close seam by hand.

5. Pin-baste the pillow sandwich together so it won't shift around as you quilt. Using stitch-in-the-ditch, machine quilt around the major shapes and border seams of the pieced block. If you use a contrasting thread on the back, you will have a two-sided, reversible quilt. Be careful every time a quilting line crosses another quilting line. Pucker is lurking.

6. After all the pillows have been made, begin sewing the blocks together by hand. Sew all the pillows across first, making 6 long strips, and then sew the strips together. The pillows are sewn together by putting rightsides together and connecting them with the toymaker's ladder stitch (Fig. 2-43). For greatest strength, work from the center out to one side, back along the side to the other end, and back to the center again. This is the slow part.

If you don't have time for the handsewing, but you still want to make a quilt present, construct all the finished pillows and send them in a big box to your friend with instructions on how to sew them together (easier—give this book to your friend as part of the gift and mark this page).

7. Borders and sides are added the same way: making a finished pillow, machine quilting it, and handsewing it to the top. Choose a machine quilting pattern from this chapter or simply stitch straight diagonal lines. When the "pillows" for the sides are large, pin or thread-baste to keep them from shifting and use the walking foot if you have one.

Additional Ideas

1. For the very lazy, sew two ribbons perpendicular to each side of each block, a third of the way from each corner. Then you can tie the blocks together instead of having to hand-sew the seams. You can also change the design at will. (Be sure to preshrink the ribbons.)

2. In the same vein, make log-cabin pillows connected by ribbons. By periodically rearranging the darks and lights, you can try all the arrangements of log cabin over the years. The same quilt will feel like a new quilt.

3. Construct a yard of string quilting (see Chapter 3). Sew it to a contrasting yard of fabric a la Johannah method. Cut apart in half-of-a-square triangles and piece blocks as usual. (Use idea also for crazy quilts.)

Note: Technically you can join finished blocks by machine but I'm not sure it's anything more than a curiosity. Loosen top tension. Decenter the needle to the left. Set the machine for the narrowest zigzag. Place the pillows rightsides together. Roll the two backing edges back slightly. Start stitching about ¾" (18 mm) from the end and leave long thread tails. Zigzag down the end, only entering the fabric on the left swing of the needle. Stop about ¾" (18 mm) from the other end of the blocks and leave a long tail. Thread the ends through a hand needle and finish sewing up the gaps with the toymaker's ladder stitch.

Ernest B. Haight's Whole-Cloth Method

Ernest B. Haight of David City, Nebraska, began quilting 40 years ago when he kibitzed over his wife's shoulders about a poorly matched cross-seam. Mrs. Haight gracefully said, "Why don't you do it?" and he did. Soon he'd enlisted the aid of his father who offered to quilt a top for each grandchild if Ernest would piece it (on a treadle machine).

When the elder Mr. Haight died, Ernest's wife began hand quilting the tops. But there were so many that Ernest began to experiment with machine quilting to make a whole quilt top. By then, he was working on a zigzag machine. Each year he makes 8 to 10 quilts for the grandchildren plus several more quilts to give away to the pastor, the organist, and friends and for wedding and anniversary gifts.

When Ernest first entered a machine-quilted quilt in the Butler County Fair in the early 1960s, it was almost refused as "*not* art" until a sympathetic official stepped in and said, "we must create a new category." The quilt won a First Premium Blue Ribbon, as have many of Ernest's orginal-designed, machine-pieced and machine-quilted quilts.

In 1971 the Stuhr Museum in Grand Island, Nebraska, held a retrospective of Ernest B. Haight's work.

In 1973 the Superintendent of Needlework at the Nebraska State Fair urged Mr. Haight to write a booklet explaining his methods in order "to get machine quilting accepted as an art form." *Practical Machine-Quilting for the Homemaker* (see ordering information in Bibliography) is highly recommended to all machine quilters for its excellent and comprehensive instructions and for its collectible value—first-hand advice from the patron saint of machine quilters.

Fig 4-7 Ernest B. Haight, the patron saint of machine quilters, at work on a 20-year-old White.

Doris Hoover, "Chicken Quilt." Variety of hand and machine techniques: satin stitch quilting, tying, hand quilting.

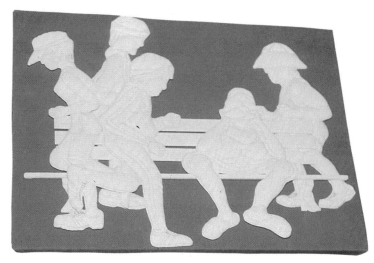

Cindy Hickok, "Some Days I Think the World Is Passing Me By." Free-machine quilting and trapunto on muslin (see Ch. 5 for Cindy's use of the same character in a different piece); 26″ x 21″. Collection of George Ehni, M.D.; photo courtesy of the artist.

Sas Colby, "Socks." Padded silk applique, machine quilted with satin stitch, 46″ x 55″. Photo courtesy of the artist.

Elizabeth Gurrier, "Boxes." Quilted with decorative stitch and free-machine quilting. Photo courtesy of the artist.

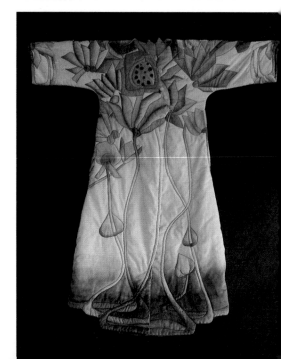

Lenore Davis, wall hanging. Machine quilting follows lines made by squeeze bottle of fiber-reactive dye, 34″ x 45″. Photo courtesy of the artist.

Joy Stocksdale, cotton velveteen coat. Machine quilted from underside, using heavy #3 pearl cotton in bobbin; design was then painted with watered-down acrylic paint (Liquitex). Photo courtesy of the artist.

dj bennett, "Wall Hanging." Batik is embellished with free-machine embroidery, then free-machine quilted to black felt, with cutout areas, 18½″ x 32″.

Merry Bean, "Washington Bicentennial Quilt." Scenes from the nation's capital, free-machine quilted in three panels, then joined.

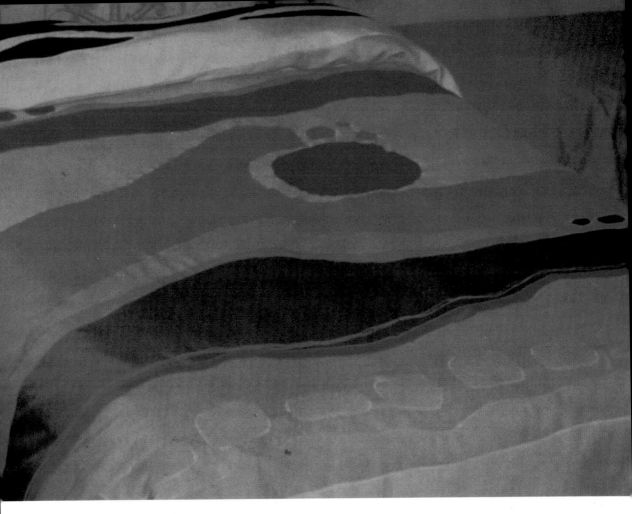

Jude Lewis, "La Playa Caliente (Warm Beach)." The finished double-bed commission discussed in Ch. 10. Photo courtesy of the artist.

Margaret Cusack, "Bloomingdale's Apple Pie." Made for cover of Bloomingdale's catalog; to create lumpy effect of pie, real pebbles inserted under surface; piecrust is upholstery fabric used underside up, 14" x 16". Photo courtesy of the artist.

Radka Donnell, "Quiet Breathing." Pieced by artist, quilted on programmed industrial machine by Claire Mielke, 89″ x 109″. Photo courtesy of the artist.

Peggy Moulton, "Have A Crabapple, Eve, Baby." Crabapple is made of small bits of fabric, stitched back and forth with straight stitch; hands have been hand quilted, 26″ x 16″ x 9″. Photo courtesy of the artist.

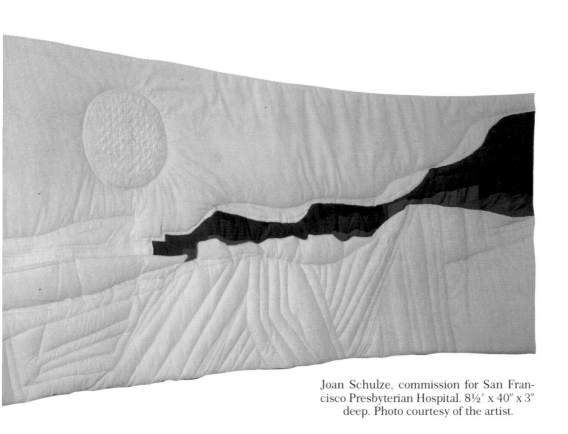

Joan Schulze, commission for San Francisco Presbyterian Hospital. 8½′ x 40″ x 3″ deep. Photo courtesy of the artist.

Joan Michaels Paque, detail. Long, trapuntoed satin piece, 5½″ x 32″. Collection of Rehr West Museum, Neitowac, Wisconsin; photo courtesy of the artist.

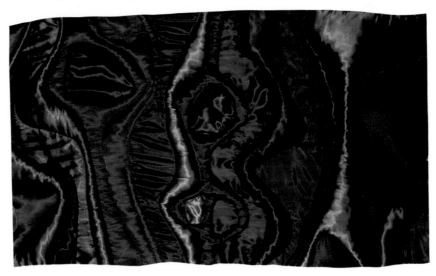

Nina Stull, closeup of "Alphabet Quilt." Translates children's drawings into fabric: satin-stitch applique, quilted with chain stitch, 69″ x 80″. Photo courtesy of the artist.

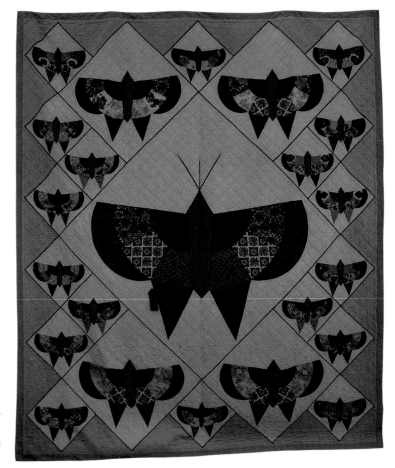

Ernest B. Haight, "Big Butterfly Quilt." Original pieced design, quilted in a diamond grid with presser foot on, 80″ x 96″.

Alice Newton, "Heart Vest." Free-machine quilted on denim, then lined.

Caryl Rae Hancock, "Sampler Quilt." Whole top machine pieced, then machine quilted with the presser foot on, 76" x 108".

One-Step Seminole Sleeping Bag
(Ch. 6).

Left, decorative-stitch-quilted Vest
for a Star (Ch. 4); *right*, Wigwarm;
background, String-Quilted Snap-
On Hat (both Ch. 6).

Fay Quanstrom, "Eric's Jungle." Oversize log cabin square made in quilt-as-you-go; center printed fabric free-machine quilted with invisible thread on top.

Projects from Chapters 5, 6, and 9. *Top to bottom, left to right:* Basic Tote, Crazy Quilt Stocking, Key/Luggage Tag, Baker's Mitt; Noel, Nametag, Catnip Kitty, Quick Message, Tooth Fairy Bag, Needlecase, Log Cabin Pincushion; Fabric Letters.

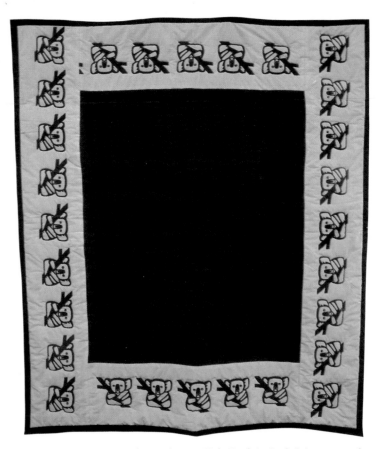

The authors, "Kali Koala's Quilt." A variety of techniques: free-machine quilting, quilting with presser foot on in straight stitch and in zigzag (see Ch. 10).

Color chart. Compare with the black and white chart (Ch. 10) to help plan relative light-medium-dark values. *From top to bottom,* the colors are red, orange, yellow, green, blue, purple, and brown. The purest hues are in the center, the darker shades on the left, and the lighter tints on the right.

Fig. 4-8 A detail of one of Ernest Haight's quilts (see color section for full quilt). "I have always been intrigued with puzzles . . . where the pieces intersect from three directions yet fit completely and perfectly. . . . To me, every quilt pattern is a puzzle, a challenge, to choose agreeable colors or prints, to work out an order of assembly, to make corners meet as they should."

First, we'll examine Ernest B. Haight's method. Read through the explanation carefully before attempting it. Then read about my experiences quilting a king-sized sheet, to see how even the simplest techniques can trick a quilter the first time. Then try it out for yourself.

1. Mark the quilt top (Fig. 4-9). After piecing, Ernest B. Haight marks his quilt top with a diagonal grid of parallel lines about 1½" to 2" (3.6 to 5.08 cm) apart (he uses cotton batting so his lines must be close). Notice that his quilt-top designs (see color section) are usually geometric with diamond or square shapes predominating; the quilting therefore echoes and integrates these shapes, instead of being slapped on top of any old design. The diamond grid is also perfect for machine quilting, as you are stitching on the bias and can manipulate the fabric as you quilt to eliminate puckers.

An easy way to find the first diagonal line from the top left corner is to fold that corner down along the opposite long edge, making a folded triangle which opens into a square, with a rectangle extending below it. Mark where the corner hits the side; connect this mark with the corner (or iron it in lightly). Do the same for the opposite corner and you have the two main quilting lines.

2. Baste in a frame. Remember, this is the secret to pucker-free machine quilting! Ernest B. Haight straight pins the backing (lining) to the quilting frames, stretches it taut but not overly so, makes the quilt sandwich, and bastes it together

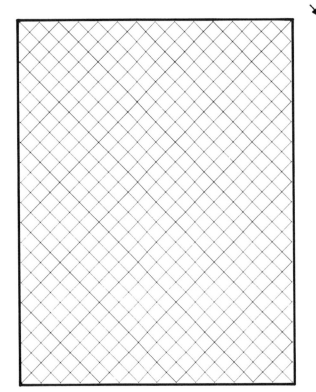

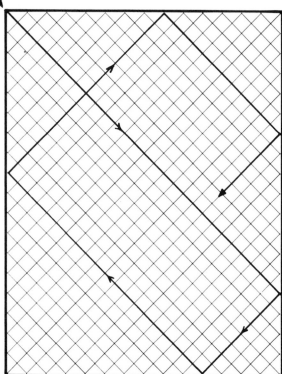

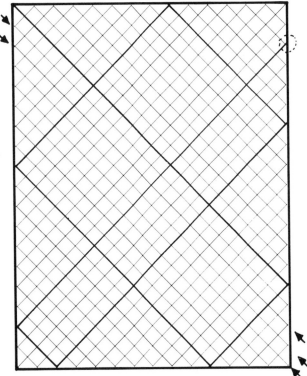

Fig. 4-9 Top left: Ernest B. Haight's diamond grid: First mark the grid on your top fabric. Form the quilt sandwich and baste securely. Right: Start at the upper left corner, stitch down the diagonal until you ricochet off the side. Turn counterclockwise and stitch down the diagonal line until you hit another side. Bottom: Continue turning the quilt counterclockwise until you run out of lines to turn to. Notice that this method places the bulk of the quilt to the left of the machine. Repeat this process from the other end of the quilt. Then move down, line-by-line, the sides of the quilt, always mirroring what you do at one end at the other end.

with about 200 safety pins for an 80″ × 96″ (203 × 244 cm) quilt (see Fig. 2-30a). As he works, the quilt is rolled onto the short frames; the whole basting process takes him three to four hours. When done, he removes the straight pins holding the lining to the frames and machine-bastes around the perimeter of the quilt sandwich.

3. Machine quilt. Haight uses a straight stitch of regular length. He changes to the straight-stitch needle plate so the quilt is not dragged into the slot, causing puckers. (You can also use a left-needle position on a zigzag plate, for the same reason.) He also uses a narrow presser foot and advises *tightening* the pressure so the quilt will feed smoothly. If your presser foot pressure is adjustable, you can do this too. Be sure to work in an open area with lots of support for the quilt behind the machine (see Chapter 1). If it drags over the edge, it will pull against the needle, causing uneven stitches, possibly puckers, and lots of impolite language.

Start stitching at the upper left-hand corner, backstitching 2–3 stitches to lock threads (Fig. 4-9). Stitch across the quilt, following the marked line, and taking your time. Your left hand spreads on either side of the presser foot to keep the working area smooth while your right hand guides the rolled-up bulk of the quilt under the head of the machine and your left elbow wrestles the rest of the quilt into position. When you reach the opposite side, leave the needle in the fabric, raise the presser bar lever, pivot the fabric 90°, lower the presser bar lever, and continue to stitch until you run out of lines to pivot towards (upper right-hand corner). Your first lines of stitching look like those shown in Fig. 4-9.

The beauty of Ernest B. Haight's quilting method is that except for the two long diagonal lines, the bulk of the quilt is always to your left and not underneath the head of the machine.

The second pass mirrors the first, by starting in the lower right-hand corner of the foot end, except that when you've turned the quilt upside-down, it becomes the upper left corner again.

Each new spiral is stitched twice, once from the head end of the quilt and once from the foot end. All starting points move down a long side from a corner. This is quite clear as you're working, although your mind may boggle looking at the overall quilting diagram. With experience, the machine quilting of a full-sized top can be done in 8 to 12 hours, and a crib-sized quilt can be finished in under two hours.

4. Bind the edges. Ernest B. Haight cuts fabric 2⅜″ (6 cm) wide along the *straight* of the grain (he prefers this to bias binding), seaming fabric together the long way until he has a long enough strip to go entirely around the quilt—about 30 feet for an 80″ × 96″ (203 × 244 cm) quilt. Fold the strip in half lengthwise, wrong sides together, and seam to the underside of the quilt, using a ¼″ (6 mm) seam. Bring the fold edge to the seam line on the topside, miter the corners, and stitch the fold down by machine. You now have a quilt made entirely by machine.

Machine Quilting a Sheet

Here's the usual advice for how to machine quilt a sheet:

It's easy. Wash the sheet. Open out the turned-over edges. Choose a batting and backing. Mark the quilt top in a diamond grid. Baste the quilt. Machine quilt. Bind edge.

Fig. 4-10 Quilting a king-sized sheet.

How *Not* to Machine Quilt a Sheet
(or learning through the mistakes of others)

Because I do so much free-machine quilting (see next chapter) and one-step quilting (Chapter 6), which are handled differently from quilting a whole top with the presser foot on, I had never tried this method before Ernest B. Haight came into my life. I decided to follow his instructions exactly, which includes the advice to practice on a "utility quilt" using printed fabric as the quilt top. I decided to quilt a king-sized sheet. That was my first of many mistakes.

Because you can learn, as I did, what to avoid from my mistakes, I catalog them here for you, without the slightest embarrassment. What I did was similar to announcing, "We're having Beef Stroganoff on Rice for dinner. Except I used tuna and I didn't have any sour cream or enough rice,"—what you serve is Tuna Noodle Casserole. I followed Ernest B. Haight's instructions exactly—except I didn't mark the quilt the way he does and I used a different size quilt top and I decided to zigzag instead of straight stitch and. . . .

Size

The size of my king-sized sheet, with the hem unpicked and opened out, was 106½″ × 107½″ (270.5 × 273 cm). I used a second king-sized sheet as backing and a ¼″ (6 mm) bonded polyester batting from a pre-cut package.

Mistake #1: Quilted, the sheet would not cover our mattress. I had to either add a large border (another sheet, cut up) or put a dust ruffle on the bottom springs. I chose the latter because it's easier.

Mistake #2: The packaged batting was not big enough for the king-sized sheet. I needed a second package, or I should have bought batting by the yard. At least I chose a sheet design that's compatible with a diamond grid, which is what the Ernest B. Haight whole-sheet method requires.

Marking

Mistake #3: I couldn't use Ernest B. Haight's clever spiral method, which requires a rectangle, because my sheet was square. If I'd planned ahead, I could have added pieces to the top and backing to make a rectangle and then the quilt would have completely covered the bed. But I was impatient to get on with the quilting, so I didn't. A king-sized sheet is enormous. I had no floor space large enough to spread out on. I worked outside on the Ping-Pong table. (Fine for summer, but what would I do in the winter in Minnesota or in the rain in Oregon? Go to the city recreation department or high school, probably, and ask to borrow their freshly mopped gymnasium floor for several hours—or work exclusively in quilt-as-you-go modules.)

The quilt folded on the diagonal was bigger than my Ping-Pong table. I gently pressed in the fold, taking care not to stretch the bias. Since I was not using cotton batting (and since I'm inherently lazy), my quilting lines could be farther apart. I used a long 3″ (7.6 cm) wide board as a marking device. It was dirty, even after I wiped it off with a rag; and my quilt had to be washed before being used. The board template was imprecise, too, since the quilt diagonal was longer than the table or the board. I probably could have carefully pinned and folded the quilt top in half and in quarters, marking two quarters and then extending the lines into the remaining two quarters. Another possibility: I could have taped cardboard together into a piece as large as our mattress and spread the top over that, using the bed as a table.

Basting

It would be easy to forget and put the backing in the quilting frames rightside up (should be, obviously, rightside down), but my sheet backing is the same on both sides. The reason hand quilters don't use cotton/poly sheets is that the tight weave resists the needle. This is of no consequence to machine quilters . . . except when pin-basting the lining to the frames. Ooh, did my finger tips get sore! Use long glass-headed pins, not regular T-headed pins. Be sure the lining is absolutely taut (but not overstretched) before spreading the batting and top on.

Mistake #4: Leave yourself plenty of time to baste. I started late in the day, not realizing until I'd pinned the long sides that I wouldn't have enough daylight to finish. The only room big enough to work in was, you guessed it, the bedroom, working over the bed. I dragged in the sawhorses and quilting frames and set up shop. Unfortunately, we could not go to bed until I'd finished many hours later.

Mistake #5: I quickly ran out of safety pins so I used straight-pins. Either thread-baste or safety-pin baste; don't expect pin-basting to hold the layers taut. Pins pop out and scratch you as you maneuver the quilt while sewing, so that your arms look like you've been attacked by cats.

Mistake #6: I stood at the short end and rolled the quilt along the long pieces to the other end of the quilting frame. I should have rolled *onto* the long pieces and *along* the short pieces. With every roll, you lose a little tautness, so the fewer rolls necessary the better. There are less rolls, obviously, along the short pieces. Every time you roll, check underneath to be sure it's still taut.

I recommend safety-pin basting; it's faster and it really holds the fabric taut. But if you don't want to buy 200 or more safety pins, consider thread-basting the quilt upside-down, stretching the top first and then adding the two layers. This way you can see that the backing is properly stretched and basted. Then when you turn it over for machine-sewing, you can control the top.

I did such a poor job of pin-basting that when I sewed my first line, it puckered on the back. I put the whole thing back on the frames again, taking out the machine quilting lines (which involved crawling under the quilt—all the kids and cats followed me as if it were a game), and rebasted with thread. Again, I did not leave myself enough time. This time I couldn't fit the 12' (3.6m) long frames into the garage so I had to leave the quilt propped against the garage overnight. Did you know birds fly around at night? Even though I'd gotten up with the sun at 5:30 AM to finish basting, they'd left messages on my quilt, which definitely had to be washed out before use.

My nine-year-old daughter Kali helped me thread-baste, a very peaceful activity for both of us. While I had the quilt on the frames, I tried hand quilting. My stitches were ridiculously long; I choose to think that it was because of the tight weave of the sheets.

Machine Quilting

I followed Ernest B. Haight's method *exactly*—except I used a walking foot and the narrowest zigzag. I also used two different colors and thread weights in top and bobbin and had trouble balancing the tensions. (I do not recommend using extra-fine machine-embroidery thread for quilting a whole top. Some of the stitches on my quilt have broken from the stress of making the bed each day and from machine washing. Regular cotton sewing thread is OK.) Everything progressed well except that I was working outside on the Ping-Pong table and it was too bright to work in the sun. ("Where'd you get that bad sunburn?" "Oh, I was machine quilting this weekend.") It was also the sticky season for live oaks so my quilt added another layer of pollen and ick to its previous dirt. Nevertheless, I love sewing outside, with the squirrels, birds, cats, and children. I spread an old sheet on the ground under me, which protected the dirty quilt some. I rigged up an L-shaped work area by putting a small board on saw horses to my left and sewing down the length of the Ping-Pong table.

I sewed from the center out to one side, all quilting lines the same direction. Then I turned the quilt upside down and sewed again from the center out. This process was repeated for the cross-quilting lines. I quickly learned to pin the bulk of the quilt that passes under the head into a fat roll. If you don't, it fights back. I also pinned along each quilting line before sewing, which took more time but was worth it in ease of handling. I found that using the slow speed on my foot pedal gave me more even stitches and that the right hand should lightly pull the bulk of the quilt along from behind the presser foot, while the left hand spreads the quilt in front of the needle. Every few inches I stopped to move more of the quilt into position; if you don't stop with the needle in the fabric, the quilt may move away from the needle and you will have a little glitch there. The lines in the middle of the quilt are the most difficult; after sewing them, each line gets progressively easier and shorter, with less bulk to fight, so that it feels like you are rewarding yourself for all that initial hard work.

In conclusion, I do *not* recommend learning on a king-sized quilt. Practice on a crib quilt.

Check your bobbin every three lines. With zigzag quilting, you use more thread than with straight stitch. It is extremely annoying to run out of thread in the middle of a line, especially since you usually are so intent on handling the quilt that you don't notice it until you finish the line. Clean your machine two or three times during this extensive quilting; you will find that the bobbin fuzz really builds up. You may also want to change the needle frequently.

A dangerous place for the inexperienced is when two quilting lines cross. At first pin-baste each line carefully. Learn to use your fingers to feel whether the backing material is thinking about bunching up and puckering at the cross-quilting lines. Quilting on the bias makes it easy to coax the fabric to go the way you want it to.

Machine quilting, as I said, is faster than hand quilting but not fast. The longest line took 15 minutes to sew and there are 88 quilting lines on my quilt. Sewing a few lines a day and allowing for normal evening interruptions like picnics, movies, volleyball, and the library, I basted the quilt one weekend and it was on the bed two weekends later. For all the mistakes, it was worth it and I enjoyed the whole process enormously, not to speak of the pleasure of sleeping under another I-made-it-myself quilt.

I spent about $25 on materials (sheets were on sale) and my quilt is reversible; to buy the same sheet factory-quilted in a large ugly pattern with a scratchy backing costs around $80, and I wouldn't have been satisfied with that at all.

Final advice

It's worth learning this whole-cloth machine quilting method. It's faster than quilt-as-you-go techniques because there are no hand-closed seams, and if you baste properly, it's the best-looking method for machine quilting a geometric pieced quilt. But start smaller than I did—a crib or lap quilt to learn on—and be sure to use a thin batt.

Other Straight-Stitch Methods

Machine quilters seem to take ultimatums as a challenge; as soon as it's generally repeated that you must do such-and-such, someone stomps defiantly to the machine and does it differently.

On the whole, it's easier and more successful to quilt whole tops on the machine with diagonal lines. But that doesn't stop machine quilters from stitching across the quilt or down it or in curved lines, if the pattern calls for it.

In particular, you may have a special print that you want to quilt. Here's how to ensure success:

1. Baste the quilt sandwich well. If you don't have quilting frames and can't borrow some, double-baste (see Chapter 2). Use the straight-stitch needle plate if you have one, or the left-needle position if you can decenter the needle.

2. Make sure it's worth the time to quilt your print. If it's surrounded by a busy design, you may not be able to see the puffiness and you'll be disappointed. Try to buy an extra ¼ yard (23 cm) of fabric to experiment on first. If outlining your print doesn't work with the presser foot on, try free-machine quilting (Chapter 5).

3. Choose the backing fabric carefully. A solid fabric is nice and can be brought around to frame the front, but it shows the goofs unless you match the top

Fig. 4-11 Try outline quilting the main elements of a print fabric. (Quilt by Kathleen Weisenberg, collection of Kjersti Weisenberg)

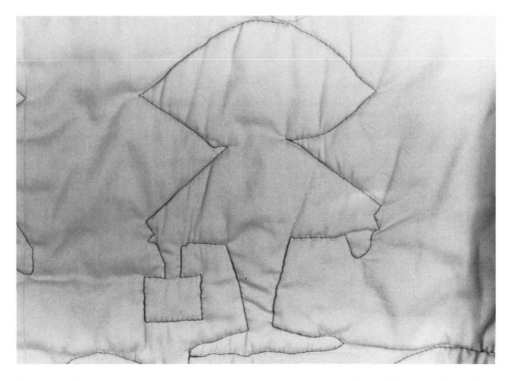

Fig. 4-12 The underside of a quilted print fabric. The sharp angles could invite a visit from Pucker.

and bobbin threads to its color. A small print for backing fabric can work well as long as it complements the top.

4. Stay away from quilting small sharp angles and complicated turns—you're only asking for a visit from Pucker. In many cases, you can stitch around the general shape, without delineating every in and out. However, if you stubbornly want to quilt each little nuance of your print, it helps to put one section or motif of the print in a hoop, put the presser foot on, and quilt. Don't try to force curves; stop with the needle in the fabric, lift the presser bar lever, move the quilt into position, lower the presser bar lever, and stitch merrily on.

5. If you are not using a hoop, choose your batting carefully, based on your experience. A thick batting looks beautiful quilted—but is harder to work without puckers. Use the open-toed presser foot so you can see where to quilt. For long straight lines down or across the quilt, work from the center out to one side, with the extra bulk under the head of the machine rolled up and pinned. Don't let the bulk of the quilt hang over behind your sewing area or it will pull away from the needle. Then turn the quilt 180° and work from the center out to the remaining side. If you are picky, pin on both sides of each quilting line before sewing. Admittedly, this takes more time, but you won't need to worry about the fabric pulling in unnatural angles.

Since the larger the area to be worked, the harder it is to handle and the more chance of error, consider breaking down a large fabric into smaller modules, adding units as shown in Chapter 6. If you don't have enough fabric to use in the center and the borders, copy the motifs onto tracing paper and outline the shapes to be used same size or enlarged as your quilting lines (See Fig. 10-13 for a good example).

Trapunto

Trapunto is the technique of stitching two layers of fabric together, slitting the back fabric, and inserting a stuffing into the slit to raise the surface of the top fabric. (It is not technically "quilting" unless you also quilt or tie the raised area.) The machine is especially well-suited to trapunto, because its stitches are sturdy and long-lasting against the strain of the raised fabric. For best results choose a top fabric that has a sheen and catches the light—silk, satin, sateen, crepes, some polyesters. If you insist on using cotton, choose a solid light-colored fabric so your work will show. For many trapuntoed print fabrics, after the motifs are painstakingly machine outlined and then stuffed, the raised areas are practically invisible except from the side.

For the backing use a firmly woven fabric such as an old sheet, good muslin, organza; or a heavy cotton such as duck. This is so that the raised area will puff up and out away from the firm foundation, instead of sinking toward the back like a crater. If you are doing a whole quilt top, mark the design on the back. For smaller pieces, work either from the back or front.

When enclosing a shape with machine stitches, overlap the beginning and ending stitches for extra strength. Make a slit in the center of the backing fabric, taking extreme care not to cut into the top fabric. Gently stuff with loose polyester batting (stuffing used for toys is best for washable quilts and clothing), using the eraser end of a pencil, a crochet hook, or any poker you can devise. If your shape is complicated, make slits in several places. Close the slit with hand stitches (herringbone works well) or with a small piece of iron-on tape.

To hide the closing stitches, the trapuntoed piece is now lined, preferably by something more elegant than an old sheet. This is also an excellent opportunity to add batting between the trapuntoed top and the new backing for additional machine quilting.

Be careful that areas of trapunto are not overstuffed and that they are balanced over the piece. A lot of stuffing in the center of a wall hanging, for example, will pull downward and make the sides wrinkle. When working trapunto over large areas of cloth, baste the two layers thoroughly together before stitching the design.

One piece of advice: trapunto looks gorgeous, but it takes a long time. If you're in a hurry, limit your hand-stuffed trapunto to accents on pockets, handbags, or small pieces. (The shape alphabet in Chapter 9 would be an apt choice for trapunto.)

A quick fake trapunto, which will not puff out as much, is to make a quilt sandwich, stitch around the shape, and cut away the excess batting outside the shape.

Italian Cording

Italian cording (like trapunto, not technically "quilting") is the joining of two layers of fabric by parallel lines of straight stitch. Unlike trapunto, the backing fabric should not be so firm that it's difficult to manipulate a tapestry needle through it, for that's how you insert the cording between the parallel lines. Thread a washable cord or yarn into the eye of a tapestry needle and carefully poke it in through the backing fabric without piercing the top fabric. Push the needle along

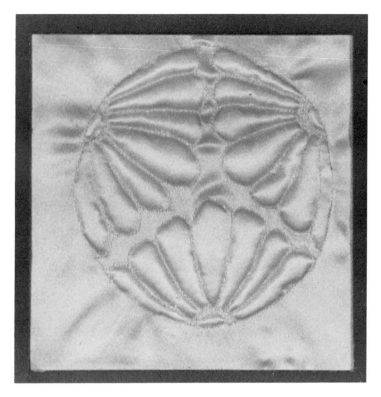

Fig. 4-13 Top: Trapunto on white taffeta. Below: How trapunto is done.

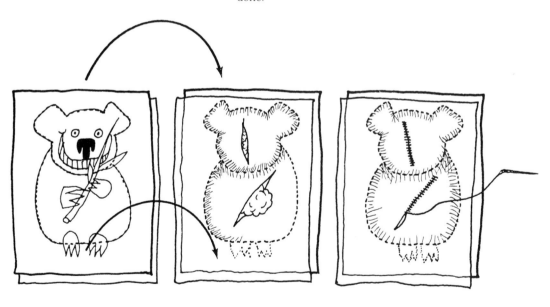

Fig. 4-14 "Family Cube" by Margaret Cusack (commercial artist), commissioned 6½" (16.5 cm) cube with portraits of a mother, father, two children, and grandparents on sides; white organza over black fabric with light areas achieved by "trapunto" polyfill. "My background is in graphic design and I began doing this work when I was between jobs, as a sort of therapy, doing something just because I wanted to explore it, with no deadlines or pressures. Gradually I began applying my graphic design techniques and skills to the fabric . . . I do my original sketch in a small postcard size format and then blow it up with an opaque projector to the final size . . . I use zigzag of varying widths and tensions. I've developed a knowledge and familiarity with my machine so that I use it like a pen or pencil at this point." [Works on a 10-year-old Singer Touch 'n Sew.]

the channel between rows of stitches. Just before curves, poke the needle back out of the backing fabric and pull through the yarn, leaving a 1" (2.54 cm) tail hanging out of the entry point. Then go back into the same exit hole and thread through the channel along the curve, coming out again when the line straightens. Do it in this inchworm fashion to have greater control over the cording; otherwise you may pull too fast and too tight and end up with a wrinkled mess. When done, cut off all the thread tails.

Fabric and upholstery stores stock various diameters of cotton cording, which are perfect for Italian cording. If the item you are making will be washed, be sure to preshrink the cording. Also experiment on a doodle cloth to see what the optimum distance between parallel lines is so that the cording won't be squished or lost. Sometimes you will need to use more than one row of cording per channel to get the effect you want.

On the edges of garments and quilts, you can cheat a little by inserting the cording like piping. Use a zipper foot to make it easier to stitch close to the cording.

A playful way to design Italian cording is to bundle an assortment of pencils, crayons, and felt-tipped pens with rubber bands and draw simple shapes. Try putting a piece of tracing paper over a magazine page you like and tracing the shapes with the pencils. Don't expect to match colors, however. Lines of thin thread color are subtle, not bold.

Note: The project for twin-needle quilting later in this chapter also uses trapunto and Italian cording.

Zigzag Quilting

One of the complaints often heard about machine quilting is that it gives a "hard line." A way around this is to quilt with a narrow zigzag (parts of both the sheet shown earlier in this chapter and the koala quilt in Chapter 10 were quilted with the narrowest zigzag). You will have to experiment on your machine to see which width you like best. When you are working small, consider using a double batt for extra loft.

Fig. 4-15 Italian cording involves stitching parallel lines on two layers of fabric and running yarn or cording between the lines and layers.

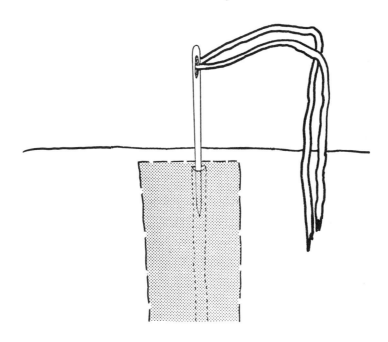

Be sure to check the thread tension on a doodle cloth when zigzag quilting, particularly when using both light and dark threads on top and bobbin. If tension is not balanced properly, loops of one color or the other show on the opposite side of the quilt, which is not always desirable. (A way around this is to use invisible thread on the top.)

On large areas, like quilting a sheet, learn to guide the fabric with the left hand spread around the needle area and the right hand stuck through the machine head opening, grasping the material behind the needle and gently coaxing it through the needle. Otherwise your zigzag stitches may be uneven, even if you're using a walking foot. Using zigzag, you will have better results setting your foot pedal at the slow speed.

For nonfrayable fabrics like double knits, you can applique and quilt in one step with a zigzag stitch. Double knits look particularly puffy in quilts because of their stretchability.

Double-Knit Placemats

Purchased placemats are often too small for a full place setting. This pattern is both large and fast to make, using leftover scraps of double-knits and washable nonfrayable fabrics. Don't use a thick batt in the middle or wine glasses may tip over. Large and small units of a scallop-edged design are alternated for the overall design.

Finished size: 17½″ × 12½″ (44.5 × 31.8 cm)
Technique: zigzag quilting
Machine setting: medium-wide zigzag
Needle: 12(80) (ballpoint needle optional)
Thread: invisible on top, regular sewing on bobbin
Seam allowance: ¼″ (6 mm)

Materials You Will Need

scraps of double knits in harmonious colors (we used blues, blue-greens, and turquoise)
1 rectangle of firm woven fabric per placemat, 17½″ × 12½″ (44.5 × 31.8 cm)
batting or interfacing fleece to match rectangle
invisible thread
tracing or graph paper

Construction

1. Blow up the design so that the larger unit is 5½″ (14 cm) wide and 4½″ (11.4 cm) tall, and the smaller unit is 5½″ (14 cm) wide and 3½″ (8.9 cm) tall.

2. Cut out three lines of the larger unit per placemat and three lines of the smaller (see Fig. 4-17). Each unit is repeated three times per line. Cut one more line of the smaller unit, but add 1″ (2.54 cm) to the height. If you don't have enough fabric for a full line, mix fabrics across the unit.

3. For each placemat place the batting on the backing and zigzag around the edges. Cut out a strip of any fabric 1¾″ × 12½″ (4.4 × 31.8 cm). Lay across one end of the batting.

4. Lay a small unit across the strip ½″ (12 mm) from the edge. Trim off extra fabric at edges. Zigzag quilt the fabric in place. Continue alternating large unit with small, as shown in the cartoon, until you've covered the placemat. Zigzag edge again.

Fig. 4-16 Zigzag quilted placemat.

Fig. 4-17 Cartoon showing placement of two units of design.

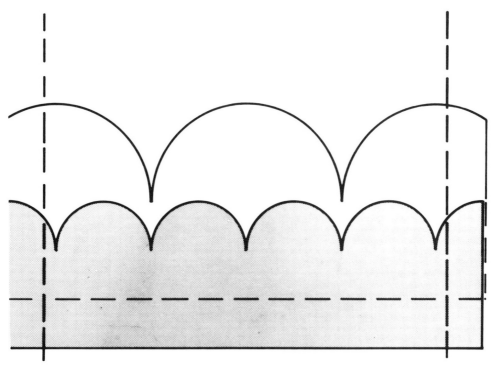

Fig. 4-18 Cartoon showing layout of design.

5. Cut 1¼″ (3.18 cm) wide strips of double knit in any harmonious color. Seam together to make a long strip for the binding. Turn in one edge ½″ (12 mm). Starting in the middle of any edge, lay the binding rightsides against the placemat, raw edges matching, and sew a ¼″ (6 mm) seam all the way around. Overlap ends ½″ (12 mm). Flip binding to the underside, mitering on the underside at corners. (See Method F, Fig. 2-50.) Pin. Stitch in the ditch from the rightside. Trim excess binding fabric.

Additional Ideas

1. Make placemats to represent four seasons of color.

2. Construct three long panels in this design to fit your mattress top, connected by border strips all of the same color.

3. Trace the outline of your table setting directly on a top fabric. Read Chapter 5; then free-machine quilt the shapes and write the names of your family on the appropriate placemat.

Satin-Stitch Quilting

As with zigzag applique/quilting, you can applique and quilt with satin stitch all in one. However the satin stitch tends to draw in the backing fabric. There are several ways to counteract this.

1. Use a heavier-weight fabric than is normally used for quilts, such as poplin, denim, or pillow ticking. Border strips can be of any fabric. If you're an experienced quilter, you can sneak by with spray-starching a lightweight backing.

2. Put typing-weight scrap paper behind the quilt, to be torn away after satin stitching (any leftover bits of paper caught in the stitches wash away with the first machine-washing).

3. Design modules not too large to be put into your hoop while satin stitching. This keeps the backing taut while stitching, but it does compress the batt so that it doesn't puff up as much. Try using a double batt.

4. Break the quilt down into manageable modules, but cut 1″ to 3″ (2.54 to 7.6 cm) extra of three layers. When you're done stitching, trim the module to the correct size for the quilt. Use the lines on your cutting board (assuming you have checked them for accuracy) for precision in measuring and add borders to the block to fill it out to the correct size. (If you don't add borders, you are limited in how you join blocks by how close the satin stitching comes to the edge of the block—see joining methods in Chapter 6.)

5. Make a lap quilt that doesn't require an accurate mattress-top measurement.

Sas Colby's "Socks" wallhanging in the color section was satin-stitch quilted using polyester thread. She first appliqued the feet to the top with a straight stitch; then made the squilt; and then satin-stitch quilted.

Satin-Stitch Lap Quilt

These satin-stitch quilted birds were inspired by the form of Jean Ray Laury's bunny quilts (see Bibliography). Leftover ribbons and trims are used for the tail feathers. Using a poplin-weight fabric minimizes puckering from the satin-stitch quilting. To increase the lap quilt to full bed size, consult Table 3-1 and add borders as specified for 14″ (35.6 cm) blocks.

Fig. 4-19 Satin-stitch bird quilt.

Finished size: 42″ × 70″ (106.7 × 177.8 cm)
Technique: satin-stitch quilting
Needle: 12(80)
Thread: 100% cotton or rayon extra-fine machine-embroidery and invisible thread
Seam allowance: ½″ (12 mm)
Machine setting: for satin stitch, medium-wide needle swing, fine stitch length

Materials You Will Need

2 yd. of 45″-wide (1.8 m of 115 cm-wide) navy blue medium-weight fabric (like poplin)
1¾ yd. of 45″-wide (1.6 m of 115 cm-wide) white medium-weight fabric
1¾ yd. of 45″-wide (1.6 m of 115 cm-wide) green polka-dot border fabric (also used for binding), light or medium-weight

3⅝ yd. of 45″-wide (3.4 m of 115 cm-wide) navy blue backing fabric, medium-weight

2⅛ yd. of 48″ wide (2 m of 115 cm-wide) batting

navy blue 100% cotton (or rayon), extra-fine machine-embroidery thread

invisible thread, navy blue regular sewing thread (used in the bobbin throughout)

white and blue embroidery floss for eyes (or use beads)

small pieces of leftover trim and ribbon (we used blues, greens, yellows, and turquoises)

Fig. 4-20 Full-size cartoon showing main elements of bird design.

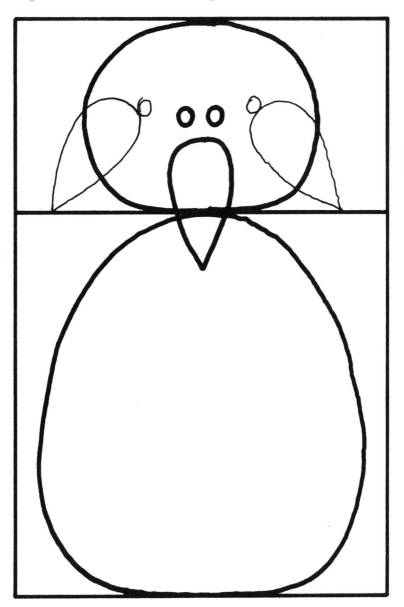

Fig. 4-21 Cartoon of block for bird quilt.

for the beaks, small amount of washable yellow fabric, vinyl, cotton, or knit; if fabric chosen is frayable, bond back to a lightweight lining with fusible interfacing

Construction

1. Preshrink all fabrics. To construct the checkerboard blocks to which the birds are appliqued, we will use the Seminole principles of fast piecing. Cut across the navy blue and white fabrics in 5″ (12.7 cm) widths. You will need 10 blue strips and 8 white. Sew the strips together down the long side in triplets—four triplets of blue/white/blue and two of white/blue/white. Cut across the white/blue/white strips every 5″ (12.7 cm), a total of 15 times. Cut across the other strips every 3″ (7.6 cm), a total of 15 times, and every 7″ (17.8 cm), a total of 15 times.

2. Make 15 blocks as shown in the cartoon in Fig. 4-22, matching cross-seams carefully.

3. To applique the birds on, cut 30 blue and 15 white rectangles slightly larger than the body. Trace the body shape onto each rectangle. Cut 15 blue and 30 white rectangles slightly larger than the head shape. Trace the shape onto each. Check Fig. 4-19 before sewing on each shape. The dark head, for example, always goes on the middle light area. Position the rectangle in place and pin. Straight stitch on the traced shape. Cut close to the stitched line. Repeat for all the heads and bodies.

4. To applique the beaks, trace the shape 45 times. Cut out and applique in place, using a straight stitch or zigzag and invisible thread. The beak position can be changed to either side or in the middle, according to your whims.

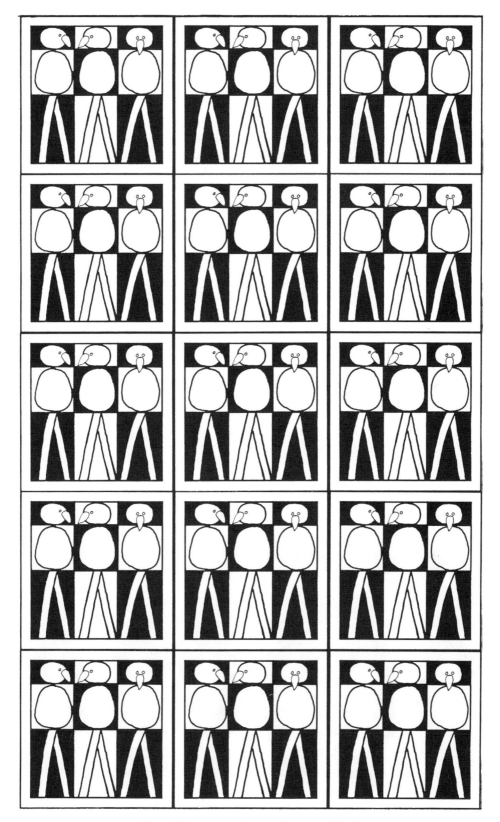

Fig. 4-22 Cartoon showing layout of blocks.

5. To make the eyes, sew French knots or a bead on either side of the beak (Fig. 4-23).

6. To make the quilt sandwich, cut the remaining navy fabric and the batting each into fifteen 16″ (40.6 cm) blocks. These are intentionally large, to allow for shrinkage in the satin-stitch quilting. Make a quilt sandwich of the navy blue fabric/batting/birds, centering the top. Pin liberally.

7. Fold each piece of trim in half and pin in place. Try to use light colors on dark areas and vice versa. Quilt and applique the trim in one step, using a zigzag stitch and invisible thread on top with navy in the bobbin. Lock the threads at beginning and end by taking three stitches in one place, before setting the stitch width lever. Perfectionists stop stitching at the bottom seam line (or stitches look sloppy on the back).

8. Replace invisible thread with 100% cotton navy thread on top. Loosen top tension slightly. Check your satin stitch on a doodle cloth. Is the tension ok? The top thread should show slightly on the back. Satin stitch around the bird heads and bodies, locking stitches to start and end as you did in Step 7. You may want to put a second row of satin stitch over the first. Clip all stray fabric threads (some pull out when tugged with tweezers).

Fig. 4-23 How to make a French knot.

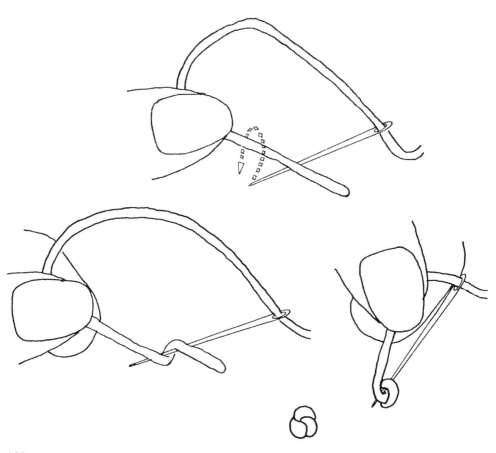

9. Cut across the border fabric into twenty-five 2″ (5.08 cm) wide strips. Rightsides together, sew a border strip to the top end of the birds. Trim even with bird block. Then sew on bottom border strip and trim. Flip out and pin in place. Sew the two side border strips. Repeat for all blocks. Trim the backing and batting to the correct size, using the border strip edges as a guide.

10. Join the blocks as shown in Method 3, Chapter 6, three blocks across and five down.

11. To bind the edge, cut across the remaining border fabric into six 3 ½″ (8.9 cm) widths. Seam the ends together to make one long strip. Plan to join ends of binding as shown on p.71. Fold the strip in half, wrongsides together, and press. Working from the back, raw edges together, sew the binding to the quilt, mitering front and back corners as shown in Method D of illustrated Miter Guide (Chapter 2). Flip binding to front and pin in place. Sew close to edge.

Additional Ideas

1. Cut out a piece of paper 4″ (10.2 cm) wide and 12″ (30.5 cm) long, the size of one bird. Make horizontal lines at 2″ (5.08 cm) and at 6″ (15.3 cm). Give the paper to a child and ask him or her to draw an animal or insect to fit that space. Use variations of the child's drawing to replace the birds above.

2. Make 24 blocks, 4″ × 6″ (10.2 × 15.3 cm), in the checkerboard way outlined above. Machine quilt each square with letters from either of the alphabets given in Chapter 9, combining O and P and leaving out X.

3. Make one 6″ (15.3 cm) block of birds dividing the space into 1″, 2″, and 3″ (2.54, 5.08, and 7.62 cm), instead of 2″, 4″, and 6″ (5.08, 10.2, and 15.3 cm). Use as the bib on a child's overalls or apron.

Twin-Needle Quilting

A fast way to bring the excitement of quilting to a plain area is to quilt with twin needles. Remember that there is only one bobbin thread underneath and that unless you loosen top tension, an unwanted ridge may be quilted into the fabric. For this reason, always check your stitching on a doodle cloth first, because you may also need to loosen bobbin tension. I had trouble stitching with rayon thread for the small sampler at the beginning of Chapter 2, using the walking foot and my serpentine stitch. Stitches were loose in some places on one line of thread. Loosening top tension did not help but changing to the wide open-toed applique foot did.

Italian cording can be done fast with the twin needles. Back the top fabric with organza or muslin and stitch rows with the twin needles. Insert cording into the space between the fabrics. The disadvantage of this technique is that the needles are a fixed distance apart (not quite ⅛″ or 3 mm), which may be too close or too far apart for your design.

You can cheat a little here on simple designs by gluing the cord to the backing fabric, putting the top fabric over it, and stitching with the twin needles, taking care not to waver over the cord.

Most decorative stitches can be worked with the twin needles. The serpentine stitch is particularly effective in machine quilting. Since the presser foot follows a straight line, even though the needle snakes back and forth, it's convenient to use in a diamond grid.

The Birthday Pillow

The stretchiness of knit Qiana shows off trapunto and Italian cording beautifully. To retain its shape without excessive stretching, we've backed it with organza and sewn it to a woven fabric, a simple pieced heart. Insert your own initial (or a loved one's) in the center (Fig. 4-24).

Finished size: 14" (35.5 cm) square
Techniques: trapunto, Italian cording, twin-needle quilting, machine-piecing, stitch-in-the-ditch
Needle size: twin needle and ballpoint or regular needle size 12(80)
Thread: 100% polyester or extra-fine machine-embroidery thread
Accessories: open-toed presser foot or pin-tucking foot, regular presser foot, zipper foot
Machine setting: straight stitch, 10-12 stitches/inch (4-5 stitches per cm)
Seam allowance: 1" (2.54 cm) around pillow, ¼" (6 mm) on heart piecing

Materials You Will Need

Side 1(Fig. 4-24):
¼ yd. (22 cm) red Qiana (or a 16" or 40 cm square, plus extra for a doodle cloth); two 16" (40 cm) squares stiff backing (organza, organdy, etc.)
16" (40 cm) square bonded polyester batting, plus extra for doodle cloth
small amount of loose polyester batting for trapunto
twin needles

Fig. 4-24 Birthday pillow, side 1. (*Collection of Mary M. Losey*)

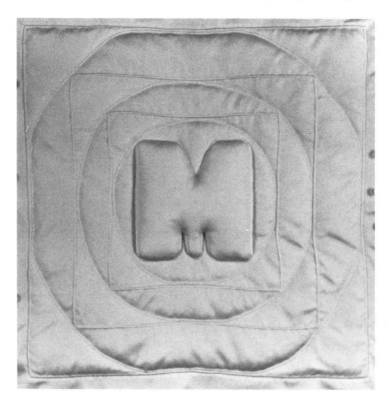

Fig. 4-25 Birthday pillow, side 2. *(Collection of Mary M. Losey)*

2 spools of red thread
cording
Side 2 (Fig. 4-25):
¼ yd. (22 cm) each, dark and light blue patterned fabric
16″ (40 cm) square stiff backing
16″ (40 cm) square bonded polyester batting
dark blue thread
Additional:
14″ (35.6 cm) square purchased pillow form
11″ to 12″ (28–30 cm) zipper
stick glue, white pencil, ruler, thumbtack, graph paper

Construction for Side 1

1. Be sure all fabrics and cording are preshrunk. Blow up the squares of the design directly onto the organza so the overall size is 16″ or 40 cm (includes 1″ or 2.54 cm seams all around). Lay your organza over graph paper or your cutting board and draw directly on the fabric. The concentric squares are 14″, 10″, 7″, and 5″ (35.6, 25.4, 17.8, and 12.7 cm), all sharing the same center (Fig. 4-26). Find the center by drawing intersecting diagonal lines. The 5″ (12.7 cm) square is drawn but not corded. Blow up your initial from the alphabet in Chapter 9 to fit within the 5″ (12.7 cm) square.

2. Run a line of glue on the organza along all the straight lines of the three squares. Cut cording the length of each line and press into place on the organza.

3. Pin-baste the Qiana over the organza. Put the twin needles on the machine and the two spools of red thread (or one spool and one bobbin used as a spool). Use

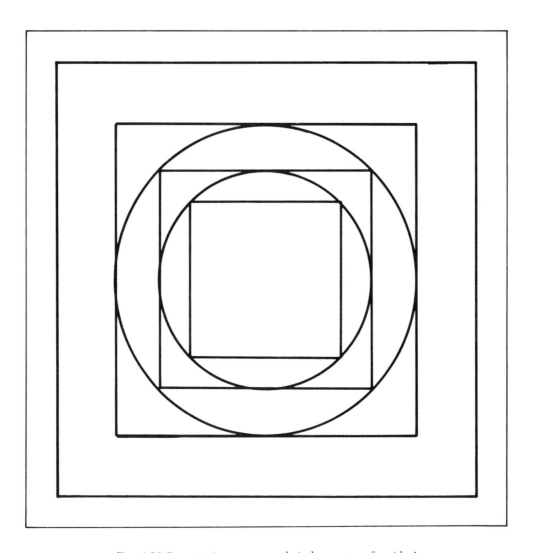

Fig. 4-26 Concentric squares and circles cartoon for side 1.

the open-toed applique foot or a pin-tucking foot. Check the tension setting on a doodle cloth; if the machine is skipping stitches, loosen top tension. Stitch carefully along each side of each square, making sure the cording falls inside the needles. You cannot stitch around a corner with twin needles. Instead, stitch as close as you can to the corners; then stop with the twin needles raised, release the presser bar lever, pivot the material, put the needles back into the fabric, lower the presser bar lever, and continue stitching. When done, pull top threads to the back and tie off.

4. To mark the circles for quilting, stick the thumbtack up through the common center of the squares. Put the Qiana face-up on a pad of newspapers. Tie some cording securely around a white pencil. Holding the point of the pencil straight down at a corner of the smallest square, stick the taut string onto the thumbtack point. Draw a circle slowly. It should touch the corners of the square and the edges of the next largest square. Repeat for all squares.

5. Change to a single needle. With underside up so you can follow the marked line, stitch around your initial, locking threads by changing stitch length to 0 and taking several stitches in one place. Stuff the initial by hand, making a slit in the back of the organza only and pushing in small amounts of loose polyester batting. (The trapunto can be done by machine but even with two batts, it won't stand out as much.) Use a whip stitch to close the opening.

6. Back the trapuntoed, corded Qiana with another layer of batting and organza backing. Pin-baste together. Put the twin needles back on the machine and twin-needle quilt the circular lines you marked in Step 4.

7. Put the zipper foot and single needle on. Stitch around the edge of the outer row of Italian cording. Trim batting and organza close to stitching.

Construction for Side 2

1. Preshrink fabrics. Cut across the grain in strips 1 ½″ (3.8 cm) wide, three strips of light fabric and two of dark. Be accurate. Cut these strips further into rectangles:

Strips		Strips	
inches	cm	#dark	#light
1½	3.8	6	—
2½	6.4	4	—
3½	8.9	3	2
4½	11.4	2	—
5½	13.9	2	2
7½	19.1	—	3
8½	21.6	—	4

From the dark fabric only cut two strips 2¾″ × 16″ (7 × 40 cm) and two, 3¼″ × 11½″ (8.3 × 29 cm)

2. To piece the heart, long strips with ¼″ (6mm) horizontal seams are made first; then the strips are seamed vertically. The sequence is, showing finished square size in inches (cm):

D	2(5)	1(2.5)	—	—	1(2.5)	3(7.6)	1(2.5)	—	—	1(2.5)	2(5)
L	3(7.6)	5(12.7)	7(17.8)	8(20)	8(20)	7(17.8)	8(20)	8(20)	7(17.8)	5(12.7)	3(7.6)
D	5(12.7)	4(10)	3(7.6)	2(5)	1(2.5)	—	1(2.5)	2(5)	3(7.6)	4(10)	5(12.7)

Start piecing the first column by sewing a dark 2″ (5 cm) rectangle to a light 3″ (7.6 cm) rectangle, which is sewn to a dark 5″ (12.7 cm) rectangle. Piece each column; then sew the columns to each other. Be accurate in seaming. Press seams to one side or open.

3. Seam the 11½″ (29 cm) strips to the bottom and top of the heart. Press seams. Seam the longer strips to the sides of the heart.

4. Make a quilt sandwich with the batting and organza. Pin-baste. Stitch-in-the-ditch around the heart. Stitch 1″ (2.5 cm) in from the outside edges. Trim batting and organza close to stitching.

5. To assemble the pillow, right sides together, machine-baste the two bottom edges of sides 1 and 2 together, matching seam lines. Press seam open. Place the zipper face down on the seam line. Pin, then stitch in place, using red thread on Side 1 and blue on Side 2. Remove basting thread in zipper area and open zipper.

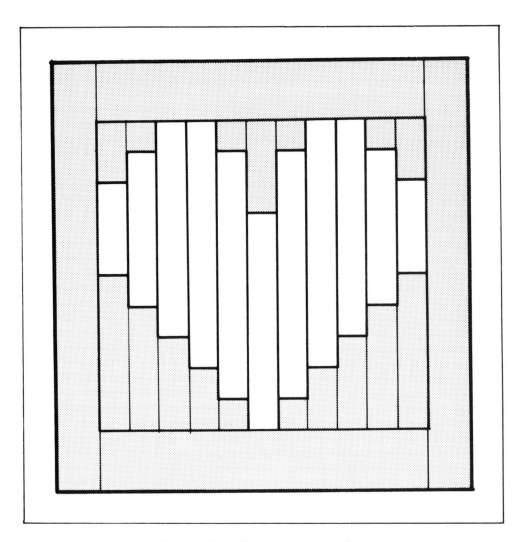

Fig. 4-27 Pieced heart cartoon for side 2.

6. Right sides together, pin-baste Side 1 to Side 2. Stitch around the three remaining sides in a 1" (2.5 cm) seam. Clip corners. Turn rightsides out. Insert pillow form and zip closed.

Decorative Stitch Quilting

If you can machine quilt with straight stitch and you can machine quilt with satin stitch, you can machine quilt with your decorative stitches. The easiest design is a vest with straight lines quilted by decorative stitches. However it is essential that you experiment on a doodle cloth first. Some stitches are temperamental and you'll want to know that *before* you start on something important.

If you can't make the stitches behave, quilt with a straight stitch first, then cover the stitching with decorative stitches. Be sure to check the underside of your doodle cloth; sometimes the heavier bobbin thread looks better than the top. If so, work underside up.

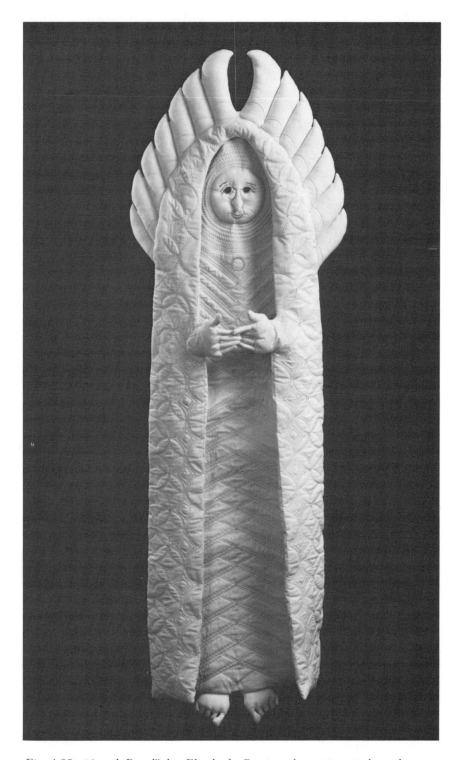

Fig. 4-28 "Angel Panel" by Elizabeth Gurrier, decorative-stitch quilting on unbleached muslin, hand-embroidered face, 67″ × 24″ (170 × 61 cm). *Photo by Robert Raiche.* "My interest in medieval history and art has influenced most of my work in form and content. Working in white allows me to place emphasis on pattern, texture and form without the interference of color to impose an emotional response." [Worked on a Universal, recently purchased a Riccar, uses cotton thread for textural quilting, polyester for strength.]

For close-quilted patterns, you'll want the decorative stitches lined up (as with serpentine) or whole, so you'll have to count on the doodle cloth how many stitches comprise one motif and make sure you begin quilting with the needle in the correct position.

I prefer to quilt first, then cut out the garment, so that shrinkage does not reduce an adult vest to child-size. If you are overweight at all, consider using a thin filler like flannel or interfacing fleece for batting rather than polyester batting; many women regret the extra bulk of the latter.

Quilted Vest for a Star

Whether your star shines in soccer, football, bicycle racing, or darts, he or she will appreciate a lightweight, warm vest for chilly morning practices—and you will appreciate that it takes only a few hours to make. We used a remnant of the pre-quilted nylon available in fabric and camping stores. Use a size 16(100) needle on nylon fabric.

Materials You Will Need

pattern for vest (or adapt a T-shirt pattern—add 2″ to 4″ (2.5 to 10 cm) for ease)
pre-quilted nylon as called for in pattern; we used ⅝ (0.60 m) yd—total cost of vest under $3
lining fabric
thread to match fabric (cotton-covered polyester for nylon fabric)
embroidery hoop
gripper snaps

Construction

1. On a corner of the pre-quilted fabric test thread tension for the decorative stitch you choose for quilting.

2. Lay out the front and back pattern pieces on the pre-quilted fabric. If your remnant has vertical quilting, have the center back seam fall on a quilting line. Overlap the side seams of the pattern at the underarm; you don't need a side seam. Mark around pattern pieces with soap or a white pencil.

3. Add three or more diagonal quilting lines 2″ or 5 cm apart on the back. Add them vertically between the quilted lines on the front (ours were added 2″ or 5 cm apart).

4. Reset the machine for straight stitch. Copy the star twice on the back of the vest with white pencil. Put the fabric in an embroidery hoop as shown in Chapter 3. You will have to take the presser foot off while you slide or tip the hoop under the needle. Stitch around both stars with a straight stitch. Tie thread ends on back.

5. Cut out the lining and vest. Rightsides together, sew everything but the shoulder seams and about 6″ (15.3 cm) on the lower edge of the back. Trim batting close to stitching. Clip corners and curved areas. Turn rightside out. Handstitch bottom opening closed.

6. On small vests, this step is awkward if you've never done it before. Be sure to use a thread color that matches the nylon vest or stitches will show. Match the nylon shoulder seams, rightsides together. Sew by hand, using a backstitch and not catching in the lining. Fold the seam inside the lining and handstitch the lining to itself, using the toymaker's ladder stitch.

7. Add snaps on the front.

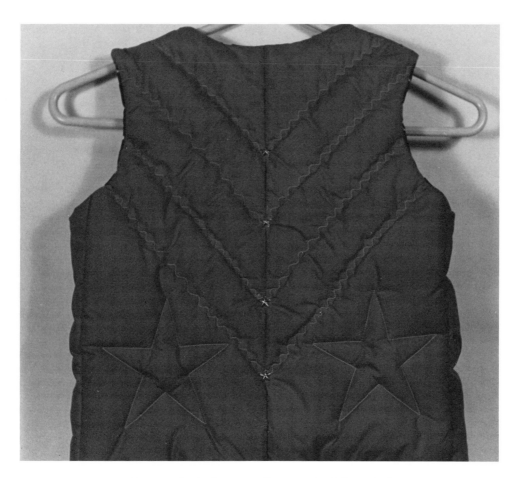

Fig. 4-29 Quilted vest. (Collection of Kali Fanning)

Tying

For quilt tops of heavy materials (such as corduroys, some denims, washable wools) and for fillers that won't shift (flannel, mattress pads, prequilted fabric remnants), the quilt sandwich may be connected by tying through the layers. There are three ways to tie on the machine: (1) with a single decorative stitch, (2) mock tying, and (3) machine-applied buttons.

Single Decorative Stitch

Practice on a doodle cloth so that you know exactly how many stitches comprise one motif. If it's not clear where to tie on your quilt top—usually the intersection of major seams—mark the top before assembling the quilt sandwich. I like to poke holes through transparent graph paper, which is placed against the quilt top, and mark through the holes with a pencil dot. The transparency makes it easy to reposition the graph paper for the next marking.

The ties should not be farther apart than about 8″ or they may break over the years. You need not end off the thread for each decorative stitch. Simply lift the presser bar lever, hold the thread down behind the presser foot with a finger, and

Fig. 4-30 Pattern for back of vest.

gently pull the fabric to the next position. When you're done with a row, preferably working parallel to the rolled-up bulk of the quilt under the head, cut the threads on front and back half-way between each stitch. Draw the top thread to the back and tie off ends in a square knot (see Chapter 2).

Mock-Tying

Mock-tying imitates the traditional method of tying. Lay a 4″ (10.2 cm) length of washable yarn on top of the quilt and perpendicular to the satin stitch you are about to use. Set stitch length at 0 and (only for beginning and ending) stitch width at 0. Press the top thread against the fabric behind the presser foot so the thread won't be drawn down into the bobbin case. Pierce the yard with the needle, taking three or four stitches. Then set the stitch width control to whatever you choose, after having experimented on a doodle cloth (as always). Satin stitch in place about four to six times; what you're doing is *bar-tacking*. Set the stitch width control back to 0 and lock the threads.

After you've attached all the yarns to the quilt, tie them in square knots.

Machine-Applied Buttons

Wall hangings and decorative objects that won't be sat upon or lain on can be tied with buttons put on by machine. Tape or glue the botton in place; the tape tears off easily after stitching. Set your machine to stitch width at 0 and stitch length at 0. If you can, decenter the needle on your machine either to the left or right. Holding the top thread securely, carefully lower the needle into one hole of the button. Stitch in place several times to lock threads. Then set the stitch width lever to make a zigzag. You will have to try several settings, moving the needle by hand on the handwheel (not foot pedal), to find the exact position for stitching each button. Satin stitch several times; then set the stitch width lever back to 0 and lock threads again.

The Ten-Hour Cuddle Quilt

One of the simplest and fastest quilt patterns is Rail Fence, which always has one strong color zigzagging through it. To make an extremely durable (and fast)

Fig. 4-31 Three ways to tie by machine: buttons (outer squares); mock tying (middle squares); decorative stitch (center square).

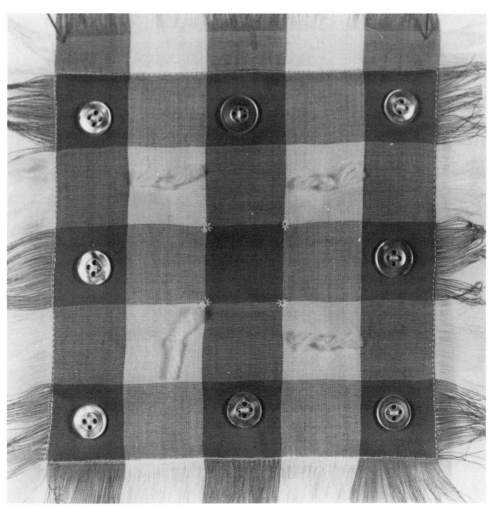

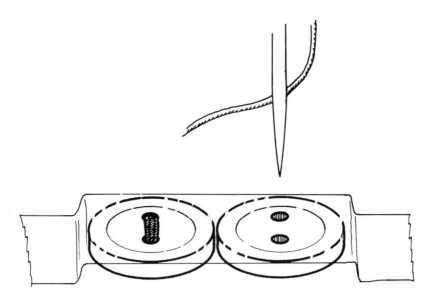

Fig. 4-32 Putting buttons on by machine is easy.

quilt, we used pre-quilted fabric on the back, polyester fleece on the inside, and tied the quilt with machine bar-tacking. (A decorative stitch can be used if it shows; it doesn't on our dark fabric.)

For the border, we used polyester batting and quilted it with Daniel's name, using the alphabet in Chapter 9. You can shave at least four hours off the making of this quilt if you do not personalize it this way.

Finished size: 30" × 54" (76 × 137 cm); 7 blocks × 5 blocks + two 6" (15.3 cm) end pieces.
Thread: "extra-strong hand quilting" cotton-covered polyester
Needle: 12(80)
Seams: ¼" (6 mm)
Techniques: machine-piecing, machine-tying
Pattern name: Rail Fence
Finished block size: 6" (15.3 cm)

Materials You Will Need

Backing: 30" × 43" (76 × 109 cm) piece of prequilted fabric
Batting: 30" × 43" (76 × 109 cm) polyester fleece, flannel, or any material suitable for tying
two strips bonded polyester batting, 32" × 7" (81 × 18 cm) for ends
Top: ½ yd. (0.5 m) each, 45"-wide (115 cm-wide) fabric (one dominant color, two less dominant colors)
four 32" × 7" (81 × 18 cm) pieces of contrasting color for ends
Binding: 110" cut 3½" wide (280 cm cut 8.9 cm wide) of contrasting color

Construction

1. Preshrink all fabric and batting for tying. Cut across the grain of the top fabrics in 2½" (6.4 cm) wide strips (I used the paper cutter). For 45"-wide (115

Fig. 4-33 The elements of the quilt top are laid out on a cutting board to avoid confusion in piecing.

cm-wide) fabric you will need six strips (this allows for waste in cutting). Double-check your accuracy in cutting.

2. Sew the top fabric strips together in long triplets, with the dominant color always on the left. Press seams open. Slice across the triplets every 6½″ (16.5 cm). Be accurate. (Note: You will have extra pieced fabric. Use for a quick gift from Chapter 9.)

3. To keep from becoming confused, lay out the blocks in a Rail Fence pattern on the floor or cutting board near your machine. The dominant color is always either to the left or on top of each block. Sew seams across the quilt first. One block will have cross-seams, one won't; put the cross-seams on top so you can be sure the pressed seams stay open. Press open the new seams. Beware of mistakes! I had to redo two rows. Double-check each seamed row by laying it in place on the floor. After sewing the seven individual rows, sew the long seams between rows, matching vertical seams of blocks and taking care to keep pressed seams open. Press new seams open.

4. Make a quilt sandwich: prequilted fabric face-down, polyester fleece between, quilt top face-up. Pin-baste; then zigzag around edges.

5. Machine-tie the left corners of the dominant color. Set the stitch length and width at 0. Take three stitches to secure the thread; then set stitch width to a medium setting (e.g., 2). Take 6 to 8 stitches (you are actually bar-tacking). Set stitch width back to 0 and secure thread again. Raise presser bar lever and pull quilt to next tying position. Later cut threads on front and back. (It doesn't take more than 20 minutes to tie the whole quilt.)

Note: If you are short of time, bind the whole quilt now. The following steps are for personalizing the quilt.

Fig. 4-34 Above, the topside of the end of the quilt; below, the underside, showing the pre-quilted backing, signature of quiltmaker, and back of other end. (Collection of Daniel J. Driscoll)

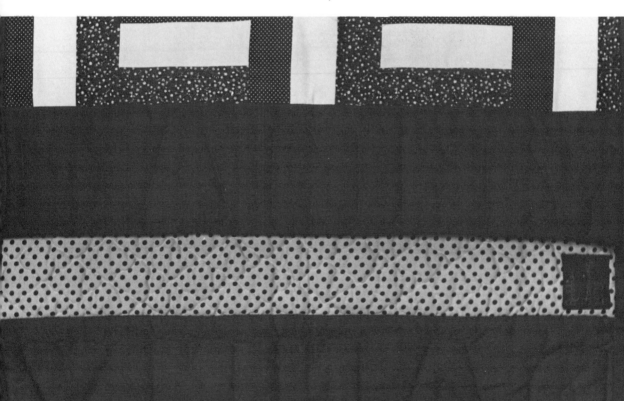

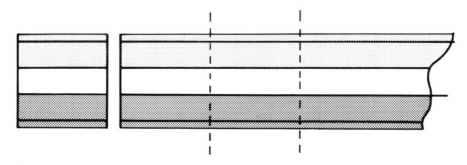

Fig. 4-35 Fabric strips are sewn together in long triplets and sliced at 6½″ (16.5 cm) intervals.

6. For each end, seam two 32″ × 7″ (81 × 18 cm) pieces the long way in a ½″ (12 mm) seam. Press open. Blow up the letters from the alphabet in Chapter 9. Copy onto the end pieces with the bottoms of the letters ½″ (12 mm) above the seam. The end pieces are 1″ (2.5 cm) longer at each end than the quilt to allow for shrinkage in step 7.

7. Place a piece of polyester batting inside each end piece. Pin-baste the ends together. Machine quilt the letters, using a short stitch length and a walking foot (optional).

8. Pin the top and batting back out of the way. Seam the end piece backing to the underside of the quilt in a ½″ (12 mm) seam. (You are connecting one layer of the end piece to all layers of the quilt.) Double-check that the letters will be arranged correctly (bottoms pointing away from quilt) and that the end piece is centered on the quilt. Press the seam lightly toward the end piece. Lay the quilt on a flat surface. Unpin the top and batting. Trim the batting even with the quilt seam allowances. Turn under the top end piece ½″ (12 mm) and pin in place. Stitch close to edge (I used a narrow zigzag). Trim the end pieces even with the quilt.

9. For a French fold binding, fold the binding in half, wrong sides together, and press. Fold in each end ½″ (2.5 cm). On the underside of the quilt, match end of binding to top end of quilt. Sew a ½″ (12 mm) seam. Several inches from the bottom end of the quilt, stop sewing. Cut the binding ½″ (12 mm) beyond the quilt and fold it to the inside of the binding. Continue sewing to end. Sew binding to other side of quilt.

10. Clip corners. Wrap binding around to front. Pin in place. Stitch close to edge (I used narrow zigzag). Optional: Use thread tails to hand-close open end of binding.

Additional Ideas

1. Make a 15″ (38 cm) wide string of patterned fabrics onto paper or muslin. Cut into six 2½″ (6.4 cm) wide strips. Seam each string-strip to two strips of solid-colored fabric of light intensity colors (so that the string strip will predominate). Construct the Rail Fence pattern, as above.

2. For a fast quilt, choose a geometrically patterned fabric of unusual beauty (perhaps a plaid or one of the gorgeous Scandinavian designs). Quilt it with mock tying at regular intervals on the pattern (so you don't have to mark the top).

Fig. 4-36 Cartoon showing Rail Fence and predominating strips.

3. Seam together leftover parts of the Rail Fence seamed strips for use in a border around a quilt. On the inside, quilt a solid-colored fabric in the baby's name and birthdate (or any adult message), arranged within an imaginary grid of 6″ (15.3 cm) blocks.

Traditional Designs for Presser-Foot Machine Quilting

To fit a design, such as the cable, into a certain existing space (not something you're designing on paper) on your quilt, such as a border, measure the length of the finished border. Estimate roughly how many repeats of the cable will fit into the border space. Divide the border measurement by the number of repeats to get the length of one cable on your quilt. Now make a paper pattern as long as one repeat and as wide as your finished border. Blow up the cable pattern to fit the space using any of the three methods for enlarging shown in Chapter 2. (If you're designing the quilt on paper, it's far easier to design the height of the border according to the given cable pattern instead of trying to manipulate the cable to fit a space.)

Don't be afraid to quilt a large rectangle or square in a traditional design and then cut it up and insert other quilted strips in it.

To design your own quilting patterns for whole quilt tops, remember to keep the quilting line continuous and straight or broadly curved nearly all the way across the quilt. Angles which involve turning the whole quilt to stitch invite problems. Wicker patterns are particularly good sources for design because they are made of continuous lines.

Industrial Machines

The phrase "industrial machines" by itself is as meaningless as "machine quilting" by itself. There are many different kinds of industrial machines: those with a heavy-duty motor and a large distance between the needle and the head, often used by upholsterers; leather and sail-makers' machines; quilting machines with built-in cams for designs; bootmakers' machines where the presser foot rotates 360°; and more. The machines, new, are expensive; used, they cost about the same as a new domestic machine.

Do you need to buy one? If you are an artist trying to make a living selling quilts or wall-hangings, and if the color and pattern of the quilt top are more important to you than the actual quilting, and if you want to sell quilts at affordable prices, and if you work almost or full time at quilting, then yes, one of the industrial machines is worth owning.

If you are not necessarily an artist but you still need to make extra money, then, yes, there is a steady demand for industrial machine quilting of quilt tops, both from individuals (and it can be done by mail) and from firms like upholstery shops and decorators. If your domestic machine groans at the bulk you're trying to push through it, then yes, an industrial machine can punch through buildings like Superman, let alone two or three thicknesses of quilt batting.

There is an underground grapevine about the availability of industrial machines. Start by asking your favorite fabric store. Sometimes they rent time on their own industrial machines, but if not, they usually have heard of someone who has an industrial machine for sale. Then call leather shops and garment factories. Soon your machine will find you.

Fig. 4-37 From top left: cable; slant; channel; variations on diamond grid.

Fig. 4-38 Top: A multineedle quilting machine at Globe Quilting Company, South San Francisco, CA. Changeable cams determine the quilting pattern. The three layers of the quilt are rolled separately to prevent slippage. Nevertheless mistakes occur and offstage a woman sits at an old Singer treadle, repairing skipped stitches. Below left: Quilted world created for a Globe ad. Right: Another type of industrial machine: the bootmaker's. The presser foot rotates 360°.

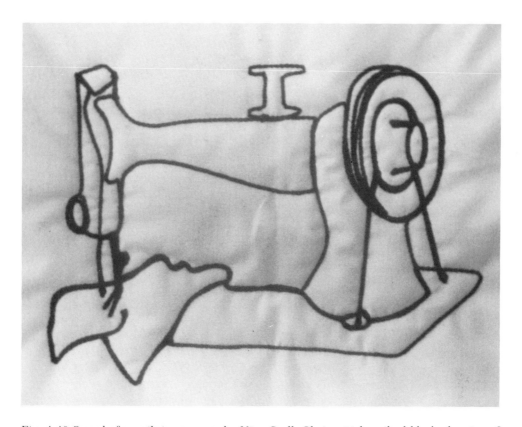

Fig. 4-40 Sample for quilt in progress by Nina Stull. Chain-stitch quilted block, drawing of Nina's chain-stitch machine, which she uses in her custom patch company, the Super Embroidery Company.

Fig. 4-39 "Bridging" by Radka Donnell, machine quilted by Claire Mielke in meander pattern. "I take my time laying the fabric pieces out on the floor. Moving close to and above them makes me arrange them differently than if I did this on a table or stuck them to a vertical surface. I let my quilts get machine quilted because I want them to withstand use by children and pets and don't want to worry about their being too fragile and precious. I feel quilts are most beautiful when they are being used, with people in front of them when they are hung, or with people wrapped in them: they belong with the daily movements of life and not in a 'higher' sphere. I know many women who have started a quilt and put the unfinished top away in a drawer because of the thought of having to hand quilt them. I want my work to inspire women to finish at least the top and have it quilted by another woman without having to feel less proud or less of an artist for doing it. Delegating the finishing work to another person has helped me to respect other people and understand the collective process of art as connecting, as sharing, and complete only when shared."

Chapter 5

Free-Machine Quilting

When you quilt by machine, you have two choices for what to do with the presser foot. You can leave it on, for the good straightforward bread-and-butter quilting techniques described in the previous chapter. Or you can take it off. This is called free-machine quilting.

Oh, the freedom that comes with free-machine quilting! You can stitch in and out of tiny little corners and around intricate curves without turning the quilt around, as you must when the presser foot is on. It's fast, it's easy, it's exhilarating.

But for success, you must put in a few playful hours of practice. And you must understand how a stitch is formed on the machine, so read Chapter 3 for how to do free-machine embroidery. An easy way to start practicing free-machine embroidery is to try writing the names of your family and friends on a scrap of cloth. Then when that becomes easy (or boring), try drawing simple shapes: a square, a circle, a triangle. When that seems a breeze, try drawing something near your machine: scissors, pincushion, thimble.

Don't worry about how it looks. You're only practicing. Enjoy the freedom, don't worry about results, and perfect your skills.

The Methods

For your first attempt at free-machine quilting, start simple on something not too important. Choose a scrap of fabric with some medium to large shapes on it, such as flowers. The scrap should be bigger than your hoop; the flowers, smaller. Make a quilt sandwich, pin or thread-baste it together, and put it in the hoop. (You may have to loosen the hoop screw quite a bit.) Set up for free-machine embroidery as usual, but use a size larger needle than you normally would for the top thread. You're going through three layers now, all of which saw at the thread, so you need a needle that will make a larger hole for the thread.

Bring up the bobbin thread and lock threads, as usual. Be sure the presser bar lever is down. Stitch around the shape of the flower and any inner details you want. Lock threads and remove the hoop. Are you happy with the quality of your stitches? If so, you're ready to free-machine quilt a quilt. If not, practice more until you're satisfied. Usually you will just need to go slower and move the hoop more smoothly.

In planning free-machine quilting, here are some considerations to keep in mind:

1. If you want to free-machine quilt a length of printed fabric, don't make it larger than about 54″ (140 cm). The bulk and weight of the quilt sometimes make

Fig. 5-1 "Duncan Envelope Bag" by Sas Colby, front; free-machine quilted letter on silk, stamp and shells hand stitched, sent through US mail as you see it; part of a book in progress called *The Art of Correspondence*. "My fabric objects are often inspired by words, or combinations of colors, or certain juxtapositions of shapes and things. I am particularly fond of incongruous combinations and the surrealists. I rarely sketch a fabric box or a book before making them, but work directly from the inspiration of the fabric and materials and the idea. Wall hangings always begin with a sketch, though the idea is often altered in translation to fabric . . . I also like the effect of writing [script] with the sewing machine on padded fabric. The element of 'something to read' is a surprise in a fabric piece; and even if it is not readily legible, the overall pattern and texture are pleasing." [Works on a 7-year-old Kenmore, using zigzag presser foot for applique and clear plastic foot for free-machine quilting.] Next page: Back of free-machine quilted letter by Sas Colby.

it difficult to maneuver the hoop. For larger quilts, plan to free-machine quilt blocks to be joined later (for details on quilt-as-you-go, see Chapter 6).

2. Does the motif you want to quilt fit into your hoop? You can always move the hoop mid-design, of course, but it's annoying. You can also free-machine quilt without a hoop, but it take lots of experience to do it well. An 8″ hoop is about as big as you can use without bumping into the head of the machine. Of course, you can turn the material around and continue stitching; but if you're working with a lot of bulk, this, too, is annoying and awkward.

3. Baste well, as you did for quilting with the presser foot on, although correctly putting the fabric in a hoop helps eliminate puckers.

4. If you choose to quilt-as-you-go and if you will be joining two blocks directly together with no lattice strips in between, you must leave *twice* the seam allowance unquilted all around. For example, for a ½″ (12 mm) seam allowance, don't quilt closer than 1″ (2.5 cm) to any raw edge, so that the seam allowance can be pressed open and lie flat without any interference from quilting.

5. There are two ways to insure that the hoop can be moved freely around the quilt, without falling off the edge.

our first visit to the Duncans in Hawaii was in 1968. Judith was keeping their house in Thai style so we removed our shoes at the door and stepped inside onto a cool polished floor. Lesley and Martha were playful toddlers all brown from the Hilo sun. The whole family met us at the airport with fragrant plumeria leis. Scott had a darkroom under the house next to the laundry room where Judith and I would go to iron and talk. I was amazed at her ability to say those Hawaiian names. They rolled off her Yankee tongue with the ease of a native: Kaneohe Kamehameha, Kalakaua, Liliukiani etc. We saw our first volcano on that trip. I remember the flames dancing high in the black fume soaked night sky, Pele's anger come to life.

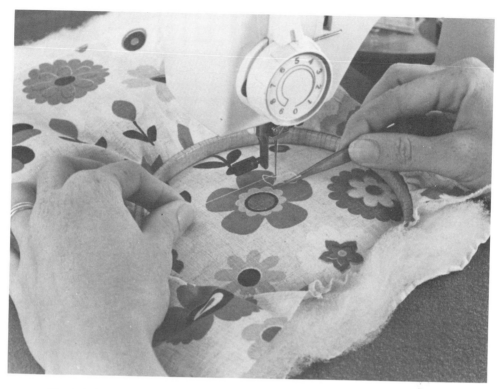

Fig. 5-2 Scrap fabric quilt sandwich in hoop to practice free-machine quilting.

Fig. 5-3 Outline the flower design for practice.

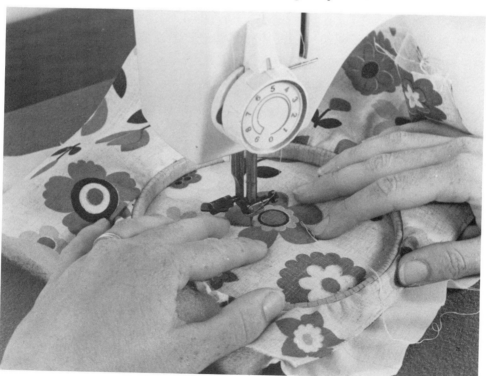

The first method is to cut the quilt about 2″ (5 cm) larger all around, to be trimmed to size after stitching. Since quilting shrinks the overall size somewhat, you can lay the block on a cutting board or graph paper and cut it precisely to size (including seam allowances, of course). The disadvantage is that you waste fabric—but these leftovers are perfect for string or crazy quilts.

The second way is to machine-baste strips of an old sheet to the outside edge of the quilt, so that the hoop can be moved partly off the quilt for free-machine quilting near the edges. To make it easy to remove the basting stitches, loosen top tension drastically. Then pull the bobbin thread when done quilting and it will easily slide out.

6. To mark the pattern for free-machine quilting when you are not quilting a print, either use pencil or transfer pencil (or possibly a water-erasable pen) on the top; or pin tracing paper to the back of the quilt and stitch underside up, so that what you see on top is the bobbin thread. Don't forget to test this on your doodle cloth. Think twice about stitching through tracing paper on the top—parts of it tear away easily but parts remain locked under piles of free-machine stitches. If you know you'll wash the piece before displaying it, there's no problem because the paper will disintegrate.

7. Choose the color of your backing fabric carefully. Since the top thread tension is loosened, you will see tiny loops of the top thread on the back. Where you lock stitches there will also be a little lump, usually unnoticeable . . . unless you use a light solid-colored fabric on back and a dark on top. Both print fabrics or the same solid color as your top thread are recommended as backing.

For small free-machine quilted items using special fabrics on which hoop marks might show, make yourself a protective fabric ring. Put a square of muslin into your hoop. Free-machine stitch near the edge of the hoop three times. Remove the hoop from the needle but don't remove the fabric from the hoop. Cut out the center circle. Now you can pin-baste the special fabric to the protective fabric without putting the special fabric directly in contact with the hoop.

The Quick Birthday Present Quilt

This quick quilt top uses leftover fabric yardage, which precludes faster piecing techniques, but it can still be made in an evening. Use one light solid-colored fabric for the letters of the child's name and prints for the other squares, which are free-machine quilted with the child's last name.

Finished size: 40″ × 48″ (102 × 122 cm)
Finished block size: 9½″ × 11½″ (24 × 29 cm)
Technique: free-machine quilting
Needle size: 12(80) for piecing and quilting
Thread: 100% cotton or rayon machine-embroidery thread
Machine set-up: 0 stitch length and width, drop feed dogs, loosen top tension
Machine accessories: darning foot (optional), walking or regular presser foot,
    8″ (20 cm) embroidery hoop
Seam allowance: ½″ (12 mm)

Materials You Will Need

¾ yd. (0.7 m) solid light-colored 45″ wide (115 cm-wide) fabric (for eight blocks; if your child has more or less letters in his or her name, adjust accordingly)

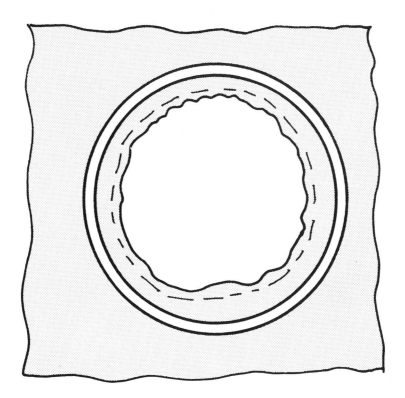

Fig. 5-4 To protect fabrics, make yourself a ring of muslin or an old sheet with a cut-out center. Put the muslin in the hoop and baste the precious fabric to the muslin. No ring marks will be left on the good fabric.

8 blocks of any harmonious prints or solids, each at least 10½″ × 12½″ (26.7 × 31.8 cm)

1⅓ yd. of ¼″ (1.2 m of 6 mm) bonded polyester batting

1½ yd. (1.4 m) backing fabric (small harmonious print best)

1 spool 100% cotton or rayon extra-fine, machine-embroidery thread in a color slightly darker than the light-colored fabric

regular sewing thread to match backing in bobbin

masking tape, ruler, pencil, scissors, pins, iron

8″ embroidery hoop

Construction

1. Preshrink all fabrics. Cut all squares 10½″ × 12½″ (26.7 × 31.8 cm). The child's name will be free-machine quilted on the light-colored fabric. Alternate light-colored blocks with the other blocks. Using regular sewing thread in top and bobbin, piece together into a rectangle four blocks by four blocks as shown in the cartoon (Fig. 5-5). Press open seams.

2. Blow up letters of child's name from alphabet in Chapter 9 or use a simple block alphabet cut free-hand from 6″ (15.3 cm) squares of paper. Pin the paper letters to the light-colored blocks.

3. Tape the backing rightside down to a hard surface. Lay on the batting and top, centering both on the backing. Pin or safety-pin the three layers together

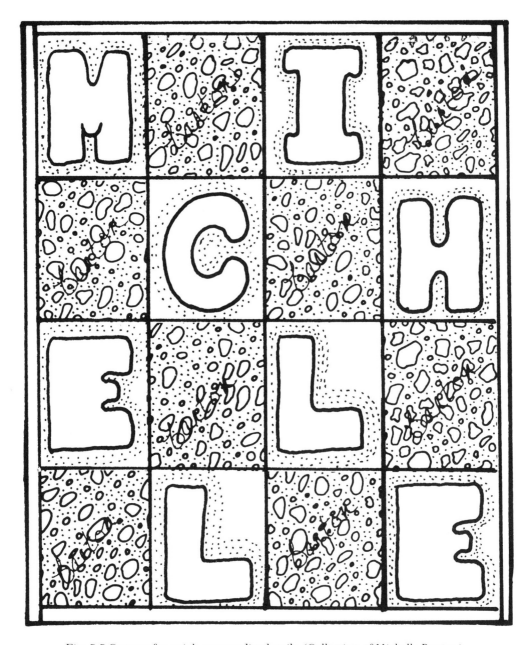

Fig. 5-5 Cartoon for quick, personalized quilt. *(Collection of Michelle Barton)*

around the edges of each block. (On a small quilt like this, you don't have to be as careful in basting.) Remove tape.

4. Put the embroidery hoop onto one light-colored block. Set up your machine for free-machine quilting, using the extra-fine thread on top and regular sewing thread on the bobbin. Free-machine quilt around the paper letters. Stitch around again three or four times close to the first row of stitching, as if you were scribbling with a crayon. (This is similar to the mock trapunto technique shown next—the letters are defined and stand out because quilting compresses the fabric around

them.) Do all the letters this way. Then put the hoop on the other squares and write the child's name in script diagonally across the block, from lower left to upper right.

5. Reset your machine for straight stitch with the presser or walking foot and regular sewing thread in the top and bobbin. Stitch-in-the-ditch of all six lengthwise and crosswise seams. Be careful not to get tucks on the back where the seams cross each other. Tie off thread ends on the topside.

6. Trim the batting even with the quilt top. Trim the backing 1¾" (4.5 cm) from the quilt top on all sides. Press backing toward its underside ½" (12 mm). Fold top and bottom edges of backing up over quilt so that 1" (2.5 cm) shows on the top. Stitch close to edge. Fold side edges of backing up over quilt, using the lapped binding shown in Chapter 2.

Additional Ideas

1. Make a doll quilt in this manner, spelling out the doll's name in miniature free-machine quilting.

2. Project your family's shadows onto paper taped on a flat wall. Cut out the shadow shapes and pin to quilt blocks. Free-machine quilt around each shadow.

3. Piece and baste a quilt as outlined above. Take it with your machine to a nursing home or children's hospital. Free-machine quilt someone's name while he or she watches you; then wrap it around the lucky person.

Mock Trapunto

Compressing the batting around a shape by stitching several concentric lines of free-machine quilting raises the shape from the background, making it look like it's been trapuntoed. Mock trapunto is considerably faster than traditional trapunto and on small pieces, like the Santa ornament in Fig. 5-6, can be stitched through a double batt for extra depth.

On small items like this, finish and stuff before stitching. You don't need a hoop for these little projects. Simply take your time in stitching, use a darning foot if possible, and keep your fingers in close, pressing the fabric against the needle plate. The shinier the fabric, the richer the effect.

For full-sized quilts, don't use a double batt. It makes the quilt too heavy.

Santa Ornament

Finished size: 4½" × 3¾" (11.4 × 9.5 cm)
Technique: mock trapunto
Seam allowance: ½" (12 mm)
Machine accessories: darning foot (optional)
Thread: 100% cotton or rayon machine-embroidery
Needle: 12(80)

Materials You Will Need

¼ yd. (23 cm) satin (enough for several Noels)
2 pieces polyester batting
white thread on bobbin
red machine-embroidery thread on top
blue embroidery thread (floss, pearl cotton, etc.)

Fig. 5-6 Santa Ornament with mock trapunto.

1. This ornament is quilted after you have made finished edges. Trace the rectangle and the letters and face of the cartoon onto the topside of the fabric (Fig. 5-7). Cut out two fabric rectangles and two pieces of batting. Pin the double batt to the underside of the top fabric. Rightsides together, sew the two fabric pieces around three and a half sides with ½" (12 mm) seam, leaving half of one side open for turning. Trim, turn, and press lightly; then handstitch the opening.

2. Free-machine quilt around the letters and the Santa face (but skip the eyes—you'll put them in later). Then free-machine quilt four or five flowing lines all around the outside and between the letters of the ornament. Don't try to stitch exactly what you see on the cartoon—those lines are only to give you an idea of what the finished project should look like. The quilting lines around the edges make the letters puff out.

3. Make the Santa eyes with blue embroidery thread (two strands of floss or pearl cotton) and French knots wound twice around the needle. Make a loop of floss or pearl cotton for a hanger.

Using Heavy Threads in the Bobbin

We machine quilters are fortunate in being able to use almost any washable thread in quilting. If we can't get it through the needle, we put it in the bobbin and stitch underside up.

Most threads can be wound onto the bobbin the usual way. If not possible, handwind the thread on. Of course unlike decorative machine stitchery, which uses thread as unusual as knitting yarn, we limit ourselves to a size compatible to the fabric and a washable thread; for example, cotton or polyester buttonhole twist, crochet or pearl cotton.

Be sure to test tension settings on a doodle cloth. You want to *tighten* top tension slightly, so the heavier thread will lie snug against the surface. If you can loosen bobbin tension on your machine, you may need to do so. Use an extra-fine machine embroidery thread on the top and a size 12(80) needle.

For a doodle cloth put the quilt in a hoop, backing fabric up. Practice free-machine quilting the design. Check the thread underneath. Does it look OK? If not, adjust the tension until you're satisfied.

One problem with using heavier threads is how to handle beginnings and endings without having ugly bumps. Solution: either design stitched lines to run into the seam allowance, to be crossed by another line of stitching that anchors the first, or make the bumps look intentional, as they are in the butterfly in Fig. 5-10.

Fig. 5-7 Full-size cartoon for Santa Ornament.

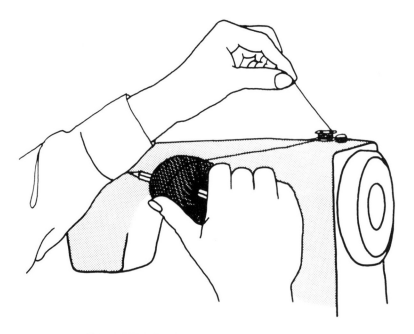

Fig. 5-8 Winding heavy threads onto the bobbin

Using the pattern of a print fabric for the quilting design is an easy way to make a reversible quilt. For example, use a bandanna on one side and denim on the other. Be sure the pattern is a fairly continuous line and that it's centered on the block. If you use your fabric in the layout given for the poncho, be sure to place your pattern on the diagonal.

Don't forget: when you finish quilting, reset your machine to normal tension.

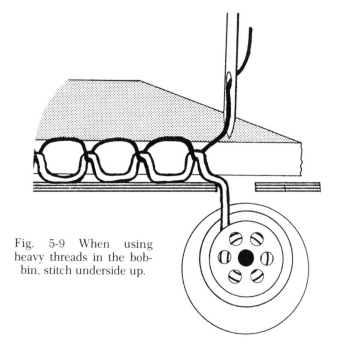

Fig. 5-9 When using heavy threads in the bobbin, stitch underside up.

Fig. 5-10 Butterfly block quilted with heavy thread.

Reversible Denim Poncho

The butterfly is a symbol of eternal life and so, in their own way, are jeans. We patch them until it's embarrassing to wear them in public and then we cut them up for quilts. Denim ages with a beautiful patina; take advantage of it by using worn dark denim in one row and worn light denim in another (or use the underside of the dark denim). Red fabric with white border strips is used on the underside of this reversible poncho.

Since the available area on old jeans is limited, we've kept the inner block size to 6″ (15.3 cm). This also allows you to use an embroidery hoop to free-machine quilt the butterfly (which is designed to be two identical continuous lines). The contrasting denim strips that frame each denim square are added first, log-cabin style, and then the butterflies are stitched.

Finished size: two rectangles, each 19½″ × 28½″ (48.2 × 72.4 cm)
Technique: free-machine quilting, heavy threads in bobbin
Needle: 16(100)

Fig. 5-11 Cartoon of butterfly; two continuous lines.

Machine setting: tighten top tension; loosen bobbin tension (experiment)
Thread: 100% cotton or rayon extra-fine machine-embroidery thread on top, crochet or pearl cotton or polyester buttonhole twist on bobbin
Seam allowance: ½″ (12 mm)

Materials You Will Need

old jeans (about 2 to 3 dark and 2 to 3 light)
1⅛ yd. (1.1 m) red fabric
⅞ yd. (0.8 m) white denim, duck, or heavy muslin
1⅛ yd. (1.1 m) batting
1 ball or spool white crochet or pearl cotton or buttonhole twist
1 spool white 100% cotton or rayon machine-embroidery thread
1 spool white regular sewing thread
3 yd. (2.7 m) folded ½″-wide (12 mm-wide) red braid for outside edge
8″ (20 cm) embroidery hoop
white pencil

Construction

1. Preshrink all fabric, including braid (make sure denim is clean). Cut out twelve 9″ (23 cm) squares from the red fabric and from the batting. Cut out six 7″ (17.8 cm) squares of dark denim and six of light denim (make sure two opposite edges of the squares run parallel to the grain of the denim). Cut out fifteen 2″ (5

cm) wide strips across the white denim. Cut out twelve 2″ × 7″ (5 × 17.8 cm) and twelve 2″ × 9″ (5 × 23 cm) strips of dark denim; cut out the same for light denim.

2. Trace a butterfly on the diagonal of each red square. In tracing you will understand how to stitch the two identical continuous lines.

3. Load the crochet cotton in the bobbin and the 100% cotton on top. Tighten top tension. Test on a doodle quilt. The crochet cotton should be held firmly against the denim. Set up the machine for a straight stitch.

4. Place a red square, butterfly-down, on a table. Place a square of batting on it next and then a dark denim square on top, centering it. Pin. Sew two light denim 7″ (17.8 cm) strips to opposite sides in a ½″ (12 mm) seam, checking Fig. 5-10 against your butterfly to be sure you have the short strips in the right place. (Note: I used the quilting guide with the regular presser foot set for ½″ (12 mm) to measure the seam.) Sew all the way from one edge of the red, over the exposed batting, over the strip, over the exposed batting to the other side. Repeat for the second strip. Flip out the two strips and pin. Sew two light denim 9″ (23 cm) strips

Fig. 5-12 Butterfly positioned in block with border.

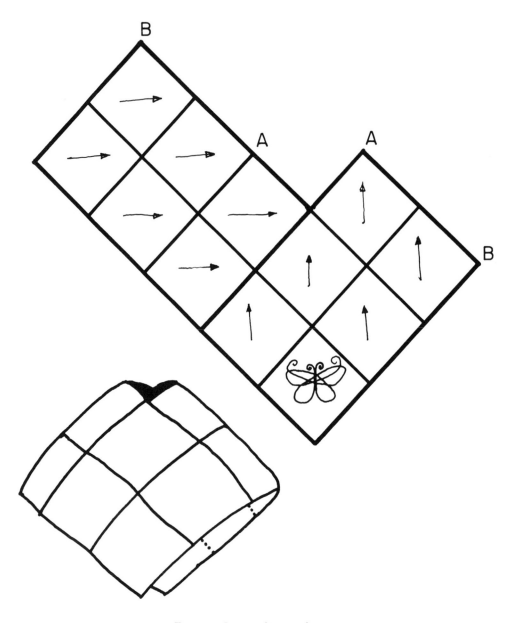

Fig. 5-13 Layout for poncho.

to opposite sides and flip out. Repeat five more blocks; then make six blocks with light centers and dark strips.

5. Change the stitch length to 0 and drop feed dogs, if you can. Take off the presser foot. Put the embroidery hoop onto the quilt, butterfly side up. You will have to loosen the embroidery hoop screw quite a bit to get it onto the fabric. Push your finger down on the fabric behind the needle, trapping the top thread. This prevents snarling in the bobbin case. Don't bother to pull up the bobbin thread. Lower the presser bar lever, stitch three times in one place to lock threads, and free-machine quilt the butterfly. Clip all threads. Repeat for all 12 blocks.

6. Reset your tension to normal. Place regular white sewing thread in top and bobbin. To sew the blocks together, lay them out in rows of dark and light, with the butterflies all facing the same way. Sew two dark blocks together by placing two strips of the white denim above and below one block, raw edges matching. Sew ½" (12 mm) seam. Flip out the top strip. Sew the other side of the top strip to a second dark block through all layers. Fold under ½" (12 mm) on bottom strip and hand-sew to block. Trim off the extra strip of white. Each rectangle of the poncho is composed of three squares each of light and dark squares. Connect a dark to a light and vice versa. Then connect between them with long white strips in the same manner.

7. The feelers on the butterflies are closer to one long edge of the rectangle than the other. Call that edge the neck edge. Turn in the white denim strips on the neck edge of each rectangle and press. Insert the end of one rectangle into the neck edge of the other rectangle, lining up the outside edges. Make sure the feelers on all the butterflies are pointing toward the neck edge. Hand sew the white denim strips on topside and underside to the white strips of the inserted strip (or topstitch by machine).

8. Sew the end of the second rectangle (into which you just sewed an end) into the neck edge of the first rectangle, as in Step 7.

9. Zigzag the white strips together all around the outside edge of the poncho. Place purchased folded braid over the outside edge and mark where the corners are. Use Method F, Fig. 2-50, to make mitered corners first and then apply the braid to the edge, topstitching it in place.

Additional Ideas

1. To make a double bed quilt, construct units in sets of four butterfly blocks, two sets on the diagonal across the quilt and three sets down, which gives you a 6" (15.3 cm) pillow tuck. Make eight full sets and ten half sets (make yourself a sloper if you don't understand). Decide whether all the butterflies will face the same way, point toward the center of the set of four blocks, or alternate directions so there is no one top to the quilt. Since this is a heavy quilt, you don't need to quilt the sides. Use white denim for a base and string or crazy-quilt old denim onto it.

2. Replace the butterfly motif in the poncho with old pockets taken off jeans. Stitching them on will quilt the block.

3. Make a poncho of twelve 8" (20.3 cm) blocks with 1" (2.5 cm) connecting bands, all free-machine quilted in the shape of traditional pieced designs such as eight-pointed star or Dresden plate.

Reminder: You can use heavy threads in the bobbin and quilt with a straight stitch or zigzag with the presser foot on, as you will do in the next project. The result looks particularly attractive on clothing.

Special Loft

Putting the quilt sandwich in a hoop and free-machine quilting compresses the three layers a lot. Using a double batt circumvents this compression somewhat, but you don't always want to use a double batt. On a full-size quilt, for example, it is too heavy.

The technique of putting only the backing fabric in the hoop and pinning the batting and top onto it, then free-machine quilting, gives the puffy effect we all love in quilts. (Incidentally, this can be done with the presser foot on, too.) This

Fig. 5-14 "Squaring the Circle" by dj bennett, 89″ (226 cm) square, white on white, worked in 8½″ (22 cm) quilt-as-you-go squares, free-machine quilted, all slightly different, twin-needle quilted on bands and borders (perfect material found in form of used sheets at rummage sale). "I begin with a good deal of thinking (usually when I can't sleep at night), but then plunge right in. I like to work directly—with what I have on hand. Pre-thinking usually inspires some collection of fabrics and threads when I see what I want; impossible to find exactly what one wants when one requires it! . . . The extreme freedom and mobility of line was a natural for free-form quilting. I'm fascinated with the effect of light upon a surface altered and manipulated through quilting." [Works on a 4-year-old Bernina, usually without any foot.]

technique is limited, of course, to blocks the size of your hoop, which means for an entire quilt you'd spend more time joining blocks than free-machine quilting. Therefore, our project is for a combination evening bag/stationery case personalized with the initial of the person who will receive your gift.

Personalized Evening Bag/Stationery Case

When you're traveling, each item must double its function. This quilted silk bag carries stationery, addresses, stamps, and envelopes and can also be used for nights out.

It is quilted underside up with heavy threads in the bobbin, using a straight stitch. The initial is free-machine quilted in the special loft way and then satin-stitched on. Before making it, be sure your stationery fits the pockets. If not, either make the bag wider or longer—or trim your stationery, a time-saving trick used by people who hate writing letters.

Finished size: (folded) 6½″ × 9¾″ (16.5 × 24.8 cm)
Needle: 12(80)
Machine Setting: free-machine quilting, stitch length and width 0, loosen top tension slightly
Seam allowance: ¼″ (6 mm)

Materials *You Will Need*

rectangle of silk, backing, and batting, each 22″ × 10½″ (55.8 × 26.7 cm); I used interfacing fleece and a lightweight cotton backing
silk or polyester buttonhole twist
100% cotton or rayon extra-fine machine-embroidery thread
regular sewing thread
silk and backing to fit hoop (for initial)
small amount of polyester batting
embroidery hoop
2 snaps
ruler, white pencil
press cloth

Note: Don't press silk with steam. Use medium-dry heat on the wrongside of the silk (or use a press cloth for the topside).

Construction

1. Sew the interfacing fleece to the wrong side of the backing fabric on the ¼″ (6 mm) seam allowance. Trim batting close to stitching. Place silk rightsides

Fig. 5-15 Evening Bag/Stationery Case with initial.

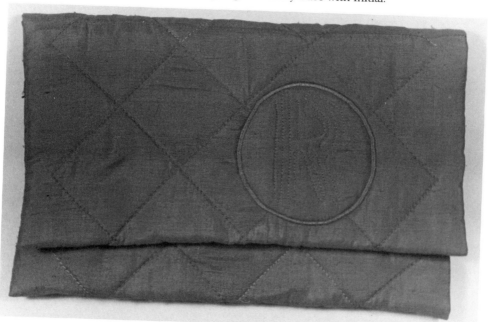

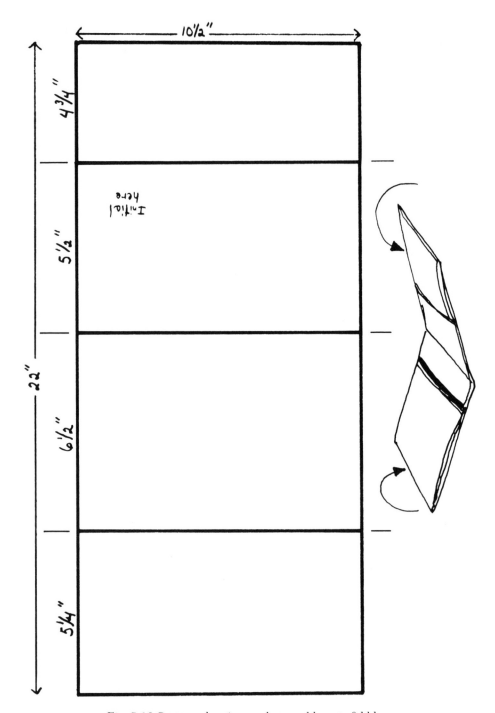

Fig. 5-16 Cartoon showing pockets and how to fold bag.

together with lining and sew all the way around the outside in a ¼" (6 mm) seam. Clip corners. Slit lining and batting only about 1" (2.5 cm) from one end. Pull bag rightside out, push out corners, and press lightly, using a press cloth. Close slash by hand with a whipstitch (this will later be hidden).

2. Mark diagonal lines 2" (5 cm) apart on the lining. Don't plan to stitch closer than ½" (12 mm) to either of the long sides. Pin the quilt securely. (*Note:* I had trouble with the silk moving around a lot and finally ended up basting the quilt sandwich, which doesn't take much time on a small item like this.) Load the silk buttonhole twist in the bobbin and the 100% cotton on top. Tighten top tension slightly and, using a straight stitch, check it on a doodle quilt. With the presser foot on, stitch the lines you just marked, lining side up. Pull thread ends to the back and tie off.

3. Blow up your initial from the line alphabet in Chapter 9 to fit a 3" (7.6 cm) circle. Trace onto the silk. Put the lining fabric in an embroidery hoop. Put the batting next and the silk fabric on top. Pin in place. (Only the lining fabric is in the hoop.) Put regular sewing thread in the bobbin; loosen top tension slightly less than normal. Drop feed dogs (optional) and set stitch length and width at 0. Free-machine quilt your initial and the circle.

4. Take the lining out of the hoop. Trim close to the circle stitching. Position the circle on the quilted rectangle as shown in the cartoon. Put the applique presser foot on and zigzag once around the circle. Then set your stitch length for satin stitches ("fine" or close to 0) and go around the circle once.

5. Turn up the two pockets as shown in the cartoon and handstitch the sides together, using a toymaker's ladder stitch.

Additional Ideas

1. Use imitation suede instead of silk and a letter from the shape alphabet (it's difficult to free-machine quilt on imitation suede).

2. Make an elegant bag of one-step string-quilting (see next chapter), using only rich, shiny, textured fabrics.

3. Using the special loft technique and the 3" (7.6 cm) circle, make yourself a hanging stuffed pendant with your initial in the middle, surrounded by tiny buttons at the edge.

Designs for Free-Machine Quilting

The main reason you would choose free-machine quilting over presser-foot quilting is that the quilting line involves many turns, angles, stops, and starts. As for finding designs for free-machine quilting, all you have to do is start looking— and record what you see. Try these: meander lines (from watching the pattern of children moving through a playground); freely interlaced lines (designed from dropping ribbons on a table); sketches of buildings in San Francisco.

Fig. 5-17 A few suggestions for free-machine quilting designs.

Chapter 6

Quilt-as-You-Go and One-Step Quilting

The term "quilt-as-you-go" is fairly new, but the concept isn't new at all. The idea is to break a large quilt into manageable blocks, make a quilt sandwich for each block, quilt each block independently, and then re-assemble the blocks into a full-sized quilt.

This method allows the quilting to be very important and intricate. As each unit is finished, we feel satisfied, as if in these busy times we've finally accomplished something. Ultimately, however, there is more work in joining the blocks than there is in quilting a whole top at once.

Joining Quilt-as-You-Go Blocks

There are six methods of joining quilt-as-you-go blocks:

1. Handle each block as if it were one layer, not three. Rightsides of top together, sew a ½" (12 mm) seam. Trim the batting to the seam line and the backing to ¼" (6 mm). Press open the seam and lay 1" wide bias binding, lace, or strips of fabric over the seam, stitching it down by hand because machine-stitching looks wobbly on the front (stitches exaggerated for Fig. 6-2). However, if you reverse the process and sew undersides together, putting the seam on the top, you can sew the strips down by machine. If you have quilted close to the seam lines, you must use this method or method #6.

2. Pin the backing and batting of both blocks out of the way. Right sides together, join the two tops in a ½" (12 mm) seam (Fig. 6-3). Press open the top seam, using a press cloth to protect the iron. Trim the batting to the seam line. Lay the two blocks on a table, rightsides down. Fold under ½" (12 mm) on one backing and lap it over the second. Pin-baste; then hand-sew the seam closed (Fig. 6-3). You can't use this method if you've stitched too close to the seam allowance. Leave two times the seam allowance free all around the unfinished block; for example, don't stitch closer than 1" (2.5 cm) with a ½" (12 mm) seam allowance.

3. Pin the top and batting out of the way. Join the backing in a ½" (12 mm) seam; press open lightly, using a press cloth to protect the iron. Trim the batting to the seam line. Unpin one top and pin it down over the batting. Turn the two blocks over and pin again from the back. Remove pins from the top side. Stitch in the ditch (right down the seam line). Turn over and unpin the remaining top. Fold it under a few threads less than ½" (12 mm). Topstitch with a straight stitch or narrow zigzag near the edge (Fig. 6-4).

4. Pin one top out of the way. Wrong sides together, join the two blocks (Fig. 6-5). Trim the batting to the seam line. Trim the fabrics to ¼" (6 mm). Press all

Fig. 6-1 "Christmas Tree" by Alice Newton, 34″ × 36″ (86 × 91 cm), center triangles one-step quilting, background tied, stuffed star hand-tacked on; design modified from quilt done by Barbara Conn and members of the American Embassy Quilting Group, Colombia, South America. "Design is everywhere, a matter of visual stimulation—or rather, overstimulation. One sees an object and begins to wonder, 'what would happen if I did this or that to it?' It is also a matter of observation or translation—one sees an object represented one way, then feels and develops another way to show (use) this same basic design. I feel that all design (inspiration) is built on past experience, whether it is of our own or peoples of ages past." [Works on 5-year-old Bernina 830, uses darning foot with glitch cut out of it.]

three layers lightly toward the top that's pinned back. Unpin the remaining top and press it under ½″ (12 mm). Lap over the fabrics and topstitch near the edge (Fig. 6-5).

    5. Work the one-step quilting in manageable modules. Lay the modules onto another backing and butt them up against each other. Cover the join with strips of fabric or bias binding topstitched in place (Fig. 6-6). If the blocks are not bigger

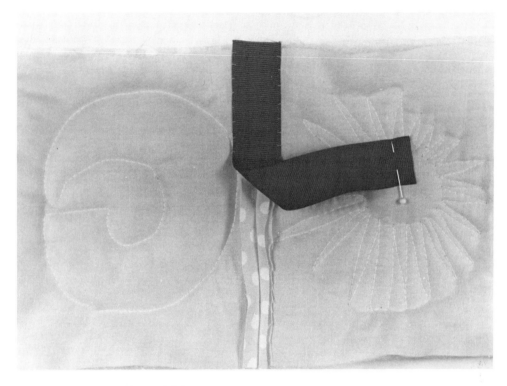

Fig. 6-2 Joining quilt-as-you-go blocks: Method 1.

than 4" to 6" (10 to 15 cm) square, you can add another layer of batting, which is quilted by the topstitching lines. The perfectionist starts and stops these lines ½" (12 mm) from the top and bottom, on the seam allowance of the cross-seam.

6. Join one-step quilting with strips of fabric by laying right sides of two strips together against both top and backing, sandwiching the quilt with the strips (Fig. 6-7). Sew a ½" (12 mm) seam. Open out the two strips and press. Match the right side of the second block's backing to the right side of the backing strip. Sew a ½" (12 mm) seam through all layers (Fig. 6-7). Press seam lightly. Lay the blocks on a hard surface, rightside up. (If the added strip is wider than two times your seam allowance (1" or 2.5 cm here), cut batting to fit from seam to seam.) Fold under ½" (12 mm) on top strip (Fig. 6-7). Pin it in place over the batting. Topstitch with a straight stitch or narrow zigzag. Optional: Topstitch the other side of the strip. (If batting was added, nothing has yet secured the batting between the strip and it will shrink in over the years of washing unless you do secure it, so machine quilt at least ¼" or 6 mm from each side.)

One-Step Quilting

In the last several years, a new wrinkle has developed in quilt-as-you-go: combining the piecing and the quilting in one operation. This, too, is sometimes called quilt-as-you-go, which can be confusing to machine quilters. There are several other techniques which are referred to as "quilt-as-you-go," so we will try to avoid confusion by consistently using this terminology:

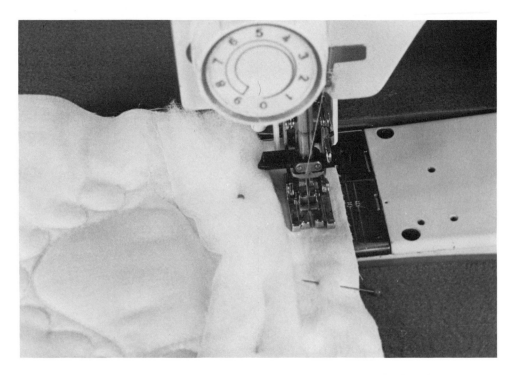

Fig. 6-3 Method 2, seaming tops: Pin-baste and then sew backs closed.

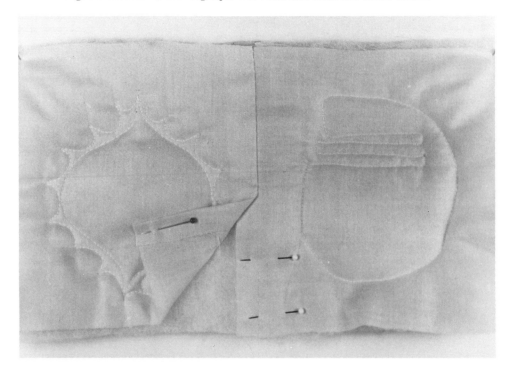

Fig. 6-4 Method 3.

Quilt-as-you-go: The process of making several quilt units smaller than the whole quilt and quilting each one before joining them together.

Finish-as-you-go: Making quilted "pillows" with finished edges which, when joined, make a whole quilt (such as the half-a-square project in Chapter 4).

One-step-piece-and-quilt (for short, one-step quilting): The piecing and quilting of the fabric is done in one operation: sometimes the entire quilt is one-step quilted, and sometimes a block at a time is one-step quilted (in which case it is also quilt-as-you-go). Do you see the distinctions now?

Log Cabin Quilt

We will demonstrate one-step piece-and-quilt with a log cabin square.

The center of the log cabin is 2″ (5 cm) square with ¼″ (6 mm) seams. If you are doing many, cut one long strip 2½″ (6.35 cm) wide and slice off each center when you need it. All the "logs" of the log cabin except the outer logs, are 1½″ (3.8 cm) wide, cut in long strips. For simplicity, we are using two solids and two prints, one set dark and one light. The outer logs are cut 2″ (5 cm) wide.

Cut a backing fabric the size of your block plus ½″ (12 mm) all around for seam allowances. Cut a batting square the same size. Optional: Machine-baste the two together ½″ (12 mm) in from the edge, using the zipper, roller, or no-snag foot so it won't catch in the batting. (This step is not necessary, but makes joining the blocks more precise and discourages the backing from shrinking and/or pucker-

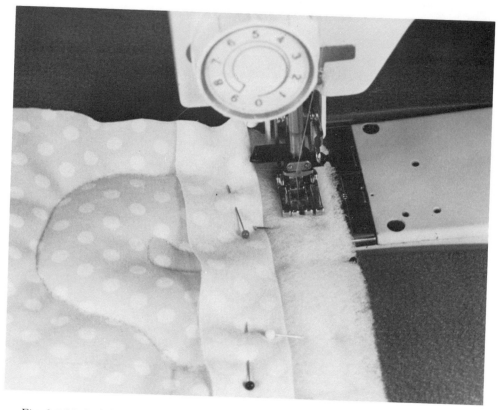

Fig. 6-5 Method 4, joining with one top pinned back out of the way, then topstitching.

ing.) Trim the batting close to the stitching. Find the center of the square by laying a ruler diagonally from corner to corner and either drawing lines with a water-erasable pen or marking where the diagonal lines cross with pins. (If you use the pen, be sure to soak your quilt in cold water when you finish it to remove the pen marks. Otherwise, the first time you wash it in hot water, the ink may seep to the surface and set.) Center a 2½" (6.35 cm) square in the middle; pin or thread-baste in place (Fig. 6-8).

The next step is simple, but calls for craftsmanship.

Place a light print along one side of the center, rightsides together and top and sides even. Pin across the strip ¼" (6 mm) in from both ends. If you cannot gauge ¼" (6 mm) by eye, use a small piece of masking tape or cut yourself a gauge from graph paper. (See the outer stitching in Fig. 6-8 for why to do this—the backside looks terrible if you don't.) Stitch with a ¼" (6 mm) seam, either back stitching at both ends or lockstitching by setting your stitch length at 0 for the beginning and ending stitches. Cut off the strip even with the center square. Flip out the fabric and fingerpress. Pin the fabric down securely, but don't flatten the batting completely. If you make no allowance for the loft of the batting, the backing will shrink in. If you've never done this before, turn your square over after each seam and check the back for tucks and creeping.

Fig. 6-6 Method 5.

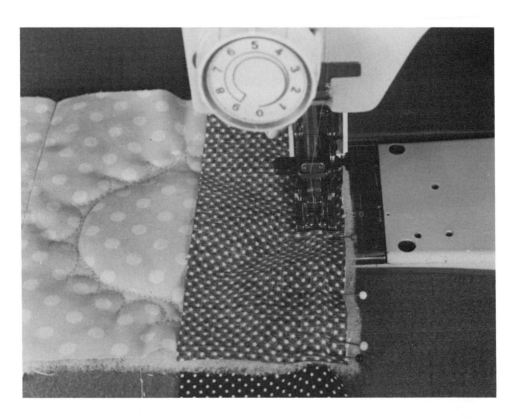

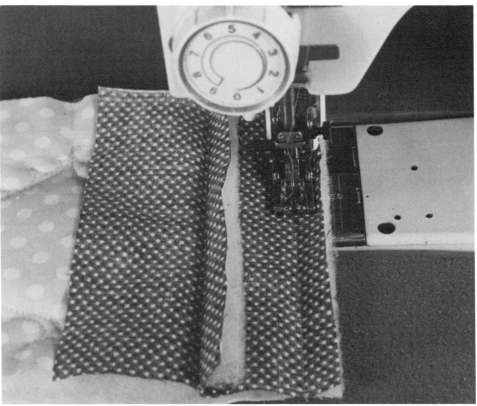

Fig. 6-7 Method 6, sandwiching the quilt between strips; attaching the strip to the next block; securing the strip to the block.

Place another piece of light-colored material along the bottom long edge, rightsides together. Stitch, using pins, a graph paper strip, or masking tape, to start and stop ¼″ (6 mm) from each edge. Continue spiraling around the center, using light colors on two sides and dark on the other two sides.

Now examine the backing side of your one-step quilting. How does it look? If you didn't pin each fabric down as you worked, thinking you could eyeball it, the backing often creeps and puckers—although pin-basting helps, and so does using a stiff backing fabric such as interfacing or using spray starch to stiffen a lightweight fabric. If you sewed from raw edge to raw edge, the intersection seam lines on the back are often a mess.

To compensate for shrinkage of the backing, I sometimes add a 1″ (2.5 cm) seam allowance all around the backing and cut the outer logs an extra ½″ (12 mm) wide. When I finish, I pin a graph paper pattern of the finished block including ½″ (12 mm) seams to the fabric block and trim to exact size.

General Guidelines for One-Step Quilting

One-step quilting adapts well to many quilting techniques and patterns, including Nine-Patch, Flying Geese, crazy and string quilts. For best results:

1. Baste the batting to the backing fabric on the seam line and then trim batting close to the stitching. If you don't do this, you cannot always easily trim the extra bulk in the seam allowance unless you rip out one-step quilting lines that extend into the seam allowance.

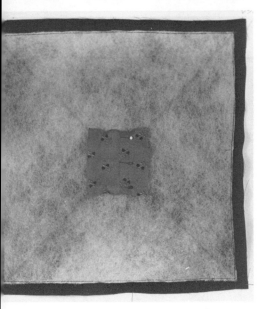

Fig. 6-8 From top: One-step Log Cabin Quilt; center 2½″ (6.35 cm) square over backing and batting. Stitching the next strip. Continue to work around the block, pinning as you work. Check the back as you work to be sure there are no creeps or puckers. The center was done with craftsmanship; the outer stitches were not.

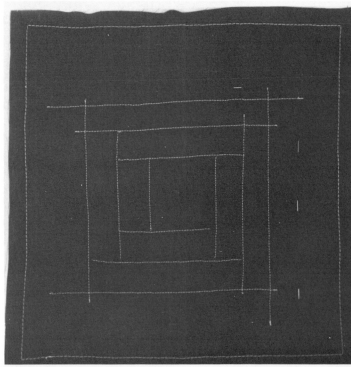

2. Use your most exciting fabrics for one-step quilting because the actual puffiness of quilting does not show up unless additional lines of quilting are added. (You may want to use a double batt.)

3. If you insert strips of batting into one-step quilting strips (such as for the sleeping bag later in this chapter) or between one-step quilted blocks, plan to add quilting lines along or across the strips or the batting will pull away from the seam line.

4. Watch the backing fabric carefully. It wants to pull in and pucker, usually because the fabric on the top has been flattened too much between seams, not allowing for the loft of the batting. The backing fabric also puckers because it is too lightweight for the technique. Either spray-starch the fabric or use a medium to heavy-weight backing fabric.

5. Use your quilting gauge as a ½″ (12 mm) seam guideline when you are one-step quilting in the middle of a batt and cannot use the guidelines inscribed on the needle plate.

6. Keep a small square of scrap paper near the machine. Before pulling the one-step quilting in progress away from the needle, slip the paper under the presser foot. Pull the fabric away to the left, holding the paper under the foot. This way the foot does not catch in the batting as you work. Use the paper to reposition the fabric under the needle.

7. If you have a low-shank machine and do a lot of one-step quilting, buy a no-snag foot, which does not catch in the batting. Otherwise, use a roller or zipper foot.

8. Consider adding selected lines of hand quilting, as you will see on the sleeping bag shown later in this chapter. The bag is technically quilted and can be used while I slowly add lines of hand quilting on the white areas.

A word of warning: Combining the piecing and the quilting in one operation is so ingenious that it's easy to run amuck with the idea. However, it doesn't always look good or wear well. If the strips being quilted are less than about 1″ apart, one-step quilting flattens the batting and you lose the puffy look of quilting. (The experienced can use a double batt to counteract this.) If the strips are huge and there is no further surface quilting, the quilt can look poorly made and the batting may shift around in the wash. Always make a sample first, to be sure you like the look. Also decide what your personal standards are. Remember my "closed fist test"? For quilts (not always for smaller items), I lay my fist on the block and if there aren't quilting lines nearby on *all* sides, I add some.

The remaining projects are based on the construction ideas in Chapter 3. Whenever a specific technique is mentioned, you can find the details there. If you don't remember how to crazy-quilt, for example, review Chapter 3.

Wigwarm

Reading in bed on icy winter nights is something to look forward to while you complete this easy-to-make project, made of warm velour. A snap on either side makes armholes or you can use it flat as a lap quilt. The size is perfect for any other blown-up traditional quilt block you want to try.

Finished size: 72″ × 40″ (183 × 102 cm)
Technique: one-step quilting
Needle size: 12(80)
Thread: ordinary sewing (cotton-covered polyester)

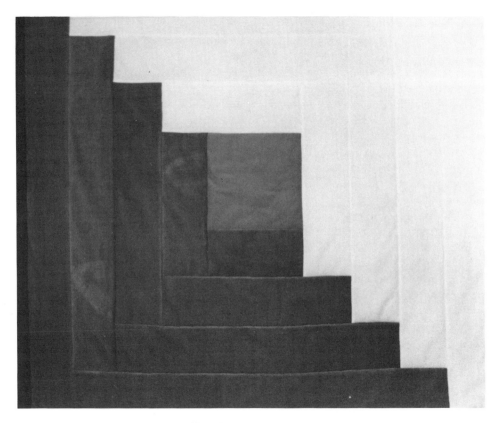

Fig. 6-9 Layout of strips.

Seam allowance: ¼" or 6 mm (Note: If you are inexperienced, use ½" or 12 mm seam allowances everywhere)

Machine setting: straight stitch of regular length

Machine accessories: zipper or roller foot, walking foot (optional)

Pattern: Log Cabin

Materials You Will Need

¾ yd. of 45" wide (68.3 cm of 115 cm-wide) white velour

2⅛ yd. tangerine velour

¾ yd. (68.3 cm) of gray velour

1⅛ yd. (1.9 m) black velour

(*Note:* Be careful when you're buying velour. To get the colors you want, you may have to buy different widths of fabric. You will then need more or less fabric; see Yardage Conversion Chart in Chapter 2.)

1 piece batting 40½" (103 cm) square and 2 pieces, each 16½" × 40½" (42 × 103 cm)

tangerine (in bobbin) and black thread

graph paper, masking tape, cornstarch

press cloth

5 gripper snaps (or use Velcro buttons)

Construction

1. Preshrink velours. If you must iron wrinkles in the yardage, do so from the underside with a press cloth or the iron will leave marks. Cut an 8½" (21.6 cm) square out of graph paper. Cut one square of tangerine velour 40 ½" (103 cm) square and one, 8 ½" (21.6 cm) square (use the graph paper for a pattern for the latter). The larger piece is the backing; find its center point by folding it, wrong sides together, into quarters. Mark center. Then unfold and pin the center of the graph paper square to the rightside center of the velour. Make the edges of the paper and fabric parallel; pin.

2. Turn the large velour square over. Place the 40½" (103 cm) batting on the wrong side of the velour. Pin around the edges. Zigzag or straight stitch around the edges, using a zipper or roller foot to keep from catching in the batting.

3. Tape the velour to a large window, batting side up. You can now see the outline of the graph paper square. Pin the 8½" (21.6 cm) tangerine velour square in place, wrong side against the batting. Remove the graph paper.

4. Cut the white and gray velour into 4½" (11.4 cm) wide strips (I used the paper cutter). For 45" (11.5 cm) wide velour you will need five strips of white and five, gray. Cut the strips so that you have one gray and one white each this long: 12½" (31.8 cm), 16½" (42 cm), 20½" (52 cm), 24½" (62 cm), 28½" (72 cm), 32½" (82.6 cm), 36½" (92.7 cm). In addition, cut one gray strip 8½" (21.6 cm) long and one white strip 40½" (103 cm) long.

5. Designate one long side of the larger tangerine square "bottom." Sew the 8½" (21.6 cm) gray strip to the bottom side of the smaller tangerine square, rightsides together, in a ¼" (6 mm) seam, stopping and starting the seam ¼" (6 mm) from each end so it will look good on the back. Flip out the gray piece rightside up and pin liberally.

6. The next gray 12½" (31.8 cm) piece is sewn across the end of the previous piece. (Don't get confused or you will have to rip out.) Repeat what you did in Step 5 for each strip around the central square, following the cartoon for color placement and always starting and stopping each seam ¼" (6 mm) from the end (Fig. 6-10).

7. Cut two tangerine and two black rectangles 16½" × 40½" each (42 × 103 cm) for the ends. Pin the rightside long edge of one black rectangle to the topside of the worked Log Cabin and the rightside long edge of one tangerine to its underside. Sew a ¼" (6 mm) seam. Repeat for the other end. Flip the ends out so the wrong sides touch.

8. Trim the graph paper square you used in Step 1 to 5" (12.7 cm) on one side. With an unthreaded needle, sew along the graph paper square 4" (10.1 cm) in from one side. Place the graph paper on one black end along the seam line. Work cornstarch through the holes of the paper to mark the quilting line, moving the paper along the seam line as needed. Mark two more quilting lines 4" (10.1 cm) from each other. Repeat for the other end.

9. Cut two rectangles of batting 16¼" × 40½" (41.3 × 103 cm). Slide one between each end. Pin liberally and zigzag or straight stitch around the edges of the ends. Machine quilt the three long lines on each black end, pinning liberally along each line. A walking foot also keeps the layers from shifting. If necessary, vacuum the cornstarch off the velour.

10. Put black thread in the bobbin. For the binding, cut 1¼" (3.2 cm) wide strips of black velour until you have a total of about 226" (574 cm). Sew the strips together on the short end and press open seams, using a press cloth. Rightsides

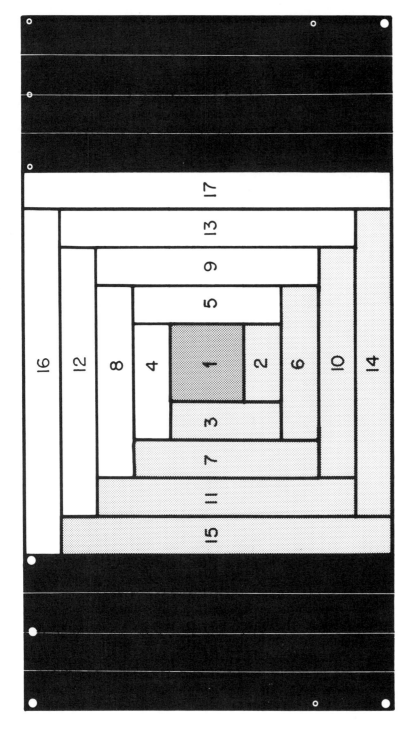

Fig. 6-10 Cartoon showing sequence of sewing strips.

together, lay the binding along one end of the Wigwarm. Turn under the raw edge of the beginning of the binding ¼" (6 mm). Sew all around the Wigwarm in a ¼" (6 mm) seam, overlapping the end of the binding 1" (2.5 cm) and trimming off extra binding. At the corners, clip to the binding as shown in Method F, Fig. 2-50. Trim corners of Wigwarm. Flip the binding over the edge to the underside and pin in place from the topside. Stitch in the ditch of the first seam. There is no need to turn under the raw edge of the velour. Trim the extra velour close to the stitching.

11. There is a new heavy-duty snap attacher on the market that is as wonderful as the old ones were useless. It is a bit expensive, but worth the dollars if you sew much. (See Resource list.) Put five snaps on as shown on the cartoon in Fig. 6-11.

Additional Ideas

1. Make the basic Log Cabin block 8" to 10" (20 to 25 cm). Make enough blocks to cover your mattress top, with long one-step quilted strips for the side and end drop.

2. Make a Wigwarm of leather and/or imitation suede, overlapping the seam lines.

3. Blow up the heart in Chapter 4, multiplying all dimensions by 3, and one-step quilting the strips to each other for a Wigwarm. Quilt the ends with the line alphabet from Chapter 9, using a name or one-word message.

Seminole Sleeping Bag

The Seminole method of piecing lends itself to many of the classic designs found in cultures all over the world. This zippered machine-washable sleeping bag opens flat and can be used as a double-bed comforter. It is constructed in two parts which are then connected. You can add hand quilting as you wish and still use the sleeping bag as you work on the handstitching little-by-little. (Use a double batt for a bag heavy enough to use for sleeping outdoors.)

Finished size: 60" × 72" plus 1½" borders (152 × 183 cm plus 3.8 cm)
Technique: one-step strip quilting
Needle size: 10/11(70)—for piecing, 12(80)—for quilting
Thread: regular sewing
Seam allowance: ½" (12 mm)
Machine setting: short straight stitch for quilting
Machine accessories: zipper foot, regular foot (or walking foot)

Materials You Will Need

4 yd. of 45" wide (3.6 m of 115 cm-wide) medium-weight cotton/blend navy blue fabric (also used for backing fabric)
⅞ yd. (.8 m) mustard fabric
⅞ yd. (.8 m) red fabric
1⅞ yd. (1.7 m) white fabric
4⅛ yd. (3.75 m) batting (you'll have lots extra for other projects)
80" to 90" (203 to 229 cm) separating sleeping bag zipper
white and navy (in bobbin) thread
cutting board or long table
clothespin (optional)

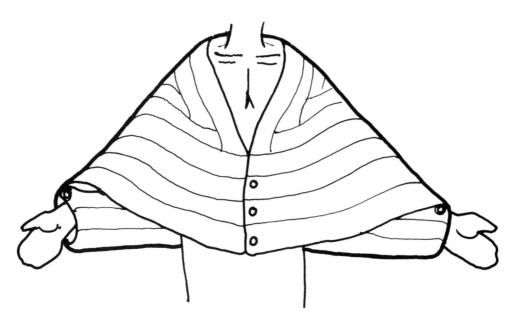

Fig. 6-11 Cartoon of Wigwarm project.

Construction

1. Preshrink fabric. (Be careful of red fabric; preshrink separately in case it bleeds.) To construct the long Seminole strips, cut across the grain of each color in 7″ (17.8 cm) wide strips. (I used a paper cutter.) You will need eight strips of white and four of each of the other colors. Sew the strips together along the long edge in this order: blue, white, yellow, white, red. You will have four sets. Press open seams. Cut across each set in 4″ (10.1 cm) wide strips. You need forty 4″ (10.1 cm) wide strips. (Use the extra fabric strips for a doodle cloth and to decorate a matching pillow case.)

2. Cut across the grain of the remaining white fabric in 4″ (10.1 cm) wide strips. Of these strips, you will need: 4 rectangles, 13″ (33 cm) long; 24 rectangles, 7″ (17.8 cm) long; 16 rectangles, 4″ (10.1 cm) long.

3. Study the cartoon. The first long strip of the motif (starting at center of quilt) matches the red ends of two Seminole strips (in a ½″ or 12 mm seam). (Reds always fall at the center of the quilt.) Add a 7″ (17.8 cm) white piece to each blue end. Repeat this strip seven more times for the entire sleeping bag. The second long strip calls for a 7″ (17.8 cm) white rectangle between two reds and a 4″ (10.1 cm) white piece at each blue end. Repeat seven more times. The third strip connects the reds with a 13″ (33 cm) white piece. Repeat three more times. Press all seams open. Arrange the strips in the correct order, according to the cartoon.

4. Cut the remaining blue fabric into two 73″ (175 cm) lengths. Cut twenty 4″ (10.1 cm) wide strips the long way. Cut the batting into 73″ (175 cm) lengths. Cut two 4″ (10.1 cm) wide strips of batting (the long way) and eighteen 3″ (7.6 cm) wide strips.

5. Make a long skinny quilt sandwich of navy backing, 4″ (10.1 cm) batting, and Strip 1. Pin liberally. Check machine tension settings on a doodle cloth, especially important when you are using two different colors of thread. Machine quilt across the long quilt everywhere white meets a color, starting at the right end

224

and working left. Quilt on the white very close to the seam. Zigzag or straight stitch one long edge.

6. Pin Strip 2 to Strip 1 on the unzigzagged edge, rightsides together, always from the center out. On the underside of the quilt add a strip of navy and pin liberally on top. Sew a ½" (12 mm) seam. Trim any batting that sticks out. Flip the two strips out and press seams lightly on front and back. Working on a flat surface (cutting board or table is best; working on floor will give you a backache), insert a 3" (7.6 cm) wide piece of batting. Pin liberally. Machine quilt the white seams, always working from the cross-seam to the raw edge. Lock the threads by setting the stitch length at 0 and taking three stitches. Reset the stitch length dial and then machine quilt to the edge. Cut thread ends on front and back when you've finished the strip. Roll the bulk of the fabric as you quilt and clip it at the edge with a clothespin (or pin the roll). This whole step takes about 20 minutes. Continue across the quilt until you've sewn two entire motifs.

7. Repeat Steps 5 and 6 for the second half of the sleeping bag, except for the very last strip. Stop quilting ⅝" (16 mm) from the raw edges and lock threads. Turn navy backing edge back ½" (12 mm) and pin out of the way. Trim batting even with backing.

8. Rightsides of the two halves together, sew a long ½" (12 mm) seam with the pinned navy backing side up. Trim the seam to ¼" (6 mm). Unpin the navy backing. Turn under raw edge and hand sew in place over seam (if you're in a hurry and not a perfectionist, this can be done by machine; stitch-in-the-ditch the seam you just made, from the topside).

9. Check the head and tail ends of the sleeping bag on a cutting board or graph paper to be sure they're straight across. Trim if necessary. Check to be sure the two sides are the same length.

Fig. 6-12 Seminole piecing.

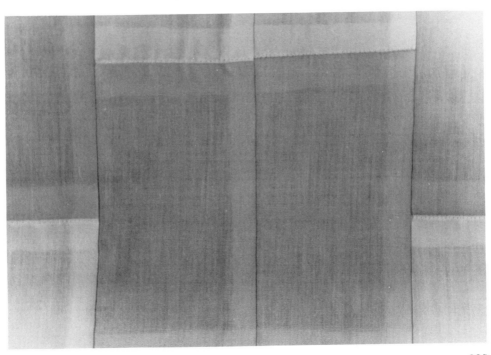

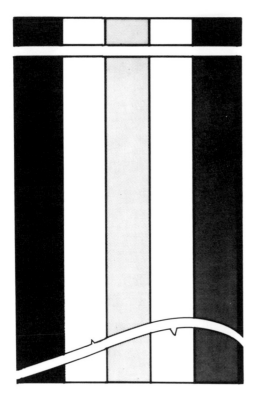

Fig. 6-13 Cartoon shows joining of five strips and then cutting set into 4″ (10 cm) wide strips

Fig. 6-14 Cartoon of strip placement.

make: 4 4 2

10. To bind the head end of the sleeping bag, cut across the grain of the remaining navy fabric in two 3½″ (8.9 cm) wide strips. Seam together across the width to make one long strip. To make French fold binding, fold strip in half, wrong sides together. Measure binding strip against sleeping bag and trim to size (no need to turn in raw ends). Working from the navy backing side, match raw edges of binding to raw edges of sleeping bag. Stitch ½″ (12 mm) seam. Trim corners off top edges of side seams. Fold binding over raw edges to topside of sleeping bag and stitch close to edge of binding.

11. To bind the rest of the quilt, cut across the remaining navy fabric in six 6″ (15.2 cm) wide strips. Seam the strips together across the widths to make one long strip. Press seams open. Fold in one raw end ½″ (12 mm) and press. Fold the strip in half, wrong sides together, and press. Working from the navy backing side, match raw edges of binding to raw edges of sleeping bag. Stitch ½″ (12 mm) seam all around the bag, mitering the corners as shown in Method D, Fig. 2-48. Just before you reach the end, trim the binding and turn in the raw end ½″ (12 mm).

Fold the binding out flat.

12. Place the opened and separated zipper parts face-down on the binding ½" (12 mm) away from the binding seam. The ends of the zipper should be 4" to 6" (10 to 15 cm) apart at the bottom of the sleeping bag (or it's difficult to zip). Let the zipper parts round across the mitered edges, instead of trying to make the zipper square at the corners. Pin the two zipper parts in place and stitch, using a zipper foot. If the zipper is too long, trim it with scissors and sew a tiny bead at the cut end near the teeth, so the zipper pull won't come off.

13. Fold the binding to the front and stitch close to the edge. Hand close the two top ends of the binding.

Additional Ideas

1. Make one motif only, bind it, and hang it behind your desk as a cheerful banner.

2. Reduce the size of the Seminole strips to 2" (5 cm) and cut them crosswise into 1" (2.5 cm) bands. Use on the yoke of a man's shirt with cream, two shades of brown, and turquoise.

3. Do one-step strip quilting as explained above in long strips of the rainbow colors, but don't further quilt each strip. When you are all done, machine quilt across the quilt with the serpentine stitch (or a straight stitch).

Crazy Quilt Stocking

The original crazy quilts were often not quilted at all. They were actually fabric collages using leftover bits of the maker's best fabrics—silks, velvets, etc. Dixie Haywood (see Bibliography) has modernized this old concept, making the building of the crazy quilt a one-step quilting procedure.

This Christmas stocking uses rich white fabrics highlighted by a fragment of old embroidery. The name of the owner and the date are free-machine quilted on one strip of fabric near the center. Additional machine-embroidery could be added along seams. This project works up so fast that you can easily make everyone in the family a new stocking every year.

This stocking has a crazy-quilted front, a plain back, and a lining.

For a clever all-machine way to line anything, see Step 7.

Finished size: 14½" (36.8 cm) high
Needle: 12(80)
Machine setting: straight stitch
Machine accessories: zipper and regular foot
Seam allowance (stocking outline): ½" (12 mm)

Materials You Will Need

⅜ yd. (.34 m) firm fabric for back of stocking (actually this is enough for three stockings)

⅜ yd. (.34 m) lightweight lining fabric

piece of interfacing, muslin, or old sheeting big enough for stocking, to use as base for crazy quilt

batting big enough for stocking

scraps of special fabrics (use a nonfrayable fabric like felt or imitation suede for the heel and toe)

8" (20.3 cm) ribbon for loop

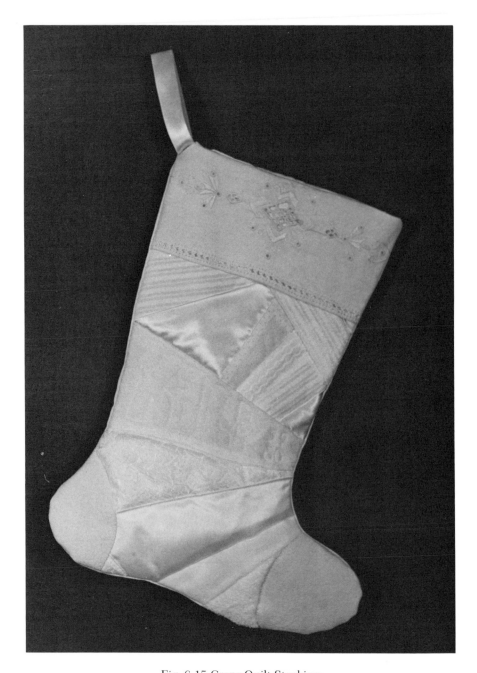

Fig. 6-15 Crazy Quilt Stocking

Construction

1. Blow up the cartoon in Fig. 6-16 so that the stocking is 14½″ (36.8 cm) high.

2. Decide which way you want the stocking to face. Cut out the base and the back side of the stocking, wrongsides together. Mark the side of the base you will sew fabric onto. Cut out batting in the stocking shape.

3. Machine-baste the batting to the stocking base on the ½″ (12 mm) seam allowance, using the zipper foot. Trim batting close to stitching.

4. Build the crazy quilt. There is no way to give specific directions for this, but review Chapter 3 for the technique. Be careful that your seam allowance for each new piece is at least ¼″ (6 mm) or the fabrics may pull apart. Make sure the pieces chosen are not too large in proportion to the stocking. Any time you reach an impasse and can't figure out how to change directions, don't be afraid to cover up previous areas of crazy quilting or to turn under the edge of a fabric and topstitch it over a line of fabrics. Seaming the fabrics together, of course, also quilts them. Optional: free-machine quilt a person's name and the year on one of the larger pieces. To fit letters into an irregular space, see Chapter 10.

5. Sew on the heel and toe of the stocking with a narrow zigzag. Turn the stocking over and trim excess fabric even with base fabric.

6. Fold the ribbon in half and pin to top back corner, raw edges of ribbon matching raw edges of stocking.

7. Here's an easy way to line the stocking; you can use the same principle to line anything. Cut out the two lining pieces. Rightsides together, stitch about 3″ (7.6 cm) down the back side of the stocking only. Open out flat and press seam lightly. Place back fabric of stocking against the crazy quilt, rightsides together.

Fig. 6-16 Cartoon for stocking.

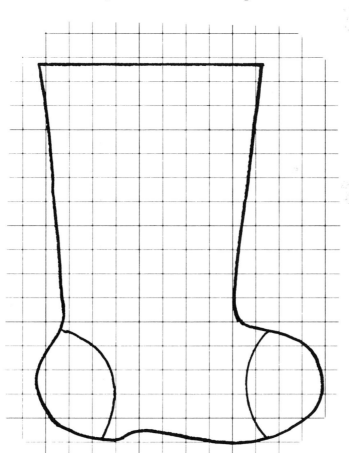

Stretch crazy quilt to fit, and pin. Stitch about 3″ (7.6 cm) down the back side of the stocking only. Open out flat and press seam lightly. (If your crazy-quilt fabrics are very precious, use a press cloth to protect them.) Place rightside of lining against rightside of stocking. Stitch across top in ½″ (12 mm) seam. Open out and press lightly (Fig. 6-17). (Optional: Topstitch on lining side.) Fold stockings in half the long way, so that rightsides of stocking and back match and rightsides of lining match. Pin. Stitch one long seam from toe of lining down all around stocking to heel of lining, leaving an opening as shown in Fig. 6-17. Clip curves. Reach through opening in lining and pull stocking rightside out. Turn under raw edges of lining and zigzag closed. Push lining inside stocking.

Additional Ideas

1. Use leftover scraps on the stocking from other projects in this book. Cover all with organza to unify the color and quilt selected lines with a white decorative stitch.

2. Using the quilt form in Chapter 5 for heavy threads in the bobbin (the butterfly poncho), crazy quilt the center 4″ (10.1 cm) squares.

3. Use a fabric with a sheen for the stocking and free-machine quilt holiday messages all over it.

Fig. 6-17 Lining the stocking. Right: Stitch and turn through opening as shown.

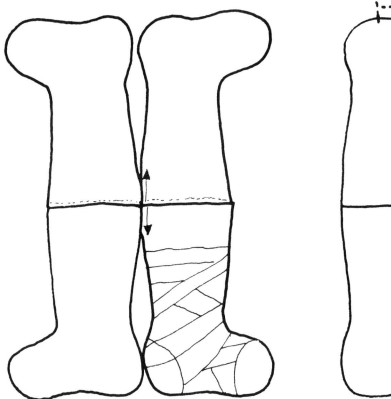
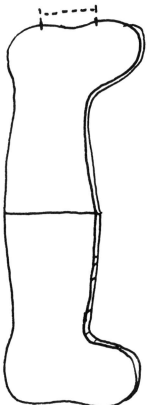

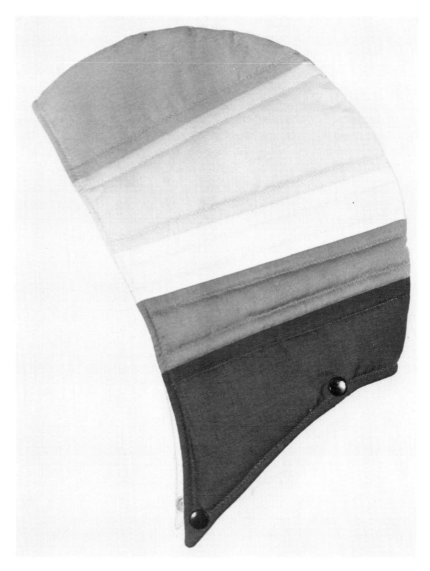

Fig. 6-18 String-quilted rainbow hat.

String-Quilted Snap-On Hat

Cheerful to look at and fast to make, this one-step quilted hat is lined with soft flannel and can be snapped onto down jackets, windbreakers, or winter coats.

Materials You Will Need

⅜ yd. (.34 m) backing fabric (old sheeting or muslin or the like)
batting big enough for two sides of hat
⅜ yd. (.34 m) flannel for lining
scraps in rainbow colors for string quilting
invisible thread on top
any thread on bobbin
label from old clothing
four snaps (or more if you plan to wear it with a specific item of clothing)

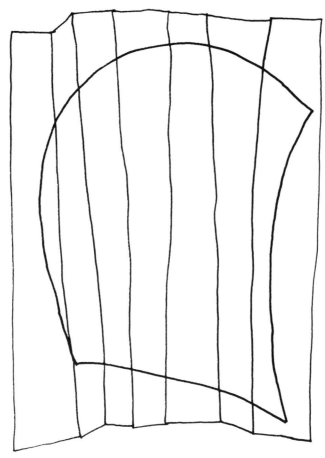

Fig. 6-19 Cartoon for hat with alternate way of string
quilting.

Construction

1. Enlarge the pattern in Fig. 6-19 so that it is about 10" (25 cm) tall. Rightsides together, cut out two sides of batting, backing, and lining. If the backing is limp, spray starch it so it won't pucker in quilting.

2. Baste the batting to the backing with a straight stitch along the ½" (12 mm) seam allowance. Trim batting close to stitching.

3. Lay strips of the rainbow colors across the hat, string quilting in the one-step method. Quilt with the invisible thread ½" (12 mm) from each seam line. The traditional order of the rainbow is red, orange, yellow, green, blue, indigo, and violet (remember ROY G. BIV?). Trim ends of strings to match backing.

4. Rightsides together, sew the center back seam of the hat. Try on the hat. If it's too big, make a deeper seam (change the lining too). Sew the center back seam of the lining. Clip curves and press seam open as well as possible.

5. Place the rightside of the lining against the rightside of the quilted hat. Sew around all sides in a ½" (12 mm) seam allowance. Clip curves and trim corners. Slash the lining at the lower back about 3" (7.6 cm) parallel to the neck edge. Pull out the hat. Press. Topstitch close to the edge, still using the invisible thread. Close slash with a hand whipstitch. Sew the clothing label (or make a label with your signature) over the slash. Put in the snaps along the back edge to match the snaps on your coat, with one snap at center bottom front of the hat.

Chapter 7

Only by Machine

Earlier we mentioned the fact that a quilt is not defined by the method used to hold its three layers together, but rather by the three layers themselves. Thus a machine-made quilt is just as much a "real" quilt as any hand-constructed one.

This extends also to the materials which can be used for the three layers.

Once you think of a quilt as a system—top, filler, backing—and not in the more traditional and rigid categories of 100% cotton top, cotton or polyester filler, cotton backing, you can look at all materials with new eyes. And of course, then the sewing machine comes into its own, because it can handle such a wide variety of materials.

In this chapter we will examine the variety of fabrics, threads, battings, and techniques allowed by your machine's versatility. Not all of these are suitable for clothing or full-size quilts, but then not everything we machine quilt is meant to cover a bed or a body. For example, quick gifts and wall hangings do not have to be machine washable so there is no reason to be limited to mundane materials.

What follows is a catalog of ideas that we hope will set free your imagination. Each of them can be done only by machine, in the sense that the sewing machine's power and versatility make them a pleasure to construct.

Fabrics

Gingham and Geometrics

Regular geometric patterns such as gingham easily lend themselves to machine quilting. Back gingham with a solid-colored fabric in a compatible color and treat the two as one top fabric. Make a quilt sandwich, basting properly. Satin stitch quilt around the gingham in 3" (7.6 cm) squares. Since satin stitch is not fast, you may want to plan larger squares of satin stitch and quilt with a straight stitch or narrow zigzag within these squares. Carefully cut only the gingham between the squares. Fringe all sides of the square as if you were making placemats. This juxtaposition of fringe with quilting is very pleasing. For a full-size quilt, break the mattress area into four or more modules so you won't have to handle a lot of bulk every time you turn a corner. Join the modules any one of the six ways shown in Chapter 6. (See Fig. 7-2.)

This same technique can be used on special fabrics such as loosely handwoven material, where the fringe of bumpy, special yarns adds texture to the quilting.

Fig. 7-1 "White Wall Quilt" by Doris Hoover, mixed materials and machine and hand techniques. "I mix hand, machine, tying, depending on the effect desired. I machine quilt when the play of light and shadow, the bas relief aspect, is primary—when a piece becomes sculptural. I also machine quilt when I am appliqueing or embroidering by machine and want one 'go-round' to serve both purposes. For quilting in larger plain areas, I quilt by hand." [Works on 5-year-old Elna Super, often quilts in modules to avoid handling entire piece.]

234

Fig. 7-2 The pattern of the fabric can determine the quilting design and technique. Here gingham is backed with white fabric and both quilted to a backing with satin stitch. The gingham is fringed, exposing the underlying fabric, and adding even more texture to the quilt.

Felt

Quilted felt looks very attractive and felt is very easy to work with. But since it isn't washable, don't use it for clothing or everyday quilts. It is especially useful for stuffed appliques and letters on large banners, and can be worked quickly since felt edges are nonfrayable and do not need to be turned under.

Napped Fabrics

The play of light on corduroy, velvet, velveteen, and other napped fabrics can be exploited by patterns that change nap direction, such as Seminole and log cabin. One-step quilting is particularly effective with these napped fabrics, as quilting across changing nap directions is tricky (Fig. 7-3).

Prequilted Fabrics

Prequilted fabrics can be combined with machine quilting in many ways. For a lightly quilted quilt, it can be used for batting without fear of shifting around. It can be used in single or double layers for the quilt itself, with additional shapes appliqued to it, such as large fabric dolls sold in panels (Fig. 7-3). It can also hide the defects in your first attempts at machine quilting—bury those puckers by backing the quilt with a second layer of pre-quilted fabric.

But don't think in strict categories. Prequilted fabric also comes in forms other than yardage. Sonya Lee Barrington of San Francisco made a short coat out of an old prequilted mattress pad.

Knits

Knit fabrics, both single and double knit, have been used in all traditional patterns by machine quilters. Use a ballpoint needle and exercise the same precision in measuring and cutting that you normally do. Since single knits tend to curl when cut in strips, you can use this characteristic in whimsical ways such as around quilted flower centers, for animal manes and fur, for monster hair-dos (Fig. 7-3).

Recycled Nylons

Nylons can be used both on quilt tops to pad appliques and for stuffing within the quilt. You can also make a face by cutting a 4″ (10.1 cm) tube of a nylon and slicing to open it up flat (Fig. 7-4). Make a tiny quilt of organza backing, batting, and the nylon. Set up your machine for free-machine embroidery (see Chapter 3). If you are comfortable drawing free-hand, stitch nylon side up. If you prefer to follow a cartoon, draw it first on the organza and stitch organza side up. If you do not like a continuous line, lock threads where needed, lift the presser bar lever, move to the new position, lower presser bar lever, lock threads, and continue

Fig. 7-3 Left: Napped fabrics change color when they change direction. Single-knit fabric cut on the bias forms corkscrews. Right: Fabric screened for dollmaking can instead be appliqued to prequilted fabric.

stitching. If you need ideas for faces, look at (or even trace) school class pictures, Sears or other mail-order catalogs, comic books, and/or newspaper and magazine ads. The completed face can be appliqued to something else, with added hair, or gathered into a circle, stuffed with loose batting, given a hairdo, and made into a small stocking-face doll.

Hair for such dolls can be made by machine in two ways:

1. Use a tailor tacking foot and loosen top tension greatly. Set up the machine for satin stitch. Stitch rows of tailor tacking around the face (Fig. 7-4). Loops can be cut if iron-on interfacing is ironed onto the back of the hair area to anchor the threads.

2. Yarn or pearl cotton is wound around a large paper clip which has been cut with wire cutters to leave a U. Place the wound clip on a bias strip of fabric flesh-colored or the same color as the thread and straight stitch down the center of the clip, stopping ½" (12 mm) from the end of the clip (Fig. 7-4). Gently pull out the paper clip a little way and wind some more yarn. Continue until the row is long enough to surround the face. Tack the strip around the face by hand or by machine. Additional rows of hair can be made to snuggle up to the first by pressing the loops together in one direction or the other and placing the wound paper clip where the loops lay. Loops may be cut when finished.

Leather and Imitation Leather

Leather and imitation leather make elegant quilts, although the former is not washable. Since the edges do not fray, you can either abut them or overlap them ¼" (6 mm). To cut accurately, use a ruler and an X-acto knife. A size 18(110) needle or a leather needle and a roller foot are helpful to prevent skipped stitches through the bulk of the quilt.

Leather, like fabric, comes in many weights. One of my favorites for quilting is the soft chamois used to wash cars. This can be found in supermarkets and auto supply stores. Also be sure to look in your local leather or sandalmaking shop, because they often sell scraps. However, choose your colors and reasons for quilting carefully. Dark colors do not show quilting lines well, so avoid them in leathers except in special and well-planned cases. You might also want to reserve leather and imitation leather for special projects, instead of bed quilts. Not only are they expensive, but these materials are heavy and can make an uncomfortably warm bedcover. Decorative wallhangings, small gifts, and clothing, however, are ideal uses for these materials, as are selected appliques. I recently saw an attractive quilt with a cotton/blend top and Ultrasuede appliques.

Transparent Fabrics

Transparent fabrics like net, gauze, organza, and plastic (available in rolls at hardware stores) are useful in pillows and wallhangings as novelty fabrics to hold down stones, shells, feathers, beads, and other found objects. Technically, unless you stitch through a batting to a backing, it's not quilting—it's more like modern trapunto. But a quick and novel thank you or a memento of a trip can be made by enclosing napkins, ticket stubs, fortune cookie messages, map fragments, and other memorabilia in plastic between lines of stitching with a message free-machine stitched to the plastic (or put on by press-on letters). This is the same as shadow quilting, where a transparent fabric is laid over felt shapes and quilting stitches outline the shapes. Again, it's not technically quilting, but it's pretty.

Ribbons and Trim

Ribbons and trim can be used in overlapping rows, quilting as you apply them. Be sure to pre-shrink them before using them. To keep small parts of trims from tangling in the washer and dryer, put them in an old nylon and pin the top closed.

Potpourri

You will discover other unusual fabrics as you prowl fabric stores, garage sales, and thrift shops. Don't miss the opportunity of using both the front and back of some fabrics.

Novelty Threads

Any thread you cannot get through the eye of a needle can be handwound onto the bobbin. Then by stitching underside up, the bobbin thread is laid on the top surface. (See more details in Chapter 5.) Always be sure to experiment on a doodle cloth first; top tension may have to be tightened. Ordinary sewing thread is used in the top and the needle size, of course, matches that top thread.

Gold Thread

Of particular beauty on quilted clothing is using gold thread wound onto the bobbin. If your quilting design is simple, use the presser foot and a straight stitch or narrow zigzag; but if the design is intricate, free-machine quilt (Fig. 7-6). The bobbin does not hold as much thick thread as ordinary thread, so check it often, so that you don't run out at a critical point.

Elastic

Winding elastic in the bobbin gives a unique effect to quilting, similar to a 19th century technique (which, incidentaly, was constructed quilt-as-you-go).

Make a quilt sandwich, using a rich fabric on top, and put it in a hoop. Set up the machine for free-machine quilting but tighten top tension slightly. Handwind the elastic onto the bobbin, taking care not to stretch it. Put it in the bobbin case as you would ordinary sewing thread.

Free-machine quilt a meander pattern. When you take the fabric off the hoop, it puckers in an interesting way (Fig. 7-7). You can use these in the centers of blocks, piecing lattice strips to all sides.

Invisible Nylon

Invisible nylon thread is favored by many machine quilters because, except under close scrutiny, all that can be seen is the depression of the quilting line, not

Fig. 7-4 Top: Cut-up nylons can be free-machine quilted and used for faces on dolls, ornaments, and even quilts. If you can't draw, use school pictures, advertisements, and the like for guidance, or trace them. Middle: Hair can be added by using a tailor-tacking foot, loosening top tension drastically. Bottom: Hair can also be added by winding pearl cotton around a large cut-off paper clip and stitching down the middle. The loops can later be cut.

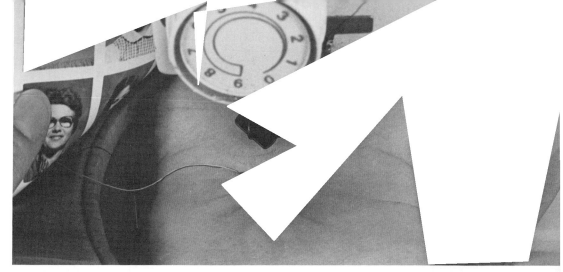

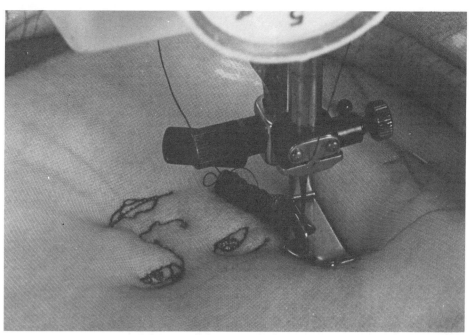

Fig. 7-5 "Chinese Dragon" by Merry Bean, free-machine quilted underside up on gold kid with invisible thread in bobbin, felt for batting, cut out and appliqued to wrong side of gold kid, frame also free-machine quilted. "Working with fabric, by hand or machine, gives me the opportunity to get lots of texture into my work whether flat or 3-D. I feel the craftsmanship is nearly as important as design. The form of presentation must be suitable to the idea of the work and I like to do things that make people smile. . . . I use quilting on all sorts of things, but I particularly like the idea of the quilt itself. For me it's an old time tradition brought up to date by starting with a modern design, taking modern drip dry materials with fiberfill batting, and sewing not by hand but by machine, quiltmaking that I feel sure would be applauded by our practical ancestors." [Works on a 10-year-old Viking 6010 and an Elna Lotus, usually stitches from underside through tracing paper so no design marks are on fabric.]

Fig. 7-6 Gold thread free-machine quilted on velvet, using the flourish under an old signature as a design source.

Fig. 7-7 Elastic is handwound on the bobbin. The quilt sandwich is put in a hoop and free-machine quilted with a meander pattern. When the fabric is taken off the hoop, it squishes up in a coral-like pattern.

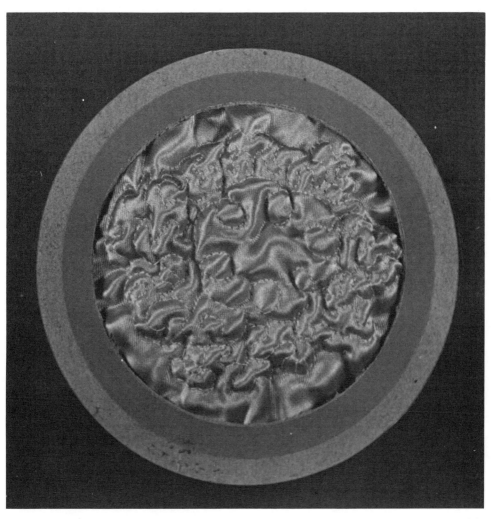

the thread itself. Invisible thread can be used in either the top or bobbin. However a hot iron will melt the thread so choose nonwrinkling fabric and/or iron only from the side opposite the nylon thread. Nylon thread comes in light and smoky colors.

Novelty Battings

Foam Rubber

Foam rubber comes in many thicknesses and is often used in shipping, so if you live near an industrial area, don't hesitate to scavenge waste bins. As long as the foam rubber is contained within two layers of fabric, you shouldn't have any trouble sewing through it (use a correspondingly larger needle for thicker foam). However, if you omit backing fabric (or paper), the foam sticks to the needle plate and is difficult to maneuver.

Down

There is nothing more luxurious than sleeping under a down comforter. The construction technique is not really quilting in that you do not pierce the filling; it's more like machine-trapunto, where you make a pocket or channel and fill it with down. The material used for top and backing must be down-proof or the little feathers work themselves out through the seams, which is why ripstock nylon is often used, backed by nylon tricot so the whole thing won't slip off the bed. Down is not difficult to handle, but it can float all over the room if you've had no experience with it. Look in the Resource section for addresses of companies which sell down by the ounce and kits for down comforters. (You can also buy pre-quilted washable Polarguard by the yard for outdoor clothing.)

Lint

My way of looking at ordinary materials has been changed by Joan Schulze's art. She machine quilts dryer lint for clothing and wallhangings. Women from all over the country send her their dryer lint. At first I snickered at the idea, until I saw the subtle marbling, the astonishing variety of colors, the traces of past lives—seeds, threads, weeds—caught in the lint (which evokes the same memories as patchwork quilts made from old clothing). Joan covers the lint with chiffon, organza, or plastic, backs it with fabric, and machine quilts (Fig. 7-9). Later she often lines a garment with silk chiffon. Now, every time I go to the dryer, I think of Joan's work. I see lint—as well as other mundane materials—with new eyes.

Innovative Techniques

Overlapping Units

Overlapping stuffed units can be connected to each other with bar tacks, buttons, or single decorative stitches done by machine. In Fig. 7-10 triangles with rounded corners are stitched, leaving an opening in the bottom edge for turning. The unit is zigzag quilted around the edge, which also closes the opening, and then bar-tacked at the top to the triangle above it. This technique could be used for a whole quilt, enlarged for a wall piece or headboard, or used as an edge for a quilt.

Other repeatable shapes can be used in a shingle effect, such as the traditional clamshell motif, flappets, etc., and either connected to each other, as shown above, or sewn to a backing in overlapping rows. This technique can be used for an entire

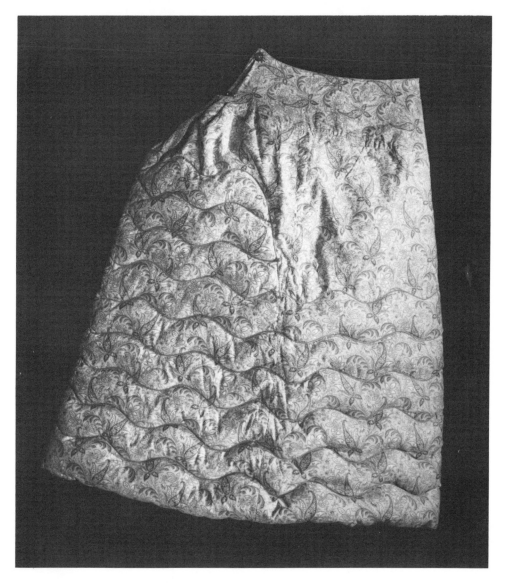

Fig. 7-8 Pink sateen skirt with brown and white paisley design quilted with a straight stitch through a cotton braid, making it appear to be chain-stitched, has channels filled with down. (c1886–1890, *photo courtesy of the Royal Ontario Museum, Toronto, Canada*)

quilt, for an edge, on capes, and on toy animals and puppets (monsters, dragons, armadillos, dinosaurs).

Stuffed Pleats

Toni Scott's outstanding book, *The Complete Book of Stuffedwork* (see Bibliography), shows various ways to play with stuffed pleats. You can either use one fabric and pleat it or join together widths of different materials to construct a new fabric. This extra raised row looks best on rich fabrics that catch the light—corduroy, velour, Qiana. Mark the pleats across the fabric, leaving generous amounts at the ends for seam allowances. Wrong sides together, sew the pleats.

Fig. 7-9 Close-up of "Quilted Lint Vest" by Joan Schulze, plastic top, dryer lint for batting, cotton backing. "The freedom to combine many techniques and materials comes from having explored each individually until it becomes second-nature. . . . What I do in each individual work cannot often be labeled as purely patchwork or applique or machine work. I feel the freedom to invent and improvise, which is a joyous thing."

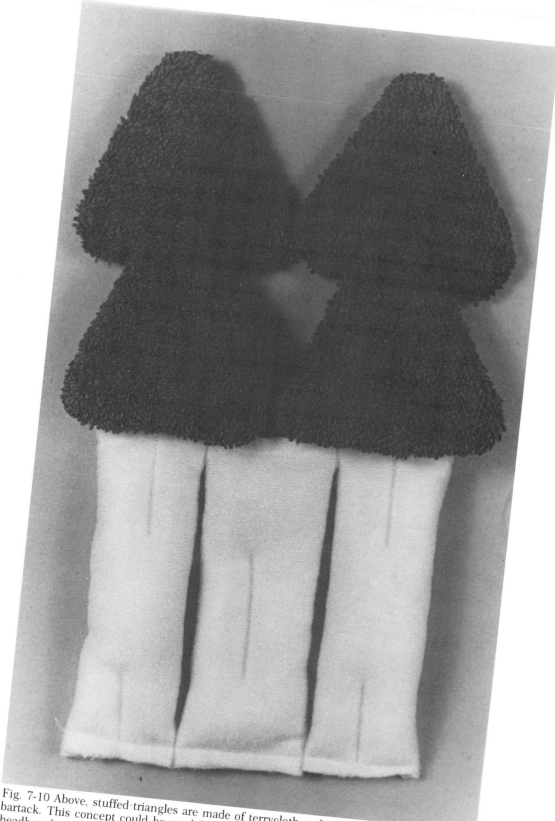

Fig. 7-10 Above, stuffed triangles are made of terrycloth and attached to each other with a bartack. This concept could be used for the side edges of a quilt or greatly enlarged for a headboard or wallhanging. Below, stuffed pleats are partially stitched to give further dimension.

With a knitting needle, stuff loose polyester batting into the long channels. For a different effect, sew all or part of the center of the pleat before stuffing (Fig. 7-10).

This technique can be used on whole-cloth quilts, in modules that change direction like the Rail Fence pattern, on the side panels of quilts, or enlarged in nonwashable items like hammocks and porch swings (perhaps stuffed with foam, packets of bean-bag pellets, or nylons stuffed tight with polyester batting or other old nylons).

As a short cut to strip pleating, use pre-quilted fabric with narrower pleats and don't stuff the channels.

Open Work

Areas framed by quilting lines can be satin stitched and cut away to leave exposed areas. This technique is not used, of course, for bed quilts but it is useful for wallhangings, picture frames, nametags, clothing, and other small items. On nonfrayable fabrics, the edges can merely be zigzagged or straight stitched before cutting away. Before cutting the background, shapes can be appliqued on top, with additional stuffing added to make a highly padded shape.

Padded Applique

Detached padded appliques can be worked two ways.

Fig. 7-11 Circle quilting on the ears as described in the text. This hat was made as a joke for a co-worker. (*Collection of Mary Nelson*)

246

One, by making a quilt sandwich, satin stitching around the edges, and cutting out the shape close to the stitching (sometimes a second row of satin stitching is needed after cutting out to tame rough edges).

The other way is by stitching the shape with a self-lining (like hidden applique) and stuffing it after turning rightside out. These detached appliques can then be free-machine quilted to another quilt sandwich or to pre-quilted fabric.

Circle Quilting

Circles are easily quilted on the machine by taping a thumbtack head-side down to the left or right of your presser foot. The distance from the point of the tack to the needle is the radius of the circle. You can either quilt circles or overlapping circles on a quilt (not too big or turning the bulk will be a nuisance) or circle-quilt finished shapes such as ears, wheels, and flower centers. Don't be shy about cutting up circle shapes after you've quilted them and then applying them with a satin stitch to other things—pockets, pillows, wallhangings.

Layered Work

Because the machine needle can practically punch through tin cans, we can layer machine quilting as thick as we want. In Fig. 7-13 Peggy Moulton, working on an old Singer featherweight, has free-machine stitched a muslin quilt in a

Fig. 7-12 Quilt circles by taping a thumbtack, point up, on the bed of your machine. Stick the quilt sandwich over it and stitch, rotating the fabric under the needle.

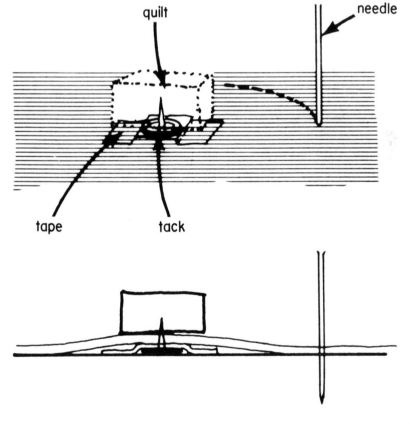

Fig. 7-13 Design sample by Peggy Moulton with layered work. "My favorite way to work is to put a piece of muslin on the wall and then just begin pinning different fabrics on it—instant results! . . . Perhaps my pearl of wisdom to beginners would be that one can do most all the machine quilting, lace, embroidery, etc., stitching without the latest expensive machine. In fact, probably the simpler, the better—we become intimidated by all the gadgets we think we should be using and find we don't need." [Works on a 50-year-old Singer Featherweight machine]

circular motion, later cutting out the centers of some of the circles. She used Italian cording on another piece of fabric, knotting the ends of the cording and letting them show. She then stuffed and appliqued this to the first piece.

New attachments, techniques, threads, and fabrics are constantly being developed for use on your machine. Keep in touch with your local fabric store for new developments. And in the meantime, enjoy the quilting versatility you can get only by machine.

Chapter 8

For Working People Only

The Quickest Full-Size Quilt of All: The Duvet

This quilt can be made in less than four hours because, to avoid piecing, you use sheets and you don't worry about workmanship: the quilt itself is hidden inside a fabric envelope. This duvet (pronounced doo-vay) or Continental quilt, doubles as a top sheet and a bedcover. As you sleep, it snuggles around you. In the morning, you simply smooth it out without tucking it in. On laundry day, you untie the hidden ties, remove the outside envelope, and wash it. The inner quilt is never washed or seen, which allows you to space the quilting lines as much as 10″ (25 cm) apart. It's also a perfect opportunity to experiment with the handling of thick batts.

You can use the same idea to hide Dacron and down sleeping bags for bed use (or old quilts, mattress pads, electric blankets, ugly blankets).

Try to use two outside sheets made by the same manufacturer. Otherwise, no matter what measurements are given on the package, the sheets will differ in turned allowance. Also if there are light colors on the outside sheets, don't use darker colors on the inner quilt, as they will show through.

Materials You Will Need

two nonwrinkle decorator flat sheets to fit your bed
two old flat sheets for inner quilt
batting size of inner sheets minus ½″ (12 mm) all around
24 ties, each 10″ to 11″ (25 to 28 cm) long, made of cotton tape (available wherever bias binding is sold), 6⅔ yd (6.1 m).
snap or Velcro tape
regular sewing machine thread
clothespins and iron

Construction of the Outside

Construction is shown in Figs. 8-2 and 8-3.

1. Preshrink all sheets. Open out hem on sheet that will be top. Although not held any longer by thread, ¼″ (6 mm) at the edge is still turned under. Sew one side of the snap or Velcro tape on the underside of the top sheet over the ¼″ (6 mm) turn-in, starting and ending tape 1″ (2.5 cm) from the sides of the sheet. Sew the other side of the tape to the rightside of the second sheet over the stitched hemline. When the two sheets are lined up at the sides, the snap positions should match.

Fig. 8-1 Duvet and matching pillow made from sheets. *(Collection of Doris C. Losey)*

2. On the underside of the top sheet at the fold line and 2″ (5 cm) in from each side edge, sew the end of a tie, stitching back and forth several times to secure each tie well. Fold the sheet lengthwise into thirds and mark (with a pin or iron) where the lines cross the fold line and the bottom edge. Sew a tie at the two marked places on the underside of the fold line.

3. For the ties at the bottom and side edges, place raw edges of ties even with the underside edge of top sheet in the same positions as the top edge (see Fig. 8-2). Sew ½″ (12 mm) in, stitching back and forth several times for each tie.

4. Turn top hem of top sheet to rightside on fold line. Pin fold in place at sides. Rightsides together, place two sheets together. Sew ½″ (12 mm) side and bottom seams (or whatever pattern in your fabric suggests). Be careful not to catch loose ends of ties in seam. Trim corners and turn rightside out. The outside envelope of the duvet is done and can easily be removed for washing.

Construction of the Inner Quilt

See Figs. 8-4 and 8-5 for construction.

1. Make sure the inner sheets are not larger than the outer sheets. If so, trim to size. (If they're slightly smaller, it doesn't matter.) To mark the quilting lines, fold one sheet in half lengthwise and iron in the crease. Fold folded sheet into lengthwise thirds and iron. Open out. Sew 12 ties to rightside of marked sheet in same position as outside fabric envelope, always matching raw edges of ties to edges of sheet. Place two sheets together, rightsides matching, and sew side seams only, in a ½″ (12 mm) seam. Turn rightside out, ironed sheet on top.

2. Pull batting through fabric tunnel, until it is ½″ (12 mm) from two open edges. Fold in ends and zigzag or straight stitch shut, letting ties hang loose. Pin along five ironed lines through all layers. Stitch down lines with a straight stitch and walking foot (or regular presser foot), using any thread you wish. Sew from right side of quilt to center, rolling and clothespinning the finished rows as you

250

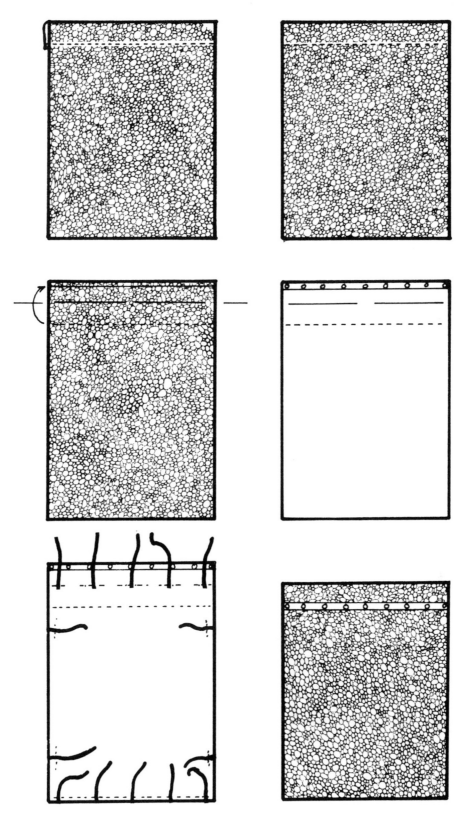

Fig. 8-2 Left to right, top to bottom: Open hem on sheet. Add snap or Velcro tape along top edge. Secure ties in position. Turn top hem of sheet to right side.

work. Then rotate quilt 180° and sew again from side toward center. It doesn't matter if your fabric puckers or creeps or the thread skips or frays—no one will see it.

3. Gather outer fabric envelope like you're putting on a nylon stocking. Push inner quilt to bottom inside of envelope. Match ties and tie in bows. Tie side bows. Tie top bows. You're in business.

Fig. 8-3 Right sides together, place two sheets together and stitch for completed duvet.

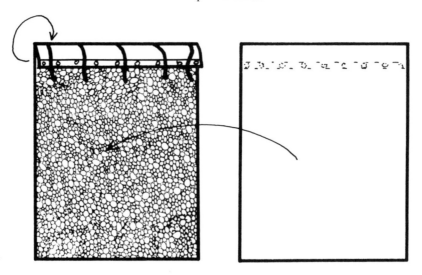

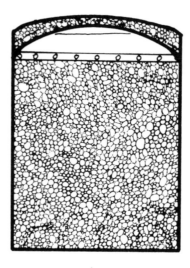

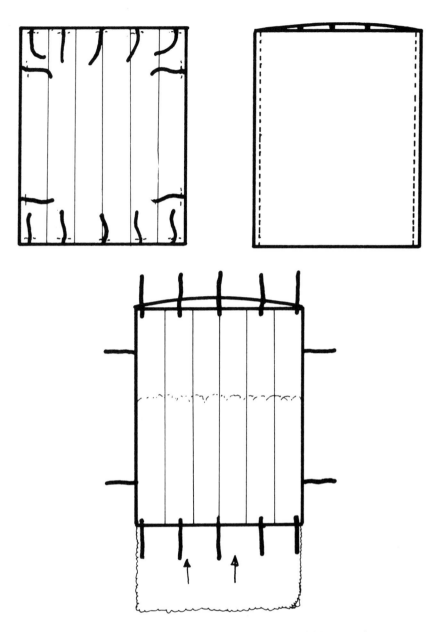

Fig. 8-4 Left to right, top to bottom: For inner quilt, fold crease lines into sheet and sew ties along creases. Lay two sheets rightsides together and sew side seams. Pull batting through fabric tunnel.

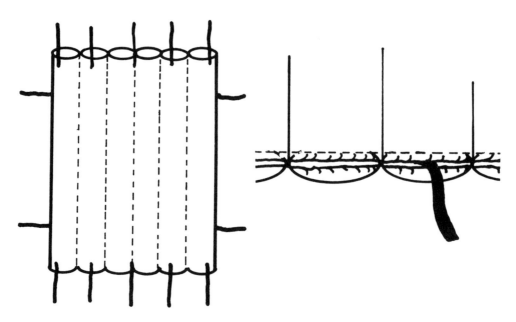

Fig. 8-5 Fold in edges of quilt, letting ties hang loose outside quilt. Pin and stitch along ironed lines, through all layers.

Working Woman's One-Night Wonder Quilt

As promised in the preface, here is a lap quilt for people who have been too busy to sew and miss it, but don't have time to read a whole lot of text or make decisions as to choice of materials, methods, and techniques. The quilt can be made in one night, but only if you follow the directions exactly. It is designed for 44″ to 45″ (115 cm) wide fabric and won't work with anything smaller, so be sure to doublecheck that your fabric isn't actually 42″ (107 cm) wide. In writing the directions, I am assuming that you know how to sew but not necessarily how to machine quilt and that you have not read this book.

Use a medium-weight fabric on the back to fight potential puckers, invisible thread on the top to hide uneven stitches, and stitch on the bias for easiest handling. The piecing of the top is done with stream-lined, time-saving methods (explained in detail in Chapter 3 if you later want to delve into more applications of them).

I suggest you choose one color, such as brown. Buy a dark and light print in that color and a solid-colored fabric for the backing. When you are done machine quilting, the backing is brought to the front in a ½″ (12 mm) frame of solid color around your dark/light print pattern.

Finished size: 40″ × 64″ (102 × 163 cm)
Each finished square: 8″ (20.3 cm)
Pattern: Checkerboard
Technique: straight-stitch machine quilting
Thread: regular sewing thread in bobbin, invisible (nylon) thread on top
Needle size: 12(80) for piecing, 16(100) for quilting
Machine setting: straight stitch of regular length (10 to 12 stitches per inch or
    4 to 5 per cm)

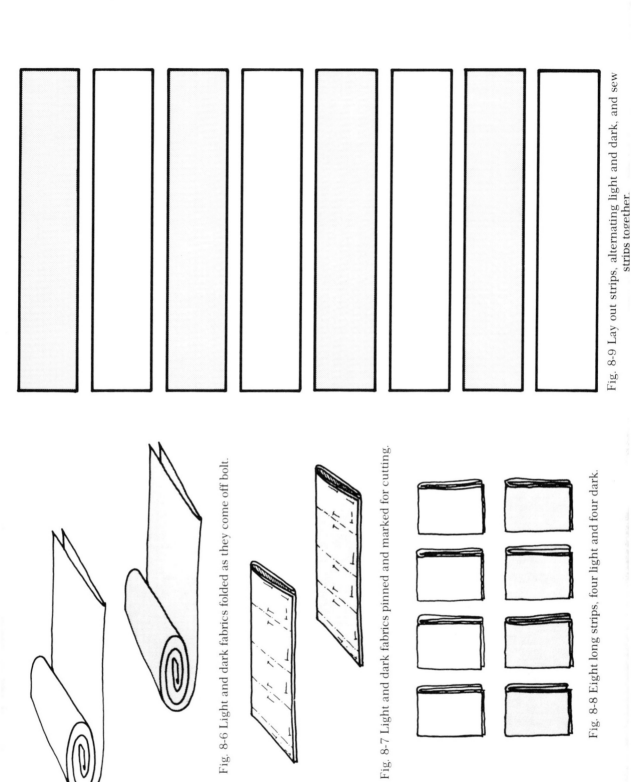

Fig. 8-9 Lay out strips, alternating light and dark, and sew strips together.

Fig. 8-6 Light and dark fabrics folded as they come off bolt.

Fig. 8-7 Light and dark fabrics pinned and marked for cutting.

Fig. 8-8 Eight long strips, four light and four dark.

255

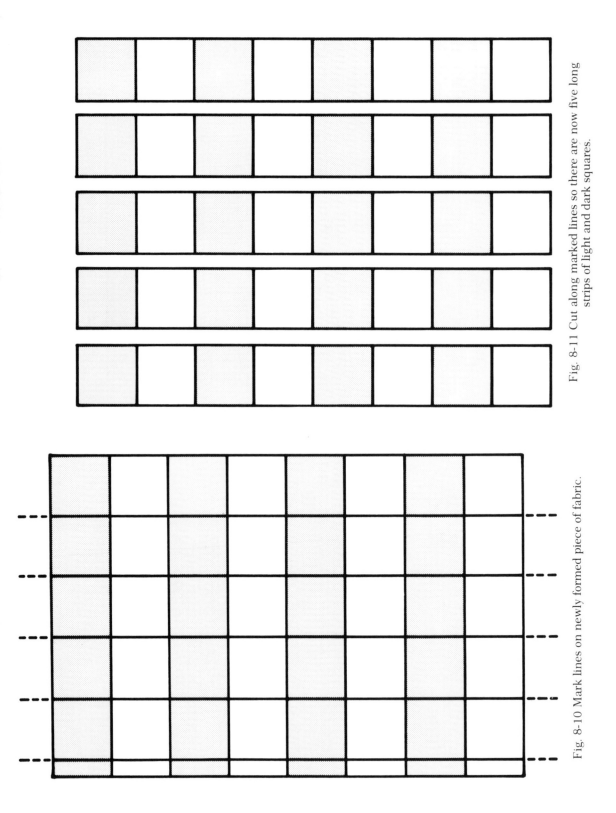

Fig. 8-11 Cut along marked lines so there are now five long strips of light and dark squares.

Fig. 8-10 Mark lines on newly formed piece of fabric.

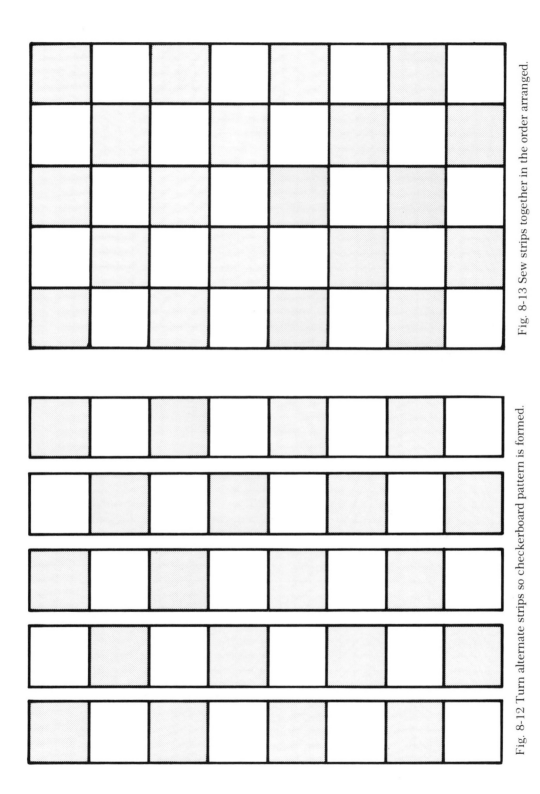

Fig. 8-13 Sew strips together in the order arranged.

Fig. 8-12 Turn alternate strips so checkerboard pattern is formed.

Optional: use straight-stitch needle plate or left-needle position
Machine accessories: regular presser foot
Seam allowance: ¼" (6 mm)

Materials You Will Need

1⅛ yd. (1 m) each of dark and light print or solid 45"-wide (115 cm-wide) cotton or cotton/poly fabric

2 yd. (1.8 m) medium-weight (such as Kettlecloth) dark backing fabric, 45"-wide (115 cm-wide), cotton or cotton/poly

1⅞ yd. of 45" wide or wider (1.7 m of 115 cm-wide) bonded polyester batting with ¼" (6 mm) loft, or packaged batt no smaller than 40" × 64" (102 × 163 cm)

pins, 40 safety pins

white pencil or soap sliver

regular pencil

1" wide masking tape

ruler

iron

scissors

clear nylon invisible thread

dark regular sewing thread to match color of backing

Construction

1. Preshrink all fabric. Cut off selvages. Straighten the ends on all fabric by pulling a thread across each end and cutting along the line it left.

2. Lay the dark fabric on a cutting surface, folded in half as it came off the bolt. Make sure the ends are exactly lined up. Fold the fold over again and pin the crosswise ends to match exactly. Pin the fold exactly along the lengthwise ends.

3. With your ruler and the white pencil or soap sliver, mark straight lines across the folded fabric. Measuring from the right end of the fabric, draw four lines 8½" (21.6 cm) apart. Pin along the lines so the four layers of fabric won't shift. Cut along the marked lines. Open out the strips and press away the fold lines.

4. Repeat Steps 2 and 3 for the light fabric, using a regular pencil to mark lines. (See Figs. 8-6 to 8-9.)

5. You now have eight long strips, half dark and half light, each 8½" (21.6 cm) wide. Use dark regular sewing thread on top and bobbin and a size 12(80) needle. Sew all the strips together along their long edges in a ¼" (6 mm) seam, alternating light and dark strips, starting with dark. Pay attention: Be sure all the ¼" (6 mm) seam allowances end up on the wrong side. Press all seams open.

6. Lay the new fabric on a cutting surface, rightside up. Mark five lines along the length of the new fabric, each 8½" (21.6 cm) wide. (If you are using a see-through ruler, put a strip of masking tape across the 8½" or 21.6 cm mark. Then you can merely slide the ruler along, marking the line on the short end of the ruler.) Cut these five long strips, but leave them in position on the cutting surface.

7. Pick up the second and fourth strips and turn each around so that the light squares are to the left, under the dark squares. This forms your checkerboard pattern (Fig. 8-12).

8. Rightsides together, sew the first strip to the second in a ¼" (6 mm) seam along the long edge. Match cross-seams by pinning exactly through the seam on both strips. Press seams open. Sew the third strip to the second. Be careful that

258

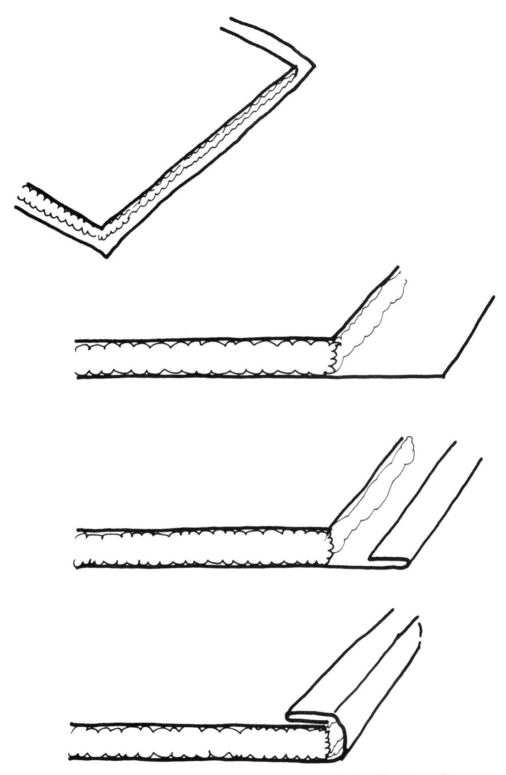

Fig. 8-14 Lay backing on hard surface. Extended edge of backing will
form a border of binding. Fold in edge of backing and bring up over top
of quilt.

you don't sew the third strip to the first. You are making a checkerboard and dark squares should never line up with dark squares. Sew all five strips together, pressing seams open (Fig. 8-13). Your quilt top is done.

9. Lay the quilt top on top of the batting. Pin each square to the batting from the center of the quilt top out to the edges. Pin all around the edges. Trim the batting even with the quilt top.

10. Lay the backing fabric wrongside up on a flat hard surface (floor, Ping-Pong table, or such). Tape the backing fabric to the hard surface around all edges with the masking tape. Lay the pin-basted quilt top/batting on top of the backing fabric, batting against wrong side of backing. Center the top between the two lengthwise and two crosswise edges of the backing. Later we will trim the backing fabric to exact size. Safety-pin the three layers together within each square to the upper right or lower left of each pin. Remove the pins. Also straight-pin all around the edges, leaving the previous pins at the edge in place.

11. Carefully remove the masking tape. Take the basted quilt to the machine. The five-squares-across ends of the quilt are the top and bottom. Change to invisible thread on the top and a size 16(100) needle. Loosen top tension a little. Start machine quilting at the top left corner of a dark square at one end of the quilt. Don't worry about backstitching, but do hold the threads behind the presser foot as you start sewing so that they will not snarl in the bobbin case. Sew diagonally down and to the right through the corner of each square until you reach the lower right corner of a dark square on the opposite side of the quilt. (You don't really need to mark this line, but if you are nervous about quilting without a guiding line, stretch a long piece of masking tape diagonally from quilt edge to edge, with one edge of the masking tape passing through the points. Sew along, but not into, the masking tape. (You can re-use the tape for each line.) Sew diagonally through all the squares on the quilt. When more than half the quilt is to the right of you, bumping up against the head of the machine, turn the quilt upside down and machine quilt from the upper left corner again. You are stitching on the bias, so the fabric is easy to handle with your fingers.

12. When you are done machine quilting, pull all the bobbin end threads to the topside. Now stitch around all four sides of the quilt near the edge, removing pins as you come to them and locking each quilting line as you pass over it. Cut off thread ends.

13. Lay the quilt on a hard flat surface again. With a ruler and the white pencil or soap, draw on the underside of the backing fabric along the edges of the quilt top. Remove all pins and safety pins. Measure 1″ (2.5 cm) out from the lines you just drew and draw new lines. Cut backing on these lines. Press backing under ¼″ (6 mm). Fold up over edge of quilt on two long sides and pin backing edge in place ½″ (12 mm) from top edge (Fig. 8-14). Stitch close to turned-under edge of backing. Now fold top and bottom edges up over quilt and pin in place ½″ (12 mm) in from quilt-top edge. Stitch in place, backstitching the beginning and end of each line. Cut thread ends. Enjoy your quilt.

Chapter 9

Quick Gifts

Giving a fabric gift that says "I made this just for you" is one of the many pleasures of machine-quilting. Because it's so fast, we can make gifts for far more occasions than the usual birthday/holiday times, as well as revive the nearly lost tradition of giving handmade presents.

The easiest way to personalize a gift is through initials, names, or special messages, which is why this chapter contains two alphabets, one for line letters and one for shapes. We also tell you how to design your own alphabets and how to manipulate letters and words to fit a space.

Some tips for nonharried gift giving and gift making:

1. Use the same principles in sewing as you do in freezing meals ahead: make extra. When you are constructing Seminole strips or crazy patch or any pieced design, make extra and use the leftovers for quick gifts.

2. When you are making these quick gifts, for example the key/luggage tag, cut out three or four of them. Then when you need a gift, you need only make the initials and sew up the sides.

3. If it's really last-minute, make a quick fabric card. Fold construction paper in half; open it flat again. Free-machine embroider a message: "thank you," "get well yesterday," "happy birthday," "especially for you." Stitch directly on the paper on the front of the card. Cut out any appropriate shape next to or below your message and glue special fabric (silk, velvet, imitation suede) behind the shape. Then fold the card, glue the back to the front, and sign the card. (In the card shown in Fig. 9-1, I free-machine quilted the shape, cut away excess batting, and glued it in place; but this extra step takes more time—ten minutes instead of five.)

With the exception of Catnip Kitty, the quick gifts in this chapter are like the patterns you buy in a fabric store—skeleton patterns only, not detailed instructions for embellishing those patterns. Any of the techniques covered earlier in the book can be used on these basic items (see the color section for how we embellished ours). Not all of them are machine-quilted, but all rely for their fastness on machine techniques.

Baker's Mitt

The bread baker at Fort Henry in Kingston, Ontario, Canada, always wears a pair of these oversized mitts as he works. Don't use polyester batting because it conducts heat. Use old towels, mattress pads, or, as here, an old ironing board cover.

Fig. 9-1 Left to right (top): Baker's Mitt, Catnip Kitty, Basic Tote; (middle) Nametag, Tooth Fairy Bag, Key/Luggage Tag, Needlecase, Log Cabin Pincushion, Sorry I Missed You Card; (bottom) Fabric Letters.

Fig. 9-2 Baker's Mitt cartoon, showing buttonhole placement.
Cut a 14″ square.

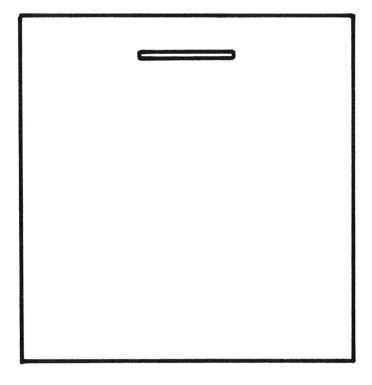

Materials You Will Need

14″ (35.6 cm) square backing fabric (use something firm but pliable like denim or duck; since it will get dirty, a dark color is preferred)

14″ (35.6 cm) square batting (remember, do not use polyester)

14″ (35.6 cm) square top (leftovers from other projects)

57+″ (145 cm) binding, ½″ (12 mm) wide, finished

Construction

1. If you are one-step quilting, place the batting on the backing and zigzag around the edge, using a 14(90) needle and strong thread such as cotton-covered polyester. Construct the top however you choose (we used one-step string quilting with leftovers from the sleeping bag project in Chapter 6).

2. Bind the edge. Optional: Put a loop at one corner for hanging.

3. Place your fist on the top center of the mitt and mark on both sides of your hand at the widest part. Make a large buttonhole parallel to the top edge (go over it at least two times for extra strength). Cut bottonhole open so your hand fits into the mitt.

Nametag

We humans are gregarious beings who are active in clubs, churches, guilds, and groups. Be kind to your cohorts, who recognize your face but don't always remember your name; make and wear a nametag.

This one can be buttoned onto a shirt front or pocket button or can be pinned on with a hidden safety pin.

Materials You Will Need

top, batting, and backing big enough to fit in your hoop

lining fabric slightly bigger than 3″ × 5″ (7.6 × 12.7 cm)

crochet cotton wound on bobbin (optional)

100% cotton extra-fine machine-embroidery thread

3″ × 5″ (7.6 × 12.7 cm) index card

embroidery hoop

a label cut off from clothing

safety pin

Construction

1. Trace a 3″ × 5″ (7.6 × 12.7 cm) card on the backing fabric. Leave ½″ (12 mm) at the top for a buttonhole and divide the rest of the space into the number of letters in your name. Blow up the line alphabet to fit the spaces. (If you have a long name, either enlarge the nametag or simply write your name in script, free-machine quilting on the front of the nametag.) Copy the letters backwards on the backing fabric, inside the traced shape.

2. Load crochet cotton in the bobbin and 100% cotton extra-fine machine-embroidery thread on top. Tighten top tension slightly. Set up the machine for free-machine quilting.

3. Make a quilt sandwich with the backing fabric face-up. Put it in the hoop. Free-machine quilt the letters. Then free-machine quilt the traced 3″ × 5″ (7.6 × 12.7 cm) outline. Remove from hoop. Trim batting and backing close to stitching. Trim thread ends.

4. Place rightsides of lining fabric and nametag together. Remove crochet cotton from bobbin; replace with regular sewing thread. Reset tension and machine for straight stitch. Stitch ⅛″ (3.2 mm) outside and all around the 3″ × 5″ (7.6 × 12.7 cm) line of stitching, backing side up. Trim corners. Slash lining 2″ (5 cm) down from and parallel to the top. Pull rightside out. Press. Whipstitch slash together.

5. Sew the top nonmoveable side of a safety pin to the label (can be done by machine satin stitch or by hand). Sew the label by hand over the slash. (My label is leftover from a pattern and says "Vogue Designer Menswear" but you could cut a label out of old clothing.)

6. Put a buttonhole at the top center of the name.

Key/Luggage Tag

Here's a fast, functional item.

Materials You Will Need

nonfrayable fabric (leather scraps, imitation suede, double knits, vinyl)
small scraps of fabric and batting for initials
invisible thread
X-acto knife or razor blade and ruler
purchased key or luggage ring (available in dime or hardware stores)

Fig. 9-3 Cartoon for Key/Luggage Tag.
Cut out center area.

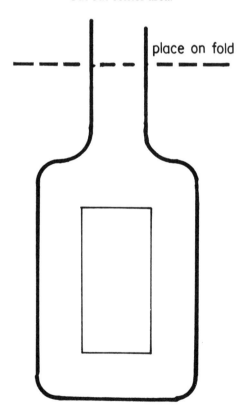

place on fold

Construction

1. Trace tag shape from Fig. 9-3 onto folded, nonfrayable fabric. Cut out rectangle from one side only, using X-acto knife and ruler.

2. Trace cutout on fabric shape (double knits are good because they puff out). Make a quilt sandwich and put in hoop. (It's easy to mass-produce these, making four or more quilted inserts from each quilt sandwich.)

3. Set up your machine for free-machine quilting, with invisible thread on the top and any thread in the bobbin. Visually divide the rectangle in two and imagine block-letter initials inside; you can eyeball this. Do mock trapunto (see Chapter 5), stitching around the rectangle a few times and around each letter a few times. Take the quilt sandwich out of the hoop and trim ¼″ (6 mm) around the rectangle.

4. Place cut-out rectangle over mock trapunto rectangle. Reset machine for straight stitch or zigzag. Stitch around rectangle with invisible thread.

5. Pull unstitched side of tag through key ring. Put wrong sides of tag together and stitch around the outside in a straight stitch or zigzag.

Fabric Letters

A common wail is, "I don't know what to give him; he already has everything." Give him the name of his company, boat, ranch, ski hut, prize horse, dog, whatever, in large fabric letters. You can hang them from a plastic rod if you wish, but I've found that people love to rearrange the letters and make funny words (especially with company names) so I now give them loose in baskets.

Children also love to play with these letters.

Note: These are slower to make than the other gifts in this chapter. Plan about one-half to one hour per letter, including enlarging time.

Materials You Will Need

graph paper
loose batting for stuffing
scraps of fabric large enough for letters
buttons

Construction

1. Blow up the shape alphabet as large as you wish. Ours were cut 7 ½″ (19 cm) tall; they shrink about 1″ (2.5 cm) in stuffing. Trace on the backside of fabric.

2. Rightsides together, stitch on the traced line. You can either leave a gap in the seam allowance for turning or stitch all the way around, slash the back and pull rightsides out, covering the slash later with press-on tape or a clothing label. Don't worry about the centers of A, B, D, O, P, Q, and R—"quilt" the centers by adding a button put on by machine (see the "O" in Chilton, Fig. 9-1). Cut ¼″ (6 mm) around stitching, clip curves, trim corners, and turn rightside out. Stuff (not a fast operation).

Basic Tote

This tote showcases whatever quilted square or leftovers you have on hand and is very fast to make. The boxed corner is worth learning for its many useful applications. If your pocket is more than 6″ (15.3 cm) high, increase the height of the bag and the length of the webbing straps.

Materials You Will Need

⅝ yd. of 36″ or 45″-wide (0.57m of 115 cm-wide) extremely firm fabric (canvas is good) for lining

⅝ yd. (0.57 m) of any fabric for outside (although we used white, I don't recommend it; it gets soiled too quickly)

2 yd. (1.8 m) webbing for straps.

bias binding for top edge

quilted pocket with top and bottom edges finished (sides will be covered)

Construction

1. Cut both lining and outside fabric 20½″ (52 cm) wide and 22″ (55.9 cm) long. Work with them separately. Place the quilted pocket on the outside fabric centered 2″ (5 cm) from the top. Stitch bottom edge of pocket to tote.

2. Cut the webbing in half. Lay one strip along one side of the pocket, turning under the raw edge of the webbing and covering the raw edges of the pocket. Stitch in place along both sides of the webbing the width of the pocket only. Bring the other end of the strip around to the opposite side of the pocket, making sure the webbing is not twisted, and sew it on the same way (Fig. 9-4). Sew the second strip to the other end of the tote in the identical position and way.

3. Place rightsides of the tote together, top edges matching. Keep webbing free. Sew the two sides in a ½″ (12 mm) seam. Press open and crease the bottom fold. Still wrongside out, bend the side seam down to meet the bottom fold. This forms a joint. Measure with your ruler so that the base of the triangle formed by the point and your ruler is 5″ (12.7 cm); see Fig. 9-5. Draw a line; pin the triangle in place. Sew along the marked line. Repeat for opposite corner. You've just made a side and bottom to your bag. Optional: Fold points to bottom and stitch in place across points through tote bottom. Otherwise trim close to stitching. Turn rightside out.

4. Construct side and bottom of lining as in Step 3. Don't turn rightside out.

5. Place lining inside bag, wrongsides together. Zigzag top edges together, keeping webbing free. Sew bias binding over top edge.

6. *Optional:* If your bag is still too limp, pinch each side edge together, catching the lining, and stitch through all layers. Repeat for all side edges, as if you were adding topstitching. You can also pinch and stitch the bottom edge.

Catnip Kitty Bag

This is what our cat looks like when he's been rolling in the catnip patch. If you make a holiday present for your pet and actually fill the bag with catnip, don't hang it on your tree or the cat will destroy your other ornaments in his zeal to reach this bag. You could also fill the bag with a potpourri mixture.

Materials You Will Need

heavy-weight cotton fabric big enough to fit in hoop (duck, canvas, light-colored denim)

lightweight backing fabric big enough to fit in hoop

polyester batting, at least 5″ × 6″ (12.7 × 15.3 cm)

ordinary sewing thread in bobbin (we used blue)

blue machine-embroidery thread

1 cup dried catnip (available in herb stores and some health food stores)

tissue paper

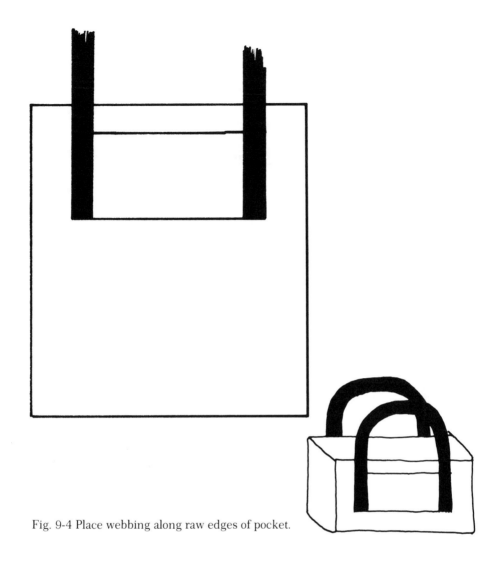

Fig. 9-4 Place webbing along raw edges of pocket.

Construction

1. You will quilt the kitty first from the underside and then cut the rectangles for the bag. Therefore, work with top and backing fabric bigger than your hoop, but trim the batting to fit inside the hoop.

2. Copy the kitty cartoon from Fig. 9-6 and the rectangle shape onto the tissue paper. Turn paper over and pin to the backing fabric, not the top fabric. Don't copy "catnip" yet, but be sure the place for it is lined up with the grain of the fabric.

3. Put the three layers (duck/batting/backing) in the hoop so that the top heavy-weight fabric lies against the needle plate.

4. Free-machine quilt the kitty. Cover all lines twice for a nice dark line.

5. Take off the hoop, turn the quilt over, and put it back into the hoop with the topside up. With a free-machine straight stitch or zigzag, write "catnip" under the kitty.

6. Remove the fabric from the hoop and trim all three layers to the rectangle shape. Tear off tissue paper.

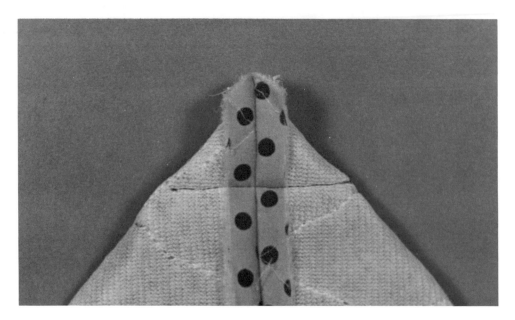

Fig. 9-5 A boxed corner.

Fig. 9-6 Full-size Catnip Kitty Bag cartoon.

7. Cut another rectangle of the top fabric. Rightsides together, sew around three and a half sides of the rectangle with a ½″ (12 mm) seam, leaving an opening for turning. Trim corners, turn rightsides out, press, fill with loose dried catnip, stitch opening closed, and give to your favorite puss.

Needlecase

This attractive little case carries my special short hand quilting needles. Mine is crazy quilted in the one-step method.

Materials You Will Need

small scraps of fabric in one color range (prints and/or solids)
5½″ × 4½″ (13.9 × 11.4 cm) rectangle, each of lightweight backing fabric (muslin, interfacing, old sheeting), batting, and lining fabric in color harmonious to scraps
4″ × 3″ (10.2 × 7.6 cm) rectangle of felt in color harmonious to scraps
two ½″ (12 mm) Velcro buttons
white bobbin
machine-embroidery thread to match scraps

Construction

1. With the straight stitch or zigzag, sew the batting and backing together around the edges. Embellish the top in whichever method you choose. Machine-embroider with a decorative stitch on top of seams if desired.

2. Sew the Velcro buttons ¼″ (6 mm) in from the four edges of the felt (Fig. 9-7). Center the felt on the lining and sew close to the edge of the felt with a straight stitch.

3. With rightsides of the needlecase against the felt, sew three and a half sides of the rectangle with a ½″ (12 mm) seam, leaving an area to turn. Trim corners and turn rightside out. Press lightly and handstitch the opening together.

Log-Cabin Pincushion

This is constructed of light and dark ribbons, with any special fabric in the center, and is very fast to make.

Materials You Will Need

½ yd. (0.45 m) each, two colors of ¾″ (18 mm) wide velvet ribbon (one light color, one dark)
4½″ (11.4 cm) square each of lightweight backing fabric and polyester batting
1¼″ (3.2 cm) square and 4½″ (11.4 cm) square fabric in color harmonious to ribbon (white satin is nice)
dark thread in top and bobbin
small amount of stuffing (or batting)

Construction

1. With a straight stitch or narrow zigzag, sew the batting to the backing around the edges. Use a light-colored (blue or pink), felt-tipped pen and a ruler to draw an X directly on the batting from diagonal corner to diagonal corner. This marks the center (and may show through if pen is too dark for fabric).

2. Center the small white square of fabric on the batting X. Sew it in place with a narrow zigzag.

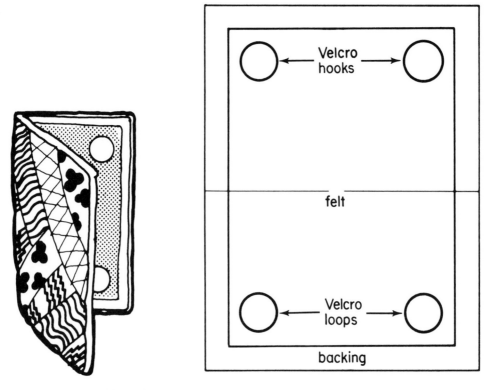

Fig. 9-7 Needlecase cartoon, showing Velcro placement.

3. For a traditional log-cabin appearance, all the dark-colored ribbon goes on two adjacent sides; all the light-colored ribbon on the remaining two adjacent sides. Sew the left edge of the dark ribbon to the right edge of the white fabric with a narrow zigzag. Trim the ribbon even with the bottom of the fabric. Sew down the right edge of the ribbon. Turn the square 90°. Sew a strip of light ribbon even at the top with the bottom of the previous ribbon; trim. Turn the square 90°. Stitch another strip of light ribbon and then a dark ribbon and continue sewing around and around, building out from the center square until you have filled in two widths of ribbon on all sides (Fig. 9-8). Sew the outside edges of the ribbon down with a narrow zigzag.

4. Rightsides together, sew the lining of white fabric to the pincushion face, leaving a place to turn. Trim corners and turn rightsides out, stuffing the cavity with more batting, and handsewing the opening closed.

Tooth Fairy Bag

I've made dozens of these special small bags and our daughter is the only one who's actually thought of delivering tooth fairy money (and saving old teeth) in them. Others use them to keep special shells, mementoes, small mirrors, thimbles, and all sorts of small treasures. They are completely machine-made. Even if you aren't planning to make one now, read the directions to learn this handy way to line anything.

For your own amusement, try to make each one different, trying all the techniques from Chapter 3. The lining is cut about one-third the size of the bag, which becomes part of the lining for a self-lining.

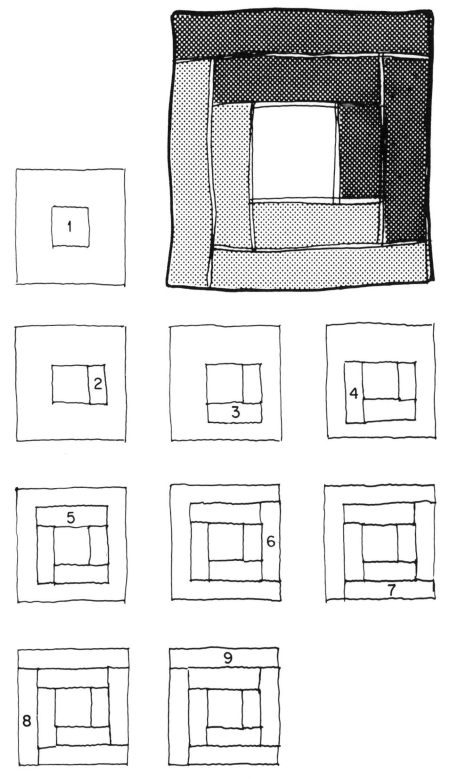

Fig. 9-8 Cartoon for Log Cabin pincushion.

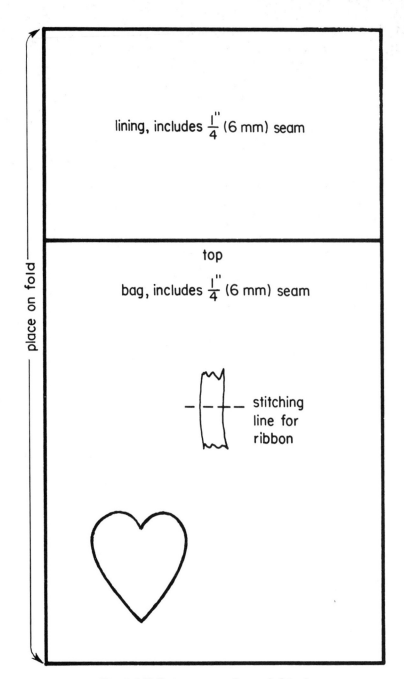

place on fold

lining, includes $\frac{1}{4}''$ (6 mm) seam

top

bag, includes $\frac{1}{4}''$ (6 mm) seam

stitching line for ribbon

Fig. 9-9 Full-size cartoon for tooth fairy bag.

Materials You Will Need

fabric for bag slightly bigger than shape in Fig. 9-9 (use something special like silk)

lining fabric (see Fig. 9-9)

16″ (41 cm) ribbon

Construction

1. If you are satin stitching a heart onto the bag, trace the bag shape on the special fabric and put the bag fabric in a hoop before actually cutting out the shape. Do any embellishing; then cut out the bag shape. Cut out the lining.

2. Rightsides together, sew the lining to the top of the bag (see Fig. 9-9) in a ¼" (6 mm) seam. Press open.

3. Find the halfway mark of the ribbon and sew it in place with straight stitches as shown by the dotted line on the cartoon in Fig. 9-9.

4. Fold the bag and lining in half, matching side seams and keeping ribbons free of stitching. Sew both side seams and the bottom of the bag in a ¼" (6 mm) seam. Turn rightsides out and press with a press cloth. Turn in remaining raw edges of lining ¼" (6 mm) and zigzag close to the edge. Poke the lining inside the bag (part of the bag fabric forms a self-lining). Place treasure inside and fold bag in half, tying closed with ribbon.

Other Quick Gifts

Other quick (but not as quick) gifts in this book include the heart pillow and placemats in Chapter 4, the stationery case and Santa ornament in Chapter 5, the

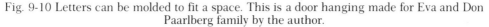

Fig. 9-10 Letters can be molded to fit a space. This is a door hanging made for Eva and Don Paarlberg family by the author.

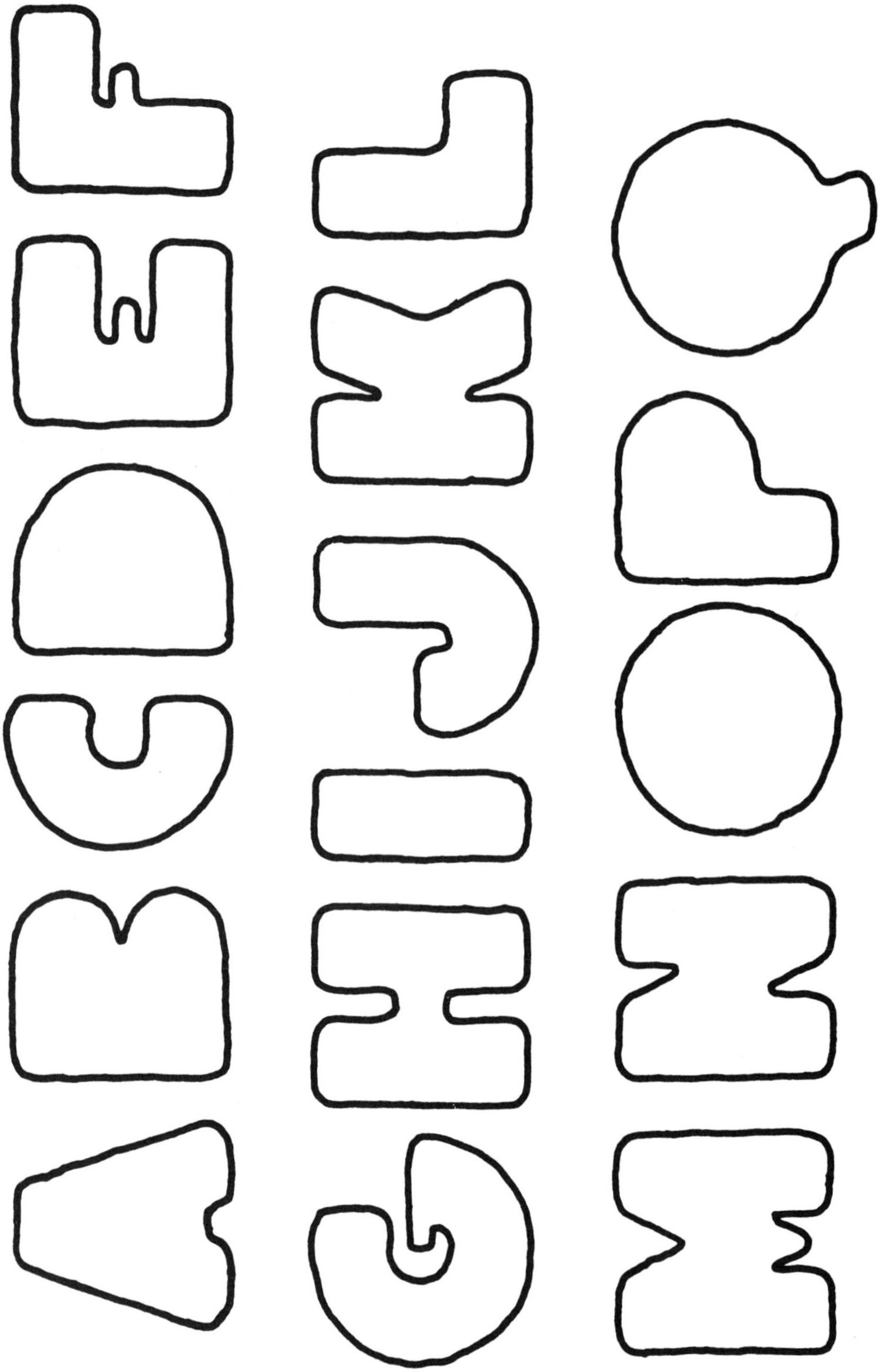
ABCDEF
GHIJKL
MNOPQ

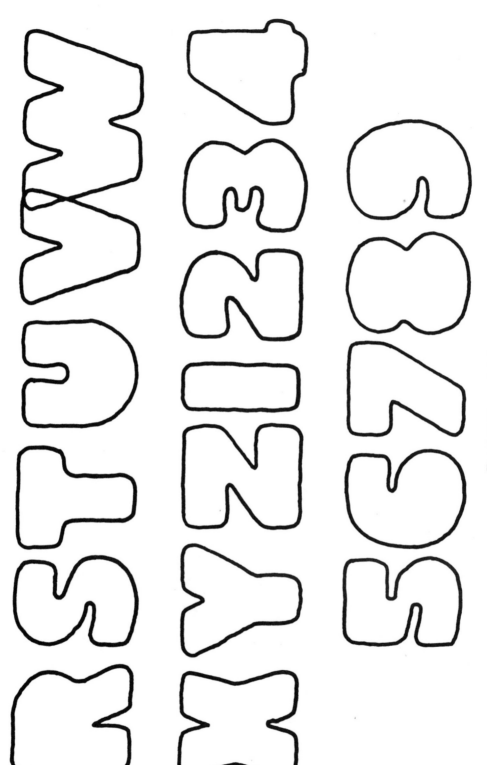

Fig. 9-11 Shape alphabet.

Fig. 9-12 Line alphabet.

Christmas stocking and vest in Chapter 6, and many of the Additional Ideas for each project.

How to Design Your Own Alphabets

Art stores sometimes give away catalogs containing sample press-on letters (incomplete alphabets). The idea is that you will fall in love with a style and buy the sheet of letters (costs anywhere from $1 to $6). However, for machine-quilting

276

purposes, lay a sheet of transparent graph paper (or use your makeshift light table) over the alphabet style you've chosen and copy the letters you need. Now you can blow up the letters to the size you need (review enlarging procedure in Chapter 2).

It is also interesting to distort the alphabet by making the size of the enlarged blocks rectangles instead of squares. Here is how to make an alphabet fit any border for a quilt. Divide the border into the same number of areas as the alphabet is divided into, even though the areas are not proportionate to the squares on the original graph paper.

Depending on the intricacy of the alphabet chosen, you can either machine quilt with the presser foot on, free-machine quilt (don't forget mock trapunto), or applique.

Letters can always be blown up to pillow size or larger and stuffed, as shown earlier in this chapter.

If you see a well-designed phrase in a magazine or as a greeting card, either blow the design up to machine quilting size or read the next chapter and design your own way to say it. I keep a file of messages I like.

And finally, letters can be manipulated to fit any interesting space. Put tracing paper over the shape and copy it. Count how many letters you must fit in and roughly divide up the space with pencil lines. Then cut out the letters free-hand from the tracing paper. You may not like your first several attempts, but keep trying. Tracing paper is inexpensive and you won't have wasted your time goofing on the actual machine-quilted item. When you're done, use a spot of glue to stick the letters down and trace them again for stitching. If you work from the underside, you can stitch right through the paper—but remember to reverse the letters or they will be backwards.

To curve a message around a circle, first copy it on a straight line. Clip between letters, keeping them connected by the line; then bend the letters around the circle perimeter.

Chapter 10

Your Own Designs

The most exciting designs—to you—are those you develop yourself. But the process of original design can also be painful and frustrating. You want to make something beautiful. You start out all enthused . . . and when you end up with something less than you wanted, you feel depressed.

Pursuing the study of design is a lifetime quest and if it sometimes feels like one step forward, three steps back, remember that even walking backwards gets you somewhere—standing still does not.

One chapter in one book cannot tap the vast subject of design. But we can give you a small start on original design specifically for machine quilting. If this opens a new world for you, find the books on design listed in the Bibliography and pursue design.

What exactly is original design?

The definition depends on what use you intend for the finished item. If your quilt will never be exhibited in a show; copied for publication in a leaflet, kit, magazine, or book; or shown beyond a circle of admiring family and friends—you can borrow and rearrange motifs from any source and call the result "original." If, however, you want to sell your design or exhibit your quilt in an Original Design category, personal ethics demand that it be developed from your own manipulation and placement of images—not something taken directly from an illustration, painting, photograph (unless it's your own), or even a traditional quilt design.

This does not mean you cannot adapt designs for machine quilting. In fact the traditional way to learn any art is to copy the masters' work, learning by doing about subtleties of form, perspective, color, and more.

This chapter shows ways to ease into original design, little by little. Expect to make many mistakes along the way—but expect to inch forward with every mistake.

One of the reasons beginners stumble along in original design is that they've never watched a professional designer hard at work. She will first make a quick sketch of an idea, jotting down possible ideas for expansion, color notes, dark and light areas. Then she'll possibly blow up the sketch, overlay tracing paper, and *simplify* the sketch, eliminating confusing lines, changing and refining shapes. This process may take days; in between she'll tack up the design on a bulletin board and eye it from time to time. Sometimes she'll look at the design in a mirror, through an artist's reducing lens, through her camera, through the wrong end of a pair of binoculars, or upside down—all to gain an objective distance from the design.

Fig. 10-1 "La Playa Caliente (Warm Beach)" by Jude Lewis, hanging done as prototype for commissioned quilt seen in color section. "I was quite unsure of myself with abstractions (I still am!) and thought it best to do a smaller sample first. It met with the approval of the couple who ordered it, so I went ahead with a quilted double bedspread. The result was 'like having an abstract painting on our bed!' according to the owners." [Works on 10-year-old Singer 758 Touch 'n Sew.]

More shapes and sketches will be added on their own little pieces of tracing paper, moved around, overlapped, merged—and always simplified, simplified. She may draw only the shapes that surround the design, to make sure that the design is well-placed.

Finally a sheet of graph or tracing paper will be overlaid on the pieces of tracing paper and, working on a light table if necessary, a final cartoon made.

The designer will now overlay tracing paper to try out dark and light areas for overall balance and then colors will be tried. Sometimes the designer will photcopy the design 10 to 30 times and try out different color schemes on those copies. (If you have children, give them a few copies to color—you may like their schemes better than yours.)

Her ideas for color come from observation of her environment (flowers, sunsets, bread mold, etc.), from magazine pages she's filed away, from fabric itself, from dreams, from historic textiles and art, from other media like painting and ceramics.

Meanwhile ideas on developing the design will be evolving, all of which she jots down in a project book, sketchbook, or the backs of old envelopes.

Finally, a full-size sample is made, checking thread and fabric behavior, suitability of technique to design, color and design aptness. Again notes are made on problems encountered, other ideas, what works and what doesn't. If the designer is pleased, she will proceed on the quilt. If she is not pleased, it's back to the drawing board for more planning.

Fig. 10-2a A design based on the paper clip.

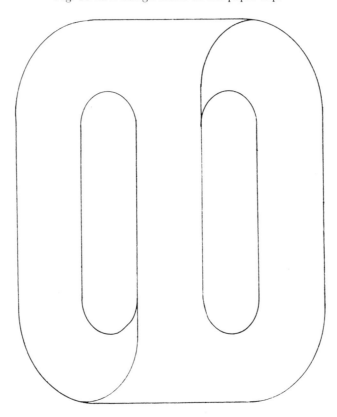

Fig. 10-2b The original is reduced and copied many times on the photocopy machine. Some lines are eliminated. The design is used as a free-machine quilting pattern.

You can see that even for the experienced, designing is hard work—but the more you do, the more successful you become, the more you want to do more.

Review the section in Chapter 2 on art tools. The tools of precision really do make designing more fun and easier—a T-square, graph paper, light table, X-acto knife, colored pens or pencils, lots of tracing paper, sketchbook, opaque projector, piles of scrap paper, visits to a photocopy machine are all helpful in making original quilt designs.

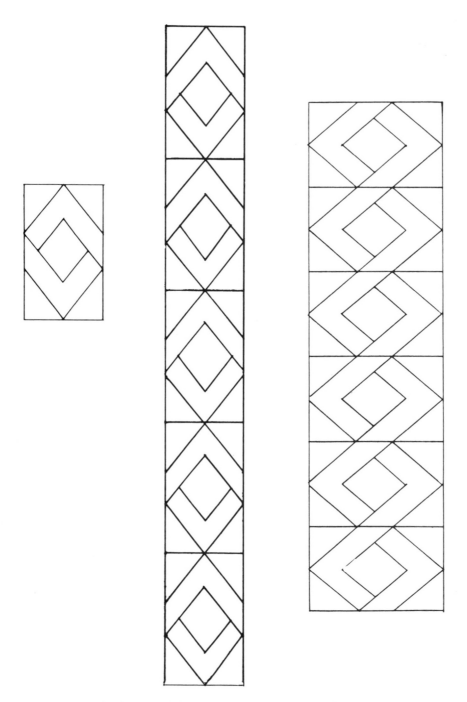

Fig. 10-3a Left, the original design, made by connecting lines on graph paper; variation of the design; turning the design.

Fig. 10-3b After photocopying, the design is pasted up.

Fig. 10-3c Borders are added.

Design Exercises for Beginners

A problem novices face in designing is too many choices. You can become paralyzed by the possibilities. As a defense against paralysis while learning, limit yourself. Choose only one shape or one symbol and play with it. What do you doodle when you're on the phone? Circle, square, triangle, spiral, heart, hexagon, crosses, or free-form? If you repeatedly doodle a shape, it must have a deep meaning for you—use and enjoy it. If you can't decide on a shape, use your name as the basic design motif. Then play with it.

"Play" is the magic word. Play with your chosen shape. If you've drawn it, cut it out and move it around, tracing it over and over. If it's asymmetrical, flop it over, turn it upside down, tilt it, overlap it. Take your shape and/or designs to the photocopy machine and make many copies. Cut these out and rearrange them.

Try your shape in these classic quilt arrangements:
1. lined-up rows of one shape (Fig. 10-4)
2. staggered rows (Fig. 10-5)
3. in a diamong-grid (Fig. 10-6)
4. in a circle (Fig. 10-7)
5. mirror image (Fig. 10-8)
6. in quarters
7. exploded (Fig. 10-9)
8. in multiples of a basic unit (e.g., basic quilt block size 6″ × 6″ or 15.3 × 15.3 cm)
9. medallion (see Chapter 3)

Now that you have manipulated one shape in many ways, look around you to find examples of that shape in your environment. Sketch or photograph what you see. Keep a file of cards, ads, magazine illustrations in your shape (in my case, I'd rather not call it The Circular File). This will give you ideas on how to embellish and vary your basic shape in quilts.

Practical Advice on Color

Once you have put yourself through these basic design exercises, you are ready to experiment with color.

This advice is for quilters who are unfamiliar with or uncomfortable about color selection. Don't bother to read this if you're an intuitive colorist or fearless about combining colors.

Just as the key word in design for the timid is "play," the key word in color is "steal." I refuse to repeat here the usual monochromatic/analagous/blah blah color schemes with drawings of wheels—these are meaningless to the novice. Find a color scheme you like and steal it. Good places to look are your garden, nature magazines, flower company catalogs, greeting cards, children's books, fabrics, and wallpaper.

Now match fabric—prints or solids—to the color scheme you've stolen. Don't forget to look at the back of your fabrics. Sometimes using the back and the front together gives a subtle blending.

Look again at the source for your color scheme. In what proportion are the areas of color? Use the same proportions for your quilt.

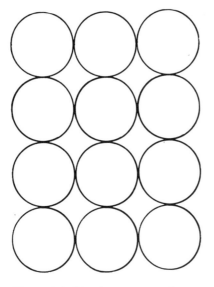

Fig. 10-4 Lined up rows of one shape.

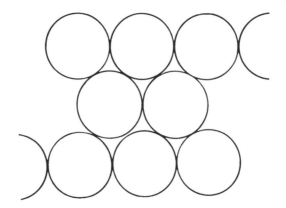

Fig. 10-5 Staggered rows of same shape.

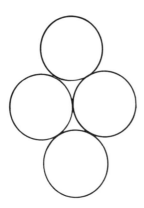

Fig. 10-6 Same shape in diamond-grid.

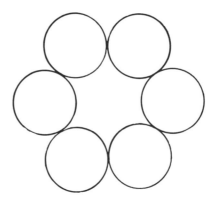

Fig. 10-7 Same shape in circle.

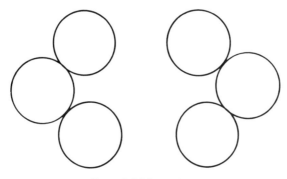

Fig. 10-8 Mirror image.

Fig. 10-9 Exploded shape.

286

Once you have chosen your fabrics, it is almost more important to divide them into dark, medium, and light piles than into color piles. Look at the color chart on the color pages compared to the same chart in black-and-white (Fig. 10-10) here if you need help. Now you can plug in the dark colors in the dark design areas and, likewise, the medium and light colors. The best quilts look as good photographed in black-and-white as in color, which only points out the importance of light/medium/dark in your fabric selection.

Use the same color scheme over and over until you feel you understand it inside out. Only by extensive experience will you begin to understand how colors blend, how different the same color can look next to other colors, how to combine prints. Only then will you appreciate what the color wheel can tell you.

One More Way To Design

One way to design a whole quilt or single quilt block is to cut out a black-and-white magazine page in which you like the dark, medium, and light values of the shapes. Then cut out a magazine page in which you like the color scheme. Trace the shapes on tracing paper and indicate dark, medium, and light areas. Now study the color page and determine whether the colors are light, medium, or dark. Plug the colors into the shapes and color with pencils, crayons, or felt-tipped pens. Now replace the shapes with your chosen shape, the one you used earlier in this chapter. Unless you want to take this new design through those design exercises to make an even newer design, you're ready to make a sample quilt block with your original design.

Print Your Own Fabric

A simple first step toward original design is to print your own fabric and quilt it. Use your chosen shape or the original design you've just developed. Printing can be done in at least six ways:

1. *Block printing* of simple shapes can be done with vegetables (potatoes are classic), by carving erasers or Styrofoam, by gluing felt shapes to cardboard, or clothesline rope to a wood block. Use fabric paints to print with (available in art supply stores or see Resource list). The color is set by ironing on the back of the painted fabric. Fabric is then washable.

Jerry Zarbaugh of Livermore, CA, suggests an alternate to block printing with fabric paints. Inko dyes, which are colorless until exposed to light, can be rolled onto your blocking device and block printed onto fabric as usual. Take out into sun and within five minutes an image appears. This image is colorfast.

2. *Fabric paints* can also be painted or air-brushed onto fabric. Thin the paints with water or extender or they will make the fabric too stiff. You can either paint first and then quilt, or quilt first and then paint. In the latter to get close to the quilting line, use a small stiff brush such as a camel's hair brush (available in art supply stores). Simple flowing shapes look best and are easiest to quilt. Joy Stocksdale's coat in the color section was done this way.

3. *Fabric crayons* look dull in the box and drawn on white paper, but as soon as you iron the design onto fabric, the colors become practically fluorescent. These crayons are available in fabric, craft, and art stores (or see Resource list). A common quilting use for them: give children in a class, Sunday school, or birthday party pre-cut squares of paper to draw on with fabric crayons. These drawings are

Fig. 10-10 Black-and-white color chart: Colors are arranged in three vertical rows with the pure hue in the center, darker to left, and lighter to right. From top down, colors are red, orange, yellow, green, blue, purple, and brown. See color pages for chart in color. Use this chart or one you make yourself to plan relative light, medium, and dark areas of your quilts.

Fig. 10-11 "Bicentennial Finery" by Lenore Davis, dyed cotton. "I used machine quilting where the line is clear or forms are clearly defined and hand quilting where soft or flat color has no clear definition and the mechanical severity of a machine-quilted line would be too strong. The soft puckering of hand quilting can be combined with the regularity of the machine line. I appreciate and design for the machine's quality of speed and regularity." [Works on Bernina 217 industrial machine and Pfaff 360, often seams fabric for dyeing, then unstitches it for quilting in long panels, to be reassembled.]

ironed onto fabric, usually framed by fabric strips, and quilted in the ditch. (Directions for heat-setting and washing are on the box.) Remember that lettering will be backwards when ironed on.

My daughter wanted a dancing-doll pillow. She drew the dancer with fabric crayons and selected the fabric. We ironed on the design, I glued on her class picture (actually I satin stitched it but the paper tore away from the stitches), and covered it with hair hand stitched on. She added an actual ribbon appliqued to the dancer's hand. I held the design up against a window and Kali drew the shape of the pillow she wanted on the underside. Rightsides together, I stitched two layers of fabric together, leaving a gap for turning and stuffing. The pillow was stuffed by Kali with loose polyester batting. She has now decided she'd like to make another pillow, changing the shape to follow the form of the dancer's flying foot more closely. Since fabric-crayon pictures can be used more than once, this will be easy to do.

Note: There are also washable felt-tipped pens, but at this writing they're harder to find, so we've omitted them here.

4. *Silkscreening* is surprisingly easy. We've done it with first-graders on T-shirts, letting the children screen the designs on. There are many different ways

Fig. 10-12 Kali's doll, showing the original drawing with fabric transfer crayons and the doll itself, made from the picture, with a school-picture face.

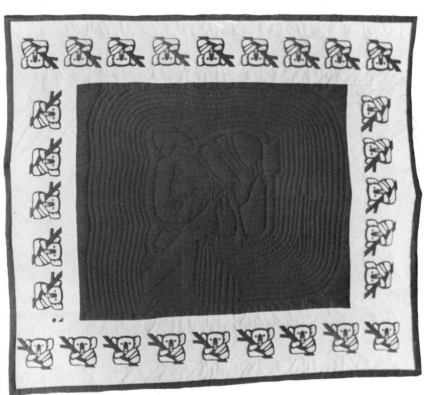

Fig. 10-13 Koala quilt, front and back. Silk-screened koalas on the borders were free-machine quilted in strips. The image was blown up for the central panel and quilted in a variety of ways (zigzag, free machine, straight stitch). Right: When a casing is not put on a quilt, you can rig hanging loops by safety-pinning 8" (20 cm) lengths (doubled) of blanket binding to the back. Quilt designed and made by the authors for Kali Koala Fanning.

to silkscreen (see Bibliography for an excellent book on the subject); here's our favorite. Trace a design you like onto acetate or drafting film (available at art supply stores) with black ink. Quilters regularly borrow designs from coloring books and greeting cards. There's no reason you can't adapt needlework designs from your overflowing library for quilting; this one was designed by Tony in honor of our daughter, Kali Koala, for our book on ethnic embroidery and applique.

The image you draw on acetate is placed on a small silkscreen (also available in art supply stores—it can be cleaned off for use over and over), a special film placed over the image, an ordinary light bulb shone through the screen, and the screen dunked in two sets of chemicals. The containers for these powdered photosilkscreening chemicals contain complete directions for use. The stencil you create this way adheres to the silkscreen. Wherever your original design had black, there is a hole through which your ink will be forced when you silkscreen. It's about as difficult as making cake from a mix; all you do is add water to the contents of the two packages and you're in business.

To actually silkscreen on fabric, the screen is set on preshrunk fabric. Lacquer-based ink is drawn over the screen with a squeegee; it only goes through the screen where you have drawn lines. (Fabric paints can be used in silkscreening, but since they are water-based, they cannot be used with photosilkscreening because they dissolve the stencil.) The screen is carefully lifted off the fabric and put down where you want the next image. When the ink is dry on the fabric, heat-set it by ironing on the backside of the fabric at a setting compatible with the fiber content of your fabric. You're now ready to quilt.

5. A collage or any 35mm slide can be printed on *heat-transfer paper* at a photocopy center with a color copier. Architects use these machines; call their offices to find out the location of the nearest color copier. The image can then be ironed or heat-bonded onto fabric (that's how many T-shirts are done).

6. *Photosensitizing* fabric is a bit more complicated but not difficult. The fabric must be coated in the dark with a photographic emulsion (available through photography stores or see Resource list). Once the fabric is coated, any object can be laid on it (grasses, lace, flower petals, etc.), taken out in the sun, and exposed. If you are familiar with the darkroom, you can also use a negative and the enlarger to print on fabric. You must fix the image on the fabric and wash it; this is not difficult and can be done in your bathtub.

Use Your Camera for Design

Again, a problem beginners face is a confusion of shapes, colors, and textures in their surroundings, making it difficult to translate what they see to what they want to put on a quilt. A camera can help in three ways—helping to look, giving some objectivity, and as a design aid.

Looking through the lens automatically puts a limit on your choice. You can only see a small rectangle, rather than a wide sweep. Walk around inside and outside your home with the camera up to your eye. Look at parts of objects, not the whole thing. Move the camera slowly around. Take your time and you will begin to see interesting angles, shapes, shadows, colors. Take black-and-white photos, color prints, or color slides. When you get them back from the photo store, put tracing paper over them (or project onto paper) and trace the most interesting shapes. Simplify, rearrange, design those shapes for a quilt.

In the process of working or after you're done with a quilt, photograph it. One reason to photograph is for your personal quilt record (see Chapter 11) and another

Fig. 10-14 "Soft Jewelry" by Joan Michaels Paque, lace laid on photosensitized fabric and exposed, satin stitched around inner and outer edge to lining. trapuntoed, 10″ × 15″ (25 × 38 cm). "My attempts are not toward perfection, for that seems infinitely unobtainable, but rather for constant growth and refinement. Mine is a trial and error approach, proceeding on the assumption that whatever works is valid . . . Each new piece or series is a whole new set of problems which dictate the solutions." (Reprinted with permission from Joan's book, *A Creative and Conceptual Analysis of Textiles*, self-published; *photo by Henry Paque*. [Works on a Singer.]

reason is to help you gain a little distance from your work. Often when you see a small picture of a large quilt, you can see instantly where you succeeded and where you failed. Make notes in your project notebook for the next time you make the same design.

And finally use your camera as a design aid. Take pictures of people and objects that are meaningful to you—family portraits, your home, your pets, your garden, your houseplants. Trace them off prints or project them onto paper taped onto the wall. Copy only the major light and dark areas—don't get bogged down in picky details. And don't be afraid to distort an image to better fit a quilt block— your cat wider than he is tall is much more charming and funnier than an undoubtedly unsuccessful attempt to portray him his exact size.

Draw Original Designs

The previous part of this chapter showed you how to adapt designs for machine quilting. But when you gain confidence, you may want to make something totally original. For this you will need to know how to draw.

You can get along perfectly well in the quilt world without knowing how to draw. However most of us who are adults and don't know how to draw suffer pangs about it. It isn't like not knowing how to knit or ride a bicycle. For those skills, we can state simply "I never learned." But with drawing, we shake our heads violently, we blush, we shiver. "I can't draw, really, I'm awful," we apologize.

Magic Words: you *can* draw! You *can* learn. It's not as if some people were born with the ability to draw and some weren't. It's not too late to learn. You didn't miss your chance to draw.

I'm not talking about being a famous artist. I'm talking about learning enough to be able to record what you need for your original designs. It may take you many years of practice, but you will improve steadily—I guarantee it.

Why bother to learn? Because it will improve your overall sense of design and color. Because it will release years of pent-up anxiety about you and drawing. Because it's relaxing and fun. Because suddenly you see and treasure quiet beauty in unexpected places, the unending diversity of human faces and bodies, the astonishing visual wealth in our world. Because part of you becomes a child again, full of wonder and joy as your eyes explore, discover, record.

How can you learn to draw? Find the drawing books listed in the Bibliography. Use them. Then carry a sketchbook and pen wherever you go. While you're waiting in doctors' and dentists' offices, at bus stops, in gas lines, draw patterns you see, shadows, paving stones, signs. You'll use very little directly and yet you'll use it all, as ideas for quilts pop into your head.

Chapter 11

Things No Other Quilting Book Will Tell You

How To Organize Your Sewing Center

A compaint often heard, particularly from working people, is "I have no place to sew. I have to set up and take down the machine every time I use it." If this prevents you from machine quilting and/or sewing, I strongly recommend that you take the time and money to set up your very own corner of your home. At the very least, you need a cardtable, a stool, and some cardboard boxes to store fabric and ideas. If you can't afford these yet, make a quilt from one of the Projects in this book and sell it. Use the money to organize your very own sewing center. If it's there, all set up, you'll sew. If you have to set up every time, you won't sew.

I say this from experience. I work in a very small room, which I've only reclaimed in the last few years. Before that, I had only a small closet and had to sew on the dining room table, which was a pain. But sewing in my little room (really, not much more than a walk-in closet) made me realize that it isn't a lot of space that we need; it's one well-organized place to throw everything, which can be as small as one corner of an apartment.

The best thing about my room is that when I quit for the day in the middle of a project—and I work messy—I can close the door on the jumble. If you work in a corner, consider making or buying a hinged room divider so you can hide your own messes.

Everyone's way of organizing is different; here's mine at its present state (the organization of my workroom changes as I change). My organizational needs fall into seven categories:

Storing Ideas

Once your eyes are opened to the world of design around you, you will begin to collect a pile of paper—notes, clippings, magazine pages, etc. Unless you organize these, they will remain an unuseable, unsightly mess. However, if you can set up a loose structure, papers can be filed as you accumulate them. My ideas are stored in three ways:

1. *Books and sketchbooks:* Most of my needlework books are on the living room bookshelves, but I move ones of current or reference interest into the sewing room as I need them. I find that when my sketchbooks are at eye level as I sit, I tend to grab them often and jot down ideas as they occur. I keep one sketchbook expressly for quilts and clothing (and one for stitchery, one for museum studies, one for general sketches). These are on short 20″ (50 cm) wide shelves on moveable brackets which I put up myself.

2. *Magazine pages, greeting cards:* These are stored in a box salvaged from behind the grocery store. (I keep telling myself someday I'll cover the ugly box with quilt wrapping paper but it doesn't seem to be high on my list of priorities.) My manilla folders are labeled: Color, Dark/Light, Texture, Pattern, Shape/Line, Quilts, Techniques (macrame, stitchery, etc.), Working Notes (from past quilts), Slopers, Cartoons From Finished Projects, Greeting Cards (I've saved them for 10 years—anything textile-related or of inspiring design), and To Be Filed.

I often add files as materials accummulate on special interests—currently I have Log Cabin and String Quilts, Lettering, Peru, Rainbows, and Machine Embroidery. These categories change. If I'm working on one large project, such as my king-sized never-ending hand quilt, it gets its own file.

Crucial to the success of this filing system is having plenty of empty file folders, to make new categories quickly and easily; having lots of scrap paper nearby to jot notes on; and not letting the To Be Filed pile overflow.

If you have a huge pile of clippings that you want to organize but can't face, don't try to tackle it all at once. Remove a handful from the pile and categorize only that layer. Little by little, you'll conquer the pile.

Friends who teach regularly staple or glue their ideas onto pages in notebooks for students to peruse. However I teach only one or two-day workshops at a time so I take the whole file box along. The portable cardboard pattern boxes sold in fabric stores are sturdy, can hold files, books, and notebooks, and have handholds for easy carrying.

3. *Display:* When I see work-in-progress, I tend to work more. When it's neatly filed away, I forget it. So I pin up my quilt blocks on the wall as I work. I pin notes to myself, quilting priorities, ideas I want to think about, quotes I like—to the curtains since I have no wall space left after the quilt blocks are up. (A bulletin board would be useful if I had room.) For pressing matters, things I have to do—like make a quilt block by such-and-such a date for the school quilt—I have a short clothesline strung up between shelves and I hang reminders there with clothespins in order of priority.

I always have one special outfit I'm working on, which I hang on the door. (Presently I'm quilting a jacket with buttons.) Often these are purchased garments I'm embellishing. I hang an old sheet behind the garment to keep the sun from fading the fabric. I'm never in a hurry with these clothes and rarely have a plan. I work a little and then study what I've done for awhile. One dress took me 1½ years to complete.

Fabric

My organization of yardage is poor. I'd love to store it on upright bolts, like in fabric stores, but I don't have enough space. Instead I use open shelves (expensive units purchased from a Scandinavian furniture store ten years ago and worth every penny—I'd eat lentils for a year in order to save enough for more of these units if I needed more storage). Cottons are in one area, solids in one stack, and prints in another, grouped by color. In order to get one piece from the middle, I have to take the whole pile down. Knits are in another area, heavy fabrics in another, special fabrics (silk, linen, 100% wool) together, and from there it's downhill toward miscellaneous chaos. I suspect I keep things in disorder so I'll be forced to sort the fabric often. I love sorting fabric.

Scraps are organized in a wonderful way, shown to me by Joan Schulze who learned it from a student in her quilting class who saw it in "Quilter's Newsletter." When I finish a sewing or quilting project, I fold excess fabric over and over into a

Fig. 11-1 How I organize scraps.

rectangle, tucking odd strings into the center. These are filed like index cards by color into cardboard catfood boxes also salvaged from the grocery store. When I need scraps of one color, it's so easy to survey what I have on hand with this method. And best of all, it takes up much less space than my previous method, throwing scraps into grocery bags (besides, every time I wanted a color, I had to empty the whole bag and then iron the crumpled scraps). Warning: Reorganizing scraps into boxes takes much longer than it looks. Don't expect to do it in one afternoon.

Threads

My extra-fine machine-embroidery threads are on two purchased plastic three-tiered thread holders, organized by color and stored on a cafeteria tray. The only problem is that dust settles on the spools and they dry out, making them brittle. First removing the nonwashable silk threads, I occasionally leave the whole tray outside overnight, letting dew soak into the threads. Other times I mist them with a plant atomizer.

My regular sewing threads are stored in a drawer of my sewing table.

Buttons

I love buttons, especially men's white shirt buttons, and love to cover garments with them (like Canadian button blankets or English pearlies' coats), quilt with them, decorate with them. I cut them off old shirts and buy them from resale stores. I have very pleasant little-girl memories of sitting by my mother as she sewed and stringing buttons onto thread for necklaces. Therefore I commissioned one of my favorite fabric artists, Sas Colby, to make me a button box.

297

Tools, Beads, and Geegaws

An $8 plastic storage box from the hardware store holds transfer pencils, chalk, crochet hooks, safety pins, beads, clock pieces, shells, and all the little miscellaneous items that we all collect.

Art Supplies

Rulers, tape, paper scissors, pens, and graph paper are kept in a drawer of my sewing table. (Opaque projector and light table are in another part of the house.) Scrap paper is in one of three stacking office trays on the table.

Sewing Machine Supplies

Pin cushion, scissors, presser feet, tape measure, needlecases, etc., are kept on a tray to the right of my machine. I like to be able to clear off my table top quickly if I want to spread out files and design on graph paper.

How To Make Time To Quilt

This section is only for those who are having trouble finding enough hours in the day to get it all done and still machine quilt. There are three steps that will help you make, not find, time to quilt:

1. *Plan* what you want to accomplish quilt-wise over the next six months. Be realistic about how much you can do in view of the amount of available time you have. If all you have is 1 to 2 hours/day or 2 to 3 sessions/week, don't expect to make everybody in your family a full-sized quilt for Christmas. However, you could make one quilt in six months or twenty-four small quilted items (one a week for six months).

One whimsical way to plan is to write a "Presume." Date your paper six months from today and write down everything you want to accomplish, quilt-wise, as if you had already done it. For example, "In September I designed an original whole-cloth king-sized quilt of Qiana, a paean to my sewing machine. In October I purchased the fabric and began quilting a little every night with one long session early Sunday mornings. I also designed and selected fabric for a friendship quilt for my sister Mary, sending out secret blocks for signing to her friends. In November when I finished the whole-cloth quilt, I machine pieced and machine quilted Mary's quilt." And so forth, for six months.

Fig. 11-2 Left: The outside of my button box, commissioned from Sas Colby, stitched with items of meaning to author. Right: Inside of my button box.

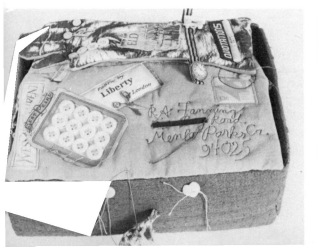 

File your Presume in the back of this book and write a note on your calendar to look at it six months from now.

Amazingly, even if you don't accomplish all you planned, you'll find you did manage to get a lot of it done in six months. Write another Presume then and continue plugging away at your quilt goals.

Once you know precisely what you want to accomplish, it's like freeing the first log from the jam and you'll have little trouble finding time to quilt.

A note for teachers: When I taught at the West Coast Quilter's Conference, I gave my students the optional homework of writing a Presume. I never intended to read these private fantasies, but psychologist Marjory Daly of Dillingham, Alaska, suggested they be turned in to me and mailed back to people January 1, of the next year. You may want to incorporate this excellent suggestion into your next class.

Incidentally, in that class this funny Presume was turned in by Wilna Lane of Chappaqua, New York: "In January I completed all my unfinished projects—these included quilting three tops, making miniature quilts to scale for a nearby museum, designing crib quilts for my new grandchild, lecturing, teaching, writing, etc. I worked 20 hours a day. The next five months were spent in a corner room of a sanitarium, where I was only permitted to weave little baskets as my diagnosis was quiltomania."

2. *Schedule* quilting times. If you have only a few free hours a day, it is unreasonable to plan to quilt every day. Interruptions are not only inevitable, but sometimes enjoyable. Don't ruin the spontaneity of life by inflexibly planning to quilt every day. But you can schedule several big two to three-hour sessions a week. Write it on your calendar; schedule it; don't let something else eat up that time. If you find yourself too weak to say "no" to interruptions in that scheduled time, sign up for a machine-quilting class, rent a studio away from home, and/or go to a friend's house to machine quilt.

Often, if you've already designed the quilt and know what to do next, you have no trouble machine quilting at night after work. But if you have to think, make decisions, cut fabric carefully after a long day, you probably won't feel like machine quilting. Try to set things up in the morning before you leave for work for that night's session. Do your designing and decision-making on weekends.

3. *Record* what you accomplish. Keep a log of the quilts and projects you make, especially if you give most of them away. Take a picture of the finished item plus detail shots (see "How to photograph your quilt" later in this chapter). From your working notes, write when you started and finished, where the fabrics and design came from, what kind of batting and threads you used, and any other notes that your heirs may be thrilled to unearth someday. Note who owns the quilt, what shows it's been in, what awards it's won. If you're really ambitious, file this record in a notebook with the sample you originally made, working notes, sketches, etc.

Then the next time you're depressed about how little you accomplish, sit down and read through your quilt record. "I've done a lot over the years," you'll realize.

How To Teach Machine Quilting

You can earn extra money (undoubtedly, to support your fabriholic habits) by teaching machine quilting, either in one-day workshops or in a series of lessons.

If you teach one-day sessions, you must choose either to help students make one completed project to learn a few basic machine-quilting techniques (such as a log cabin one-step quilted pillow); or to survey the wide variety of machine-quilting

Fig. 11-3 Teaching the first quilt-as-you-go class.

techniques, showing your own samples and demonstrating on your own machine rather than having students make a complete project. Which approach you choose depends on the experience of your students. The inexperienced and the young will probably prefer making one completed project; other teachers and experienced machine quilters usually prefer being bombarded with ideas that they can later develop at home for their own original quilts and/or class projects.

If you teach a series of classes, you can both show techniques and help students make a full-size sampler quilt or several projects. There are so many choices of subject matter that you could teach the same group of students for years and not duplicate yourself: The Machine and Log Cabin Variations, String Quilt Variations, Survey of Machine Quilting, Free-Machine Quilting, Seminole Piecing Variations, Original Design in Quilting, Friendship Quilts, Machine Applique, are just a beginning.

There are three places often used for series classes, with pro's and con's for each: adult education and community college home ec rooms, a home (yours or somebody else's), or stores (fabric, quilt, sewing machine, sewing schools).

1. Adult ed and community college home ec rooms.

Pro's: The administration rounds up the students for you. There is usually plenty of room to cut fabric and enough machines for everybody. Film, slide, and opaque projectors are often available for use. Students are usually devoted types who take your classes again and again.

Con's: The pay is sometimes small. The sewing machines have sometimes been ravaged by high school students. The classes are cancelled if less than a large number of students show up (under 15 to 20 sometimes, whereas you can sometimes afford to teach as few as four students without such restrictions). For adult ed you usually must teach at night, when you're tired (and some people are afraid to come out at night). For community colleges you must usually have a state teaching license.

2. A home (yours or somebody else's).

Pro's: You can easily fit up to 25 students in a middle-sized living room, two to a cardtable. (Don't worry about sewing machines pulling too much power—but plug the iron into another room's outlet.) There is no overhead such as rent and you can keep the entire class fee. During the day a babysitter can be hired to play with small children in the backyard or in another room, so that young mothers can attend. People learn to machine quilt on their own familiar machines. You do not always have to charge money—you can barter interesting things and services in exchange for classes. I've traded stays at vacation homes, artwork, dental work, babysitting, and more for machine-quilting lessons and I treasure these exchanges more than money.

Con's: Someone always walks off with your best scissors. You feel compelled to clean before class and you must clean afterwards. You probably will want to provide coffee and tea and it's amazing how much toilet paper 25 students use. You must advertise and hustle to find students.

3. Stores (fabrics, quilt, sewing machine, sewing schools).

Pro's: The storeowner will advertise your class via mailing lists, flyers, and posters, ads in newspapers, etc. There is usually plentiful working space and store machines to back up broken student machines. If you're teaching on store machines, you know what they can do (technically, you should get a sales commission on any machines sold because of your machine quilting class). Supplies are readily available. It's inspiring to be surrounded by fabric. Teachers are usually given personal discounts on supplies.

Con's: You must split the fee with the store owner (usually 75% to you, 25% to owner). Although most store owners are wonderful, some are reptiles. You meet some strange people with stranger machines.

How much to charge for classes? This depends on the type of student and frankly, what the traffic will bear. Check around to find out what similar craft classes cost. In 1980 a teacher usually charges a minimum of $100 + travel expenses for a one-day six-hour workshop ($5 to $10/person). A six-session class of two to three hours each usually costs $5 to $7, per person per session, which means you, as a teacher, must set a minimum number of students you'll teach. (I won't teach less than eight.)

Where to find ideas for teaching? This book and others, the well-known ladies' magazines, the specialty magazines like "Treadleart" and "Quilter's Newsletter." Two places train teachers for machine embroidery and quilting (see Resource list). Demonstrators for the various brands of machines travel through from time to time; ask your fabric store owner to let you know when. Attending quilt and embroidery conferences is always exciting for the exchange of ideas with other teachers and participants. Once you start teaching, you'll find students a source of some of your best ideas.

Remember that a good teacher tells her students what they will learn, shows them the subject (via visual aids like samples, slides, books and magazines, drawings, photocopied or dittoed instructions, etc.), has them learn by doing, and then sums up by telling them what they did learn. Also a good teacher is always at some new threshold of learning herself, sharing her new discoveries with her students.

How To Buy a Sewing Machine

My one key advice in buying a new machine is: don't hurry. A sewing machine is a major tool and must be selected with great care. All brands are not the same, no matter what a salesperson will tell you. Take the time to do each of the following and the machine you eventually buy will last a lifetime:

1. Go to the public library and look up the yearly issue of "Consumer Reports" that rates new machines. (Ask your reference librarian for help if you need it.) In some ways, these reports are like comparing apples and oranges, but at least you will find out which models of which brands you can expect to malfunction. Look at the machine chart in Chapter 1 for features desirable to machine quilters.

2. Talk to consumers about their preferences—other machine quilters, sewing and home ec teachers, quilt guild members, home sewers. This can be amusing, because those who love their brand of machine are usually wildly enthusiastic about it and will make unfounded snipes at other perfectly good brands. If possible, machine quilt on as many models as you can before buying one. Find out which machines have terrible repair records. As for my own preference, I've sewn on all machines and have four or five favorite brands, each with some unique feature. I'd like one of each but my bank account objects. Three features I could not do without: (1) easy portability (some so-called portable machines weigh a ton—compare weights of machines when you're shopping; (2) free-arm—I use it constantly; (3) a wide range of stitches for all possible sewing situations. I feel it is worth buying the top-of-the-line model of the brand you've chosen, even if you have to get a loan to do so.

3. At the store, make the salesperson machine quilt (not just sew pretty stitches on one or two layers of fabric) on your machine—not a floor model—before leaving the store. Contrary to popular delusion, the floor models are often the finest tuned in the store. Make sure yours, fresh from bouncing around in a factory box, is in as good a shape as the demonstrator machine.

4. Don't cut corners in buying a machine. Top-notch machines cost money. To stay in top-notch shape, they need top-notch repair people, who truly care about sewing machines. Nothing is more frustrating than buying an extremely expensive machine at a discount store for $100 less than the fabric store charges—and taking home a machine out of tune that never sews right and is never really fixed correctly. Establishing a close relationship with a good fabric/sewing machine dealer will bring you years of pleasure in your machine quilting.

How To Photograph a Quilt

Remember that photography has little to do with the subject; it has to do with the quality of light. You are not photographing a quilt; you are photographing dark and light.

Therefore, the first question to ask yourself is, "Where is the light source? What is it doing to my quilt?"

Quilts are textiles; textiles have texture; texture is varieties of ups and downs, hills and valleys, bumps and smooths—in short, dark and light shadows. Light falling directly on a quilt washes out the shadows, the very texture of the quilting. Light from the side, however, accentuates the shadows, the texture, the quiltness.

Most quilts photographed on a bed with overhead lighting or head-on flash look terrible. They could just as easily be sheets and you can't see most of the pattern because near the floor it's usually dark.

It is far better to use that powerful lightbulb in the sky, the sun, as your light source. However, the same principles apply outside as in. If the sun falls directly on your quilt, the texture will be washed out. Hang or drape your quilt outside in full (not dappled) shade or if you prefer to photograph in the light, before 10 AM or after 4 PM when the sun creates a low soft side-lighting perfect for quilts. (Some people advise to photograph at noon in full sun. This, too, is side-lighting—from the topside—but it gives a harsh quality to the color slide. My favorite photography time is 10 AM on an overcast day.)

Fill your viewfinder with the quilt, turning the camera, if necessary, to photograph a quilt longer than it is wide. We are interested in details of the quilt, not the barn you hung it on. Get as close to the quilt as you can. If your camera will stay in focus, take another shot even closer up, a detail of the quilting or of one quilt block.

If you are taking color slides, you can buy a silver polyester tape at film supply stores (or use black electrician's tape—but it sometimes sticks in the slide projector) to mask out unwanted areas (such as that barn) on your slides. Put the slide on your light table (or jury-rig a light table as shown in Chapter 2) so you can see what you're doing. Cut small pieces of tape to lay over the unwanted areas. Do this on the side of the slide with the printing (name of film company) so that you can label the other side of the slide. (I'm also told you can paint red nail polish onto unwanted areas with a small stiff brush, but I haven't tried it.)

There are two situations which call for special handling: if the quilt is predominantly white and if the quilt is very dark (black, navy blue, purple). If you're working with a small pocket camera, shoot these quilts slightly from the side. If you're using a 35mm single-lens reflex, your built-in meter is trying to make that white quilt 18% gray. To counteract the meter and let in more light, open up, either by changing the f/stop (e.g., change from f/11 to f/8) or the shutter speed (e.g., change from 1/125th to 1/60th of a second). Otherwise your white quilt slides will be too dark. (My mnemonic device for remembering doesn't make sense but it works for me; I say to myself "WHIP!"—white: open up.) For very dark quilts, do the opposite: close down a stop (e.g., either f/8 to f/11 or 1/60th to 1/125th).

Some very large quilts are better photographed hung sidewards so they don't drag on the ground. For your own quilts, consider putting a casing for hanging both on the top and along one side. For photographing quilts with no casing, cut blanket binding about 8" (20 cm) long, double the pieces, and safety pin them along the top back edge so that a pole can be slipped through the blanket binding loops. You can also safety pin one half of a long Velcro strip to the back of the quilt, tacking the other half to your hanging surface. The Velcro is so strong as a hanging device that museums use it all the time. Try not to have your friends hold up the quilt for photography. They giggle and wiggle and their hands and feet stick out at the edges of your quilt photo. If you can't find a place big enough to hang your quilt, drape it but study the quilt and ladies' magazines to see how they do it.

If there is any breeze, I safety pin invisible thread to the bottom corners and tape the thread on paint cans which are outside the picture frame.

For 35mm cameras, start with a speed of 1/60th of a second and match your f/stop to that speed. Unless you are very experienced, any slower speed may give you a fuzzy picture caused by camera shake or the wind blowing your quilt. When there is a lot of light and you have a choice of closing down the f/stop or speeding up the shutter speed, choose the former. Try to get as close to f/16 as you can, for the sharpest details of texture in your quilt. This is especially important if your quilt is draped, not hung. Otherwise parts of the quilt may be out of focus in the photo. (The wider open the f/stop, the smaller the depth of field. When your quilt is draped, the side closest and farthest from you may be out of focus, with only a small part of the center in focus.)

As for film, companies are bringing out new faster color films all the time. Any information I give here would be dated tomorrow. Check with your film store about the best film for your needs. Tell them what kind of light source it will be—indoor lighting is usually tungsten; outdoor is obviously the sun—and whether you're shooting black-and-white, color prints, or color transparencies (slides).

A useful trick: if you have one kind of film in the camera and wish to replace it with another (say, outdoor film to be replaced by indoor), note what frame number you're on. Rewind the film back into the cannister, listening carefully so that you hear the tongue of the film click loose of the reel. Stop winding so that the film tongue is left protruding out of the film cannister. Remove the roll of film from the camera and put a piece of masking tape on the cannister with the date and the last frame number shot. Put in the other roll of film, change the ASA rating if necessary, and you're in business. When you reload the half-used film, keep the lens cap on as you click through to your previous frame number. Waste a few frames by clicking one or two past where you left off, so that you won't have any unintentional double images.

As for using flash, if you can, bounce the flash off a low ceiling or adjacent wall. Head-on flash washes out all texture.

Since most museums will not allow flash, I use an indoor Ektachrome film that can be "pushed"—that is, instead of setting my camera at the given ASA rating, I set it at double the speed (320 instead of 160). Even in poor lighting, I can then get decent shots. When turning in the film for developing, I tell the film people what I've done and they process accordingly. However, I usually don't load film in my camera until I see what the lighting source in the museum is—sometimes it's light coming in a window with no overhead lights.

Incidentally, if you wish to submit slides of your work for magazine or book publication, juried shows, etc., it's far cheaper to take several shots of one piece than to make duplicates of one slide. Mark each slide with your name and address, title and dimensions of piece, and "top."

Photography is a vast subject and the more deeply you immerse yourself in it, the more you realize how little you know. Like machine quilting, experience is the key, which usually means shooting rolls of terrible pictures before you begin to succeed.

For the other photography nuts who are curious: we have two Olympus OM-1 bodies and a Mamiya 2¼" (5.7 cm) twin-lens reflex used mostly for black-and-white studio shots. For small objects we shoot indoors with two 3400 photofloods draped with old translucent curtains for a softer light. We always use a tripod and a cable release when shooting at home. We don't have enough lights for full-sized quilts, so we shoot outdoors in the early morning, hanging the quilts against the garage on a device Tony made. We use the 28mm lens the most for quilts but often have to mask out the sides of a slide. We also have 50mm, 2X extender, and 200mm lenses plus close-up rings. We recently bought a slide duplicator because of our enormous slide library of artists' work and because we send out so many slides of our work for magazine articles and books.

How To Organize Group Quilting

A truly unique family or community heirloom can be created when machine quilters join together. You can also raise a good bit of money for a worthy cause—school, guild, church, library, and other groups. (But be sure selling raffle tickets is legal in your state.)

The diversity of a group quilt can also be its downfall, unless you plan well. You may receive so many different colors and odd-sized quilt blocks that when you put them together, you have a hodge-podge, not something memorable.

Therefore, the most important aspect of a group quilt is planning. Break the overall quilt down into manageably sized blocks. Plan the overall color of the quilt. For best results buy all the fabric yourself, preshrink and cut it (using generous margins on the blocks—1″ or 2.5 cm, or more). This will give continuity to the quilt when all the completed blocks are returned.

Send along a letter to participants with precise instructions: Is the block to be embroidered, appliqued, machine quilted? In exactly what colors (and remind participants to use colorfast colors)?, how big are the margins? If you send out quilt-as-you-go blocks, how close to the margin can they quilt? Do you want participants to sign and date their blocks? Is the whole project a surprise for someone? When are the completed blocks due back?

As a courtesy when the quilt is done, send another letter to everyone enclosing a color print of the finished quilt and a diagram showing who did what.

Some traditional ideas for group quilts are:

1. *Album quilts:* signatures of friends, group members, famous people are written on fabric in indelible ink (available at art supply stores).

2. *Friendship quilts:* everyone makes a block for a friend.

3. *Theme quilts:* blocks reflect something you all have in common like bicycles, an occupation, rockhounding, music, historical homes in miniature, etc.

4. *Geographical:* scenes from your town, a graphic map of your area or neighborhood.

5. *Mementoes:* .guests at a wedding sign their names on fabric blocks to be made into a quilt for the newlyweds; children in Sunday school make pictures with fabric crayons which are ironed onto quilt blocks; students in a machine-quilting class make and assemble blocks in class and draw lots for the winner of the quilt.

If your group quilt is to raise money, allow several weeks or months after completion of the quilt for display of it. Notify the local papers where and when the quilt will be hung—libraries, schools, churches, and banks are all likely to welcome exhibiting the quilt for you. After the quilt is raffled off, notify the papers who won and how much money was raised. (Technically, the money spent on materials for the quilt should come out of the money raised for it but participants often chip in for the materials.) Recently, a group raised $1300 for their church by displaying a quilt for one weekend only and selling raffle tickets.

A note to teachers: Roberta Horton's theme quilts are well-known through the pages of "Quilter's Newsletter" (see cover photographs on March 1978 and subsequent issues). She keeps interest high in her on-going 10-week quilt classes by drawing lots at the end of each session for the quilt made during the classes. Students put their names in a bowl, once for every class attended, so that perfect class attendance increases a student's chance to win the quilt. Those who have missed more than two weeks of class cannot participate in the drawing.

Roberta advises that the more limitations built into the design of the quilt, the better. After many years of teaching, she has settled on 14″ (35.6 cm) blocks with 3″ (7.6 cm) border strips between them, and the backing brought to the front in a 3″ (7.6 cm) border. The blocks are actually cut 15″ (38 cm) and later trimmed to the correct size because students seem to fill out the 14″ (35.6 cm) block better this way. The entire class decides on the theme in the first class, but only one person buys the fabric. The first five weeks of each three-hour class are spent designing and piecing the top; the last five weeks, hand quilting.

(Note: One of the themes was stained glass, out of which an interesting technique and book arose—see the Bibliography.)

How To Care for Machine-Quilted Quilts

As you finish each quilt, make a muslin or fabric sack for it, so that each unused quilt can be rolled and stored in the sack in a dark, cool, dry area.

The enemies of quilts are dirt, creases, damp, some chemicals, and direct sunlight. Keep your quilts clean—no problem with machine-quilted quilts, which can be washed and dried in home machines. Try to roll your quilts. If necessary to fold, try to do so on a seam line. Put a note on your calendar once a month to unfold, hang out for airing, and reroll stored quilts (I can't think of a more pleasant household task). Try to refold stored quilts a different way each time.

Don't store quilts in plastic bags. Moisture may collect inside and rot your quilt. Also I was told that a woman who stored a quilt in a large green plastic bag had it mistakenly picked up and carted off to the garbage dump.

Most tissue papers and newsprint are acidic and will destroy the quilt fibers over a number of years. (See the Resource list for the address of acid-free tissue paper.)

If you have wall space, hang the quilts you're not using. But be sure direct sun does not fall on them because some of the fabrics will fade.

To remove dust, batting lint, dog and cat hairs, pin net over the quilt and vacuum the whole thing. This protects the quilting stitches from being sucked into the vacuum cleaner and possibly broken by the strain.

How To Buy and Sell a Quilt

In buying an original quilt, keep in mind that you're paying for three things: the artist's time, materials, and special vision. Therefore you can expect to pay substantially more than you would for a department store comforter.

After your first rush of love for a quilt and its design, examine it as objectively as you can—from a distance, if possible. Then look at it up-close to see how the workmanship is, especially between seams and on the bindings. Ask the artist how to care for the quilt and if that information isn't on a label on the back of the quilt, write it down in a notebook (or put it in the envelope you stapled in the back of this book). Ask the artist if he or she will repair any parted seams or defects in sewing that develop in the first year of ownership.

If you can't afford a quilt you ache to buy, try forming an informal co-op with friends. Divide the price into equal parts; everyone gets to display the quilt in his or her home for a proportionate number of months. Members can sell their share in the quilt for whatever the traffic will bear, as long as other co-op members agree, but the display time per home remains constant.

To sell a number of quilts in a store, make a prototype first and keep track of your time and how much the materials cost. Keep your design simple and easily repeatable, so that you change colors and textures, but you do not change the basic design. Remember that in business, every penny counts—try to buy all of your supplies at wholesale costs, for which you'll need a resale number. If you don't know which state agency issues resale numbers, ask either your reference librarian or any friendly shopkeeper.

Theoretically, the price of your quilt to a store is figured by your time multiplied by $x/hour (you set the rate—minimum wage is about $3) + cost of materials, doubled. The store will then raise the price again to the customer. Realistically, this sometimes means you're charging $300 for a crib quilt, which is not in the budget of most shoppers.

However, if you streamline your design and do all machine work, you can get a fair price for your machine quilting.

To sell custom-made quilts directly to people, be sure you talk extensively with the buyers before you start. Find out exactly what they want—what colors, size, materials, where the quilt will be displayed. Make a mock-up of the design and/or a sample block and check that with the buyers also. This will also give you a chance to estimate how much time it will take you to make the quilt.

Try to use a basic quilt layout (see beginning of Chapter 3) so that your design time does not stretch into no-pay hours. If it does, reserve the right to sell the design again (use it in another quilt or sell the design to a ladies' magazine).

To find customers, leave notices (preferably with a photo of one of your quilts) in hairdressing salons, doctors' and dentists' waiting rooms, church and public bulletin boards, waterbed and folding-foam bed stores, and any other place frequented by people who can afford your quilts. Advertise in local shopper newspapers. In the beginning you might arrange a show of your quilts in a library, medical clinic, or small compatible restaurant. After that, if your quilts are pleasing and affordable, customers will find you by word of mouth.

(Note: Janie Warnick gave me much valuable advice on selling a quilt.)

How *Not* to Hang a Quilt Show

Since I've never hung a quilt show, I can't give you first-hand information on that; but I have been to dozens of quilt shows, ranging from mediocre to excellent, and I can tell you how *not* to hang a quilt show.

1. Do not have improperly displayed quilts. We want to see them hung full-face, with an identifying number and/or name and an accompanying booklet with information on who made it, when, and something that makes the quilt special ("her first quilt, made in so-and-so's class," "won First Prize at the State Fair"). No quilts should be dumped on tables for pawing through by people attending the show. Also, there should be enough light and space between rows of quilts for photography.

2. Do not frustrate us with lack of information, attention, or time. Have plenty of hostesses around with white gloves on so we can look at the backs of the quilts and ask questions. Schedule the show for at least two days so it won't be too crowded.

3. Do not over-hustle us. Keep the merchants in a separate area and make sure they all relate to quilting. I resent getting a pitch for vacuum cleaners at a quilt show.

4. Do not show 200 similar or already-seen quilts. Have a range of antique and modern quilts, traditional and contemporary design. And *please*, include some of the exciting machine quilting that's being done all over the country (and world).

5. Do not project a harried, disorganized, "this-show-is-a-burden-to-stage" image. Put up many directional signs within a mile of the show. Have adequate parking. Organize the entrance so that we don't have to stand in long lines. Greet us; make us feel welcome. Put up signs pointing to exhibits, restrooms, food, merchants. Have on-going demonstrations of quilting, sign-ups for classes, lectures. Have chairs for us to rest on. Make your show a celebration of quilts.

Chapter 12

Problem Solving and Miscellaneous Tips

This chapter binds the whole book together. You will find directions for: an easy dust ruffle; making a standard pillowcase; taming a Slippery Quilt; fabric care; stain removal; dye chart; ways to relax; a short treatise on workmanship and personal standards; and a final word.

Easy Dust Ruffle

This dust ruffle covers three sides of the bed.

Materials You Will Need

old mattress pad (the size of your mattress)
two old flat sheets (the size of your mattress—dye them if they're the wrong color)
string or cord or #5 pearl cotton, mattress width + two times length

Construction

1. Measure the distance from the bottom of your mattress (where it hits the box springs, if you have them) to the floor. Add ½" (12 mm) turn-under and ½" (12 mm) seam allowance. Cut off the bottom and top hems of your sheets (unless you have extra time—then you can open them out). Cut strips as wide as your mattress/floor measurement off the length of both sheets. Rightsides together, seam strips together across widths in ½" (12 mm) seams, making one long strip. Press seams open. Turn under two crosswise ends of long strip so no raw edges show. Stitch close to edge. Turn under ¼" (6 mm) on one long raw edge and press. Turn another ¼" (6 mm). Stitch close to edge of hem.

2. Lay cord or string on underside of strip along long ½" (12 mm) seam line of raw edge. Run a line of wide zigzag over the cord, being careful not to pierce the cord. Gather dust ruffle by pulling cord.

3. Rightsides together, lay ruffle on mattress pad. Distribute ruffles evenly around three sides of mattress pad. Pin. Straight stitch ½" (12 mm) seam. Put dust ruffle on bed. (The mattress pad goes between box springs and top mattress.)

Standard Pillowcase

Materials

⅞ yd. (0.8 m) medium-weight 45"-wide (115 cm-wide) fabric per case

Construction

1. After preparing fabric, turn under ¼" (6 mm) across the fabric and stitch. If you are adding any decorative work, sew it on now, leaving 2½" (6.4 cm) free on the end you just stitched.

2. Fold fabric in half lengthwise, rightsides together. Stitch across the unstitched end and down the side in a ¼" (6 mm) seam. Clip corners.

3. Turn open end inside 2½" (6.4 cm) and stitch close to edge (your bobbin thread will show on right side). Turn rightside out, poke out corners gently, and press.

This whole process takes less than 20 minutes, if you're wondering if it's worth your time. You also can make more beautiful cases than you can buy. Ours are all different colors.

For king-sized pillowcase, measure length of pillow and adjust length of fabric accordingly. The rest of the procedure is the same. They are longer, but not much wider, than standard pillowcases.

How To Tame a Slippery Quilt

Quilts made of satin, tricot and some knits (and all quilts slept under by children, regardless of fiber content) tend to slide off the bed at night as you move in your sleep. Stitch the cut-off end of a contour or flat sheet or of an old blanket to the bottom underside of your quilt. Then tuck the extra flap over and under the mattress and you'll have no more problems.

Fabric Care

Table 12-1 details caring for fabrics used in quilting.

Remember: the compleat machine quilter puts a care label on the back of her quilts, telling how to wash and dry them (for future heirs).

Stain Removal

Time and heat are your two worst enemies with stains. Try to treat stains immediately. It is worth sending for the U.S. Department of Agriculture's Home and Garden Bulletin No. 62, "Removing Stains From Fabrics" (40¢ from Superintendent of Documents, U.S. Gov't Printing Office, Washington, DC 20402, Stock #001-000-03481-2). Your public library probably already has this in their pamphlet file under Laundry and Cleaning. Also see the Laundry/Marker Test in Chapter 2.

Ballpoint pen: Sponge with rubbing alcohol, or spray with hairspray; let dry before washing.

Blood: Chew ball of white thread and blot on spot; or dissolve meat tenderizer in cold water and blot spot; don't let it dry before treating, if possible.

Candle wax: Rub spot with ice cube; scrape off with blunt knife.

Chewing gum: Same as for candle wax.

Coffee, tea: Machine-wash and dry.

Crayons: Rub with shampoo; handwash; or place paper towels over wax and iron with warm iron; sponge remaining stain with turpentine and wash.

Egg: Use drycleaning solvent, flush with water, and then apply liquid hand dishwashing detergent and a few drops of ammonia; flush thoroughly with water.

Table 12-1. Fabric Care Chart

Fiber	Machine Washing	Machine Drying	Ironing	Dye Class	Beware
cotton/poly	warm	low	warm	union	
100% cotton	hot water	regular	hot	fiber reactive direct	shrinks a lot
100% polyester (e.g., Dacron)	warm water	low	low-moderate	disperse acid	
nylon (e.g., Qiana)	warm	low	cool (melts under high heat)	acid disperse	picks up colors from other fabrics in wash
rayon	hand-wash	drip-dry	low-moderate on wrong side	fiber reactive direct	
linen	hot	regular	hot	direct	
silk	hand-wash	or dry-clean	medium on wrong side-no steam	fiber reactive acid	water spots
wool	hand-wash/cool water	or dry-clean	medium with press cloth	acid	shrinks drastically if exposed to heat (hot water or hot dryer air)

Felt-tipped pen: Use drycleaning solvent, rinse with water/ammonia solution, then water; repeat process until stain is removed (final traces may be removed by chlorine bleach).

Grease: Sprinkle with talcum powder, then brush off.

Hemline: Rub with vinegar solution (¼ cup white vinegar to 1 cup water).

Lipstick: Rub with ice cube, blot with lighter fluid; or rub with petroleum jelly before washing.

Nail polish: Use nail polish remover (but not on acetate).

Pencil marks: Grease Relief; Windex diluted 1:1 in water and applied with old toothbrush.

Rust: Take to drycleaner (home solutions may discolor fabric).

Scorch marks: Sponge with peroxide; let dry in sun; wash.

Transfer pencil: Soak with liquid detergent before machine-washing.

Urine: Soak in enzyme pre-soak before washing or blot spot with vinegar solution (¼ cup white vinegar to 1 cup water).

Wine (red): Sprinkle immediately with salt, soak with cold water, rub out stain, then wash.

Dye Chart

Dyeing is easy and always an adventure. However, most popular written instructions seem to imply that you can dye any fabric with any dyestuff. Not true. These are the major classes of dyes. Choose a class according to your fabric/fiber. After that, it's about as difficult as making frozen orange juice. Follow the complete directions on the dye package.

Fiber Reactive
>   Trade names: Procion (cold-water M series), Fibrec, Hi-Dye, Reactive Dye
>   Fiber: cotton, flax, viscose rayon, silk
>   Easy to use, brilliant colors

Disperse
>   Trade names: Celliton, Dispersall, Poly-dye
>   Fiber: acetate, nylon, all polyesters
>   Brilliant color, set with iron (transfer crayons are actually disperse dyes in wax form)

Acid
>   Trade names: Kiton, Acid
>   Fiber: silk, wool, nylon
>   Especially good on silk and wool

Direct
>   Trade names: Clorantine, Calcomine
>   Fiber: cellulose fibers (cotton, viscose rayon, linen)
>   Extremely light-fast (won't fade); has a true black

Union
>   Trade names: Rit, Putnam, Cushing
>   Fiber: especially for fabric blends like cotton/poly
>   Trouble with colorfastness; set by steam; hard to get dark colors; easy to use

Vat
>   Trade names: Inko, indigo

Fiber: any fiber

Sets with light (like the sun)

Notes on dyeing: Old sheets are easy to dye; permanent press sheets are impossible. There is no one good book on dyeing, but worth owning is the *Straw Into Gold Catalog* (see Resource page) for its dye information pages.

The Problem-Solving Clinic

Table 12-2 details a wide range of problems you may encounter in machine quilting, with the solutions that many hours of quilting and teaching have taught me.

Ways To Relax

Spending hours in any one position is hard on aging bodies, no matter the activity. But particularly, bending over a machine for hours, hypnotically watching a needle pierce a quilt, is hard on the neck and back.

Alberta Humphreys showed me a simple relaxation technique that feels wonderful after machine quilting. Sit up straight; have a friend stand behind you and firmly clasp over your ears and under your chin. Have the friend pull straight up gently. That's all there is to it, and it works.

Slow gentle stretching exercises are also excellent. Richard Hittleman's *Yoga 28-Day Exercise Plan* (see Bibliography) is a good start on yoga.

We also run 10 to 20 miles/week for the increased energy and good health we feel.

Workmanship and Personal Standards . . .

How much of a perfectionist should you be? If there's one pucker on the back of your quilt, should you lose sleep over it?

Only you can set your own personal standards. Mine are modified according to the purpose of the quilt. If it's for a show, I'm strict with myself: no puckers, no overlapping stitches, thread ends must be hidden, no thread burbles on the back where I've locked stitches, quilt must pass Closed Fist Test and hang straight.

But if it's a present or a quilt for ourselves, merely to enjoy sleeping under, not to examine minutely, I do the best I can at the time and don't worry about the mistakes.

If standards of excellence are preventing you from producing, don't be a perfectionist. Instead bring to each new quilt the knowledge you've learned from mistakes.

. . . And a Final Word

We've covered many techniques in this book and I hope you're filled with enthusiasm and ideas. However, if you've learned only these four things, I'll be happy:

1. The proper way to baste for pucker-free machine-quilting.

Table 12-2. The Problem-Solving Clinic

Problem Caused by	Solution

THREAD PROBLEMS

Upper thread breaks

the machine is not threaded properly	re-thread
needle inserted wrong way round or at wrong height	insert properly
upper tension too tight	loosen
thread is caught below spool on spindle or in nick of spool	use tapestry needle (see Chapter 2); turn spool upside down
thread too dry and brittle	buy better thread; leave outside overnight
thread is cheap and poorly made	buy better thread
thread too thick for needle or material	change thread and/or needle—see chart, Chapter 1
needle bent or blunt	change needle
presser foot not lowered	lower presser foot
burrs on edges of needle plate hole	file with emery cloth
material too thick or dense (e.g., leather)	use heavier needle
take-up lever not in highest position when removing fabric from machine	set take-up lever in highest position

Top thread loops show on back

bobbin tension too tight and/or upper tension too loose	re-adjust
threads used in top and bobbin of uneven weight or tensile strength	use same thread for both or hide loops by using small print on back

Lower thread breaks

lower tension too tight	loosen
thread is unevenly wound on bobbin or brought up incorrectly	read your instruction manual
burrs on edges of needle plate hole	file with emery cloth

Lower thread loops show on top

upper tension too tight and/or bobbin tension too loose	re-adjust
threads used in top and bobbin of uneven weight or tensile strength	use same thread or use heavier thread (and larger needle) on top

Threads jam at start of sewing

top thread not held securely behind presser foot for first few stitches, pulling it into bobbin snarl	hold thread
cat or baby walked on unattended machine's foot pedal	watch out; get a canary
presser foot not down at start of sewing	lower presser foot

Stitches are skipped or uneven

bobbin innards are linty and clogged	clean and oil
broken threads in bobbin case	clean and oil
needles being used are not made expressly for machine	use correct needles
wrong type needle for material being used	change to ballpoint, sharp or leather needle—see Chapter 1
machine incorrectly threaded or needle inserted wrong	check threading and needle
fabric(s) were not touching the needle plate at moment the stitch was formed	press down on fabric near needle with fingers

THREAD PROBLEMS (continued)

needle bent or dull or has burrs	change needle
needle plate hole too large; material being dragged down into it	use left-needle position or straight stitch plate
thread too thick for size needle being used	change needle size
upper tension too tight	loosen
your machine is old and hates polyester thread	change brands of thread, use cotton thread, or buy new machine
in middle of quilting line, you didn't stop sewing with needle in fabric; quilt weight dragged material away from needle	when you stop quilting, leave needle in fabric
you're pulling the quilt through too fast or too slow	practice to achieve an even feed of material

NEEDLE PROBLEMS

Needle breaks

material has been jerked during sewing, bending needle and causing it to hit presser foot or needle plate	practice even feeding of material
upper tension too tight for machine	loosen
needle mounted incorrectly	re-mount correctly
you sewed over pins	no-no
material too thick and dense for your machine to handle	forego thick material or buy better machine

Needle falls out

screw holding needle in too loose	tighten screw
needle screw hits embroidery hoop repeatedly while working near edge of hoop	move hoop on fabric or rotate hoop so closest edge is in front of needle

FABRIC PROBLEMS

Top material puckers

incorrect needle point for material	change to ballpoint, sharp, or leather needle
thread too thick for material	use thinner thread
upper and/or lower tensions too tight	loosen
stitches too long for weight of material	shorten stitches
fabric jerked away from needle at end of stitching, gathering and puckering fabric	pull fabric gently to left side, pinching ends of threads
fabric needs stabilizer (paper, interfacing, etc.) to withstand heavy stitching	use stabilizer
fabric cut off-grain for piecing	straighten fabric grain and cut pieces on-grain
needle plate hole too large for material	use left-needle position or straight-stitch needle plate

Backing puckers (tucks)

backing not taut enough while basting quilt	baste properly—see Chapter 2
fabric creeps ahead until it reaches a cross-seam, where it folds over itself	use fingers as tools; use walking foot
needle plate hole too large for material	use straight-stitch needle plate or left-needle position

QUILT PROBLEMS

Three layers end up uneven

presser foot tension too tight, pushing fabrics at uneven rates	use walking foot; baste properly; loosen presser foot tension

Quilt hangs unevenly

no allowance made for shrinking during quilting	cut backing 1″ to 3″ (2.5 to 7.6 cm) larger than called for; trim later
quilt improperly basted	baste properly—see Chapter 2
fabrics for top and/or back cut off-grain	cut on-grain
fabrics not preshrunk before working; at first washing, everything shrinks	learn from your mistakes—preshrink everything

2. The liberating aspects of using tracing paper to manipulate images for your own designs and to examine the areas around your images (the negative space).

3. To design the light, medium, and dark areas of your quilts, traditional or contemporary, first—before you plug in color.

4. To savor your machine as *the* tool to mold fiber and fabric.

And now there's only one thing left to say:

Glossary

Applique: One fabric sewn on top of another, usually larger, fabric.

Bar Tacks: The sewing machine stitch length is set at 0, the stitch width near its widest, and the needle takes 4 to 6 stitches in the same place.

Basting: A quick sewing together of the three layers of a quilt, with no attempt to be neat since the stitches will be removed later.

Bearding: The migration of polyester batting fibers through the top fabric, leaving a white mold appearance.

Block: A basic unit of a quilt, normally rectangular, which is repeated to form the quilt.

Cartoon: An age-old term for a simplified line drawing which can be transferred to some other material—such as fabric, for making a quilt.

Casing: A long rectangle of fabric sewn along its two long sides only to the top back side of a quilt, through which a rod can be inserted for hanging (for photography, put a casing along one side of the quilt too).

Chaining: In piecing, sewing the seams of similar parts one after the other without stopping to cut the threads between until you're done.

Channel Quilting: Parallel rows of straight quilting, usually stitched along the grain, not on the bias.

Concentric: All arranged about a common center; shapes of diminishing size fit inside each other, such as the rings formed when you toss a pebble into a pond.

Diamond Grid: On a quilt, intersecting perpendicular lines usually stitched on the bias so they appear to be diamonds instead of squares.

Double-Baste: To sew the backing to the batting in long sloppy stitches; then to sew the top to the basted backing/batting.

Drop: On a bed, the distance from the mattress top to the floor.

Fingerpress: Instead of using an iron to press seam allowances, you press them with your finger.

Finish-As-You-Go: In quilting, to break the item down into manageable units, to finish the edges, and then to quilt each unit before working on the next unit.

Flexible Ruler: A metal-reinforced rubber ruler that bends to any shape.

Free-Machine Quilting: Removing the dual action of the feed dogs and presser foot so that the quilt may be moved backwards, forwards, sidewards, anywaywards.

French Curve: A draftsman's plastic tool which helps make smooth curves.

French Fold Binding: An extra-strong and easy way to bind an edge by folding the binding in half before construction; the finished edge has four layers of binding fabric on one side and two on the other.

Grid: A pattern of connected squares or rectangles.

Hidden Applique: Sewing a lining all around an applique shape, slashing the lining, pulling out the rightside of the applique, and then applying it to the background fabric (the slash and lining are hidden and the edges look perfect).

Johannah Method: Fast ways to piece developed by Barbara Johannah; see Chapter 4.

Ladder Stitch: A toymaker's stitch to connect the gap of two fabrics when an item is turned rightside out; see Fig. 2-43.

Lap Quilting: In hand quilting, working without a frame or hoop, pinning along the line to be quilted to hold the quilt sandwich taut.

Lattice Strips: Fabric rectangles that join each block in a quilt.

Loft: The depth of the batting, anywhere from ¼" to 3" (6 mm to 7.6 cm).

Machine Quilting: Read previous 316 pages.

Miter: To join two perpendicular edges at the corner in a 45° angle; see the Miter Guide in Chapter 2.

One-Step Piecing and Quilting: The quilt is constructed all at once, laying pieces to be joined on the batting and backing, and sewing through all layers.

Outline Quilting: Surrounding a shape on a quilt with a row of quilting stitches, usually ¼″ to 1″ (6 mm to 2.5 cm) outside the shape.

Parallel: A will never meet nor cross B anywhere, even if you extended lines from here to China; A is parallel to B.

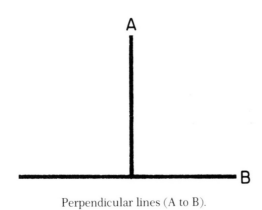

Parallel lines.

Perimeter: Distance around edge of any shape.

Perpendicular: A is at a 90° angle to B; A is perpendicular to B.

Perpendicular lines (A to B).

Pieced: Two fabrics joined together by a thread seam.

Pounce Powder: Powdered charcoal or chalk which is rubbed through holes in paper, transferring the powder and the design to the fabric underneath the paper.

Prepare Fabric: Preshrink it, iron it, straighten the ends by pulling a thread, and straighten the grain (all explained in detail in Chapter 2).

Preshrink: To machine-dry wet new fabric so that any possible shrinkage occurs before construction of the quilt.

Quilt Sandwich: Three layers—top, batting, backing (also called a squilt).

Quilt-As-You-Go: To break an item down into manageable units, quilting each unit and later rejoining the seams to make a whole.

Regular Stitch Length: 10 to 12 stitches per inch (4 to 5 stitches per cm).

Satin Stitch: See zigzag.

Scale: In comparing two or more objects or patterns, the relative largeness or smallness of one to another; in using fabrics, refers to how large the pattern is on the fabric compared to the amount of fabric which will show on the quilt.

Scarf: Groove in the sewing machine needle above the eye into which thread is pushed when a stitch is being formed.

Sloper: A blueprint of a bed, giving all measurements (mattress width and length, distance to floor, pillow tuck allowance).

Squilt: A quilt sandwich, composed of three layers (top, batting, backing)—it's a squilt until the quilting is done; then it's a quilt.

Stabilizer: An interfacing used behind limp or stretchy material so it won't pucker in stitching.

Stitch-In-The-Ditch: Machine quilt along and through seam lines in the top of the quilt.

Template: An object to trace around (cup, cardboard shape, hand, etc.).

Tuck (Pillow Tuck): Extra amount added to quilt length, to be tucked under and over the pillows.

Utility Quilt: A nonprecious functional quilt often made of printed fabric for the top (e.g., a sheet).

Value: The lightness or darkness of a color in relation to the colors surrounding it; if photographed in black-and-white, would the color be light, medium, or dark?

X-Acto Knife: A razor-like blade set into a holder that makes cutting easy.

Zigzag: The sewing machine needle swings from side to side and makes a line of lightning bolts; satin stitch compresses the stitches together to make a wide solid line.

Bibliography

Of the many books on quilting, these are the most exciting to me. If you love quilt books, too, read all the entries because there are several little-known self-published gems in here. Books discussed in the text are indicated by an asterisk. Most quilt books are in the 746.4–6 section of your public library. Your library can get you almost any book on inter-library loan. (Note: A good source of mail-order quilt books is Barbara Bannister, Alanson, MI 49700. Write for catalog.)

The Sewing Machine

Bakke, Karen. *The Sewing Machine as a Creative Tool*. Prentice-Hall, 1976, $4.95.

Bartley, Regina. *The Joy of Machine Embroidery*. Henry Regnery, 1976, $4.95.

Bray, Karen. *Machine Applique*. Self-published (21 Birch Dr, Walnut Creek, CA 94596). 1978, $6.50.

Butler, Anne. *Machine Stitches*. BT Batsford Ltd, London, 1976, $9.95.

Clucas, Joy. *Your Machine for Embroidery*. G. Bell & Sons, London, 1975.

Devlin, Nancy. *Guide to Machine Quilting*. Starshine Stitchery Press (434 Benfield Rd, Severna Park, MD 21146), 1976, $11.95.

*Fanning, Robbie. *Decorative Machine Stitchery*. Butterick Publishing, 1976, $9.95, $5.95. Available autographed from PO Box 2634, Menlo Park, CA 94025.

———. "How To Select A Sewing Machine." *Better Homes and Gardens,* December, 1979.

———. "How To Make Extra Money By Teaching Machine-embroidery Classes." *The Mother Earth News.*

*Graham, Lucille Merrell. *Creative Machine Embroidery*, Vol. 1–3. Self-published (PO Box 291, Bountiful, UT 84010), $9/volume.

Gray, Jennifer. *Machine Embroidery, Technique and Design*. Van Nostrand Reinhold, 1973, $12.

*Haight, Ernest B. *Practical Machine-Quilting for the Homemaker*. Self-published (David City, NE 68632), 1974, $2.

Holt, Verna. *Machine Embroidery and Yarn Stitchery on the Sewing Machine*. Self-published (700 S. Jones Blvd, Las Vegas, NV 89107), 1974, $7.98.

*Lee, Barbara, and S. Gail Reeder. *Successful Machine Applique*. Yours Truly Inc. (PO Box 80218, Atlanta, GA 30366), 1978, $4.95.

Lillow, Ira. *Introducing Machine Embroidery*. Watson-Guptill, 1967, $6.95.

Murwin, Susan Aylsworth, and Suzzy Chalfant Payne. *Quick and Easy Patchwork on the Sewing Machine*. Dover Publications, Inc., 1979, $3.

Skjerseth, Douglas Neil. *Stitchology*. Seth Publications (PO Box 1606, Novato, CA 94947), 1979, $3.95.

Swift, Gay. *Machine Stitchery*. Charles T. Branford Co, 1974, $9.75.

Wood, Kaye M. *Machine Embroidery and Applique Lessons for Junior and Senior High School Sewing Classes, 4H and Other Groups*. Self-published (4949 Rau Rd, West Branch, MI 48661), 1978, $6.

Historical Quilts

Bacon, Lenice Ingram. *American Patchwork Quilts*. William Morrow & Co, 1973, $16.50.

Bath, Virginia Churchill. *Needlework in America*. The Viking Press, 1979, $25.

Bishop, Robert, and Elizabeth Safanda. *Gallery of Amish Quilts*. EP Dutton, 1976, $9.95

Brackman, Barbara. *An Encyclopedia of Pieced Quilt Patterns*. Vol 1: One-Patch, Non-Square Block, Multi Patch, Strip Quilt. Self-published (500 Louisiana St, Lawrence, KS 66044), 1979, $5.50.

Conroy, Mary. *300 Years of Canada's Quilts*. Griffin House (461 King St West, Toronto M5V 1K7 Canada), 1976, $7.95.

DeGraw, Imelda G., curator. *Quilts and Coverlets* (exhibition catalog). The Denver Art Museum (100 W. 14th Ave Parkway, Denver, CO 80204), 1974, $7.

Finley, Ruth E. *Old Patchwork Quilts*. Charles T. Branford Co, 1929, 1957, $7.25.

Lubell, Cecil. *Textile Collections of the World*, Vol. 1: US and Canada. Van Nostrand Reinhold, 1976, $30.

The McCall's Book of Quilts, Simon and Schuster, 1964, $8.95.

Mainardi, Patricia. "Quilts: A Great American Art." *MS. Magazine*, December 1973.

———*Quilts: The Great American Art*. Miles and Weir (Box 1906, San Pedro, CA 90733). 1979, $3.25. Reprinted with illustrations from her outstanding article in the Winter 1973 The Feminist Art Journal, which is extinct.

Meeker, L.K. *Quilt Patterns for the Collector*. Self-published (3145 NE 27th, Portland, OR 97212), 1979, $4.35.

Mitchell, Jean. *Quilt Kansas!* Helen Foresman Spencer Museum of Art (The University of Kansas, Lawrence, KS 66045), 1978, $6. Prepared for the 1978 Kansas Quilt Symposium.

Nelson, Cyril, compiler. *The Quilt Engagement Calendar*. EP Dutton, yearly, $6.95.

North Carolina Country Quilts: Regional Variations (exhibition catalog). The Ackland Art Museum (University of North Carolina at Chapel Hill), $5.

Orlofsky. Patsy and Myron. *Quilts in America*. McGraw-Hill, 1974, $24.95.

Quilter's Choice/Quilts from the Museum Collection. Helen Foresman Spencer Museum of Art (The University of Kansas, Lawrence, KS 66045), 1978, $6.

Safford, Carleton L. and Robert Bishop. *America's Quilts and Coverlets*. EP Dutton, 1972, $25.

Shogren, Linda. *Log Cabin Compendium*, $2.50, and *Quilt Pattern Index*. The *Index* tells what books and magazines have which patterns, $5.45. Both from Quilting Publications (566 30th Ave, San Mateo, CA 94403).

Southern Comfort: Quilts from the Atlanta Historical Society Collection (exhibition catalog). Atlanta Historical Society (PO Box 12421, Atlanta, GA 30305), 1978, $5.

Traditional Quiltmaking

Beyer, Alice. *Quilting*. Original 1934 edition reprinted by Easy Bay Heritage Quilters (PO Box 6223, Albany, CA 94706), 1978, $8.

Beyer, Jinny. *Patchwork Patterns*. EPM Publications (1003 Turkey Run Rd, McLean, VA 22101), 1979, $15.95.

Bond, Dorothy. *Embroidery Stitches from Old American Quilts*. Self-published (34706 Row River Rd, Cottage Grove, OR 97424), 1977, $4.50.

Colby, Averil. *Quilting*. Charles Scribner's Sons, 1971, $12.50.

Gammell, Alice I. *Polly Prindle's Book of American Patchwork Quilts*. Grosset and Dunlap, 1973, $6.95.

Hechtlinger, Adelaide. *American Quilts, Quilting, and Patchwork*. Stackpole Books, 1974, $12.95.

Ickis, Marguerite. *The Standard Book of Quilt Making and Collecting*. Dover, 1949, $3.50.

McKim, Ruby Short. *One Hundred and One Patchwork Patterns*. Dover, 1962, $2.50.

Pforr, Effie Chalmers. *Award Winning Quilts/The History and How-To of Old Quilts and New Patterns*. Oxmoor House, 1974, $9.95.

Contemporary Quiltmaking

General

Brown, Elsa. *Creative Quilting.* Watson-Guptill, 1975, $11.95.

Chase, Pattie, with Mimi Dolbier. *The Contemporary Quilt/New American Quilts and Fabric Art.* EP Dutton, 1978, $19.95, 10.95.

Gutcheon, Beth. *The Perfect Patchwork Primer.* Penguin Books, 1973, $6.95.

Hall, Carolyn Vosburg. *Stitched and Stuffed Art.* Doubleday, 1974, $12.50.

Heard, Audrey, and Beverly Pryor. *Complete Guide to Quilting.* Creative Home Library/ Better Homes and Gardens, 1974, $12.95.

James, Michael. *The Quiltmaker's Handbook/A Guide to Design and Construction.* Prentice-Hall, 1978, $6.95.

*Laury, Jean Ray. *Quilts and Coverlets/A Contemporary Approach.* Van Nostrand Reinhold, 1970, $9.95, $4.95.

Leman, Bonnie. *Quick and Easy Quilting.* Hearthside Press Inc. (Great Neck, NY 10021), 1972, $7.95.

Quilting and Patchwork. Sunset Books, 1973, $1.95.

Short, Eirian. *Introducing Quilting.* Charles Scribner's Sons, 1974, $7.95.

Specialized

*Bradkin, Cheryl Greider. *The Seminole Patchwork Book.* Self-published (3534 Altamont Dr, Carmichael, CA 95608), 1978, $4.50.

Gutcheon, Beth and Jeffrey. *The Quilt Design Workbook.* Rawson Assoc, 1976, $7.95.

*Haywood, Dixie. *The Contemporary Crazy Quilt Project Book.* Crown Publishers, 1977, $4.95.

*Horton, Roberta V. *Stained Glass Quilting Technique.* Self-published (1929 El Dorado Ave, Berkeley, CA 94707), 1977, $4.80.

Johannah, Barbara. *Quick Quilting/Make a Quilt This Weekend.* Drake Publishers, 1976, $6.95 (out-of-print).

*Johannah, Barbara. *The Quick Quiltmaking Handbook.* Pride of the Forest Press (PO Box 7266, Menlo Park, CA 94025), 1979, $8.95.

*Larsen, Judith LaBelle, and Carol Waugh Gull. *The Patchwork Quilt Design and Coloring Book.* Butterick Publishing, 1977, $7.95.

Puckett, Marjorie, and Gail Giberson. *Primarily Patchwork.* Cabin Craft (Box 561, Redlands, CA 92373), 1975, $8.95.

Puckett, Marjorie. *String Quilts 'N Things.* Orange Patchwork Publishers (PO Box 2557, Orange, CA 92669), 1979, $9.

Timmins, Alice. *Introducing Patchwork.* Watson-Guptill, 1968, $7.95.

*Wittman, Lassie. *More Seminole Patchwork.* Self-published (2221 76th Ave, Bellevue, WA 98004), 1979, $5.

Related Arts

Avery, Virginia. *The Big Book of Applique.* Charles Scribner's Sons, 1978, $17.50.

Blair, Margot Carter, and Cathleen Ryan. *Banners and Flags/How to Sew a Celebration.* Harcourt Brace Jovanovich, 1977, $16.95.

Botsford, Shirley J. *Between Thimble and Thumb.* Holt, Rinehart and Winston, 1979, $8.95.

Foose, Sandra Lounsbury. *Scrap Saver's Stitchery Book.* Countryside Press, 1977, $8.95.

Raymo, Anne, and Holly Vose. *Sew-Up Art.* Quick Fox, 1976, $4.95.

*Scott, Toni. *The Complete Book of Stuffedwork.* Houghton Mifflin Co, 1978, $14.95.

Shears, Evangeline, and Diantha Fielding. *Applique.* Watson-Guptill, 1972, $10.95.

Clothing and Accessories

Aiken, Joyce, and Jean Ray Laury. *The Total Tote Bag Book.* Taplinger Publishing Co, 1977, $12.50.

Aulson, Pam. *The Placemat Plus.* Self-published (PO Box 87, Wenham, MA 01984), 1978, $1.50. Uses purchased fabric placemats to make clothing and decorative objects.

Ericson, Lois, and Diane Ericson. *Ethnic Costume.* Van Nostrand Reinhold, 1979, $14.95.

*Fanning, Robbie and Tony. *Here and Now Stitchery from Other Times and Places*. Ethnic embroidery and applique. Butterick, 1978, $9.95. Available autographed from PO Box 2634, Menlo Park, CA 94025.

Johnson, Mary Elizabeth. *Pillows*. Oxmoor House (PO Box 2463, Birmingham, AL 35202), 1978, $12.95.

Laury, Jean Ray, and Joyce Aiken. *Creating Body Coverings*. Van Nostrand Reinhold, 1973, $4.95.

Nicholas, Annwen, and Daphne Teague. *Embroidery in Fashion*. Watson-Guptill Publications, 1975, $16.95.

The Personal Touch II. Frostline (Frostline Circle, Denver, CO 80241), 1977, $2.95. Personalized skiwear.

Porcella, Yvonne. *Five Ethnic Patterns*. Self-published (3619 Shoemake Ave, Modesto, CA 95351), 1977, $3.50.

Tilke, Max. *Costume Patterns and Designs*. Frederick A. Praeger, 1957, $49.95.

Drawing

Edwards, Betty. *Drawing on the Right Side of the Brain*. JP Tarcher, Inc. (9110 Sunset Blvd, Los Angeles, CA 90069), 1979, $8.95.

Nicolaides, Kimon. *The Natural Way to Draw*. Houghton Mifflin Co, 1975, $4.95.

O'Neill, Dan. *The Big Yellow Drawing Book*. Hugh O'Neill and Assoc. (Nevada City, CA 95959), 1974, $3.50.

Design

Bates, Kenneth. *Basic Design*. Funk and Wagnalls, 1975,$2.95.

Bothwell, Dorr, and Marlys Frey. *Notan*. Van Nostrand Reinhold, 1968, $3.95.

Lantz, Sherlee. *Trianglepoint*. Viking, 1976, $12.95. Interesting challenges at end of book.

Marein, Shirley. *Stitchery, Needlepoint, Applique, and Patchwork, Complete Guide*. Viking, 1974, $12.95.

Proctor, Richard M. *Principles of Pattern for Craftsmen and Designers*. Van Nostrand Reinhold, 1969, $4.95.

Reiss, John J. *Colors*. Bradbury Press, 1969, $6.95. Children's book.

Russell, Pat. *Lettering for Embroidery*. Van Nostrand Reinhold, 1971.

Ranucci, E.R. and J.L. Teeters. *Creating Escher-Type Drawings*. Creative Publications (PO Box 10328, Palo Alto, CA 94303), 1977, $6.25.

Schoenfeld, Susan. *Pattern Design for Needlepoint and Patchwork*. Van Nostrand Reinhold, 1973, $11.50.

Short, Erian. *Embroidery and Fabric Collage*. Sir Isaac Pitman and Sons, Ltd, 1967, $10.50.

*Tubau, Ivan. *How to Attract Attention with Your Art/A Guide for Graphic Artists*. Sterling, 1970, $4.95.

Wadsworth, John W. *Design from Plant Forms*. Universe Books (381 Park Ave South, New York, NY 10016), 1977 (originally 1910), $4.95.

Warnick, Janie. *Twenty-Six Ways to Use One Design*. Self-published (91 Baywood, San Mateo, CA 94403), 1977, $3.50.

Miscellaneous

Katz, Ruth. *Footwear: Shoes and Socks You Can Make Yourself*. Van Nostrand Reinhold, 1979, $8.95.

Robinson, Stuart and Patricia. *Exploring Fabric Printing*. Mills and Boon Ltd, 1970.

*Valentino, Richard, and Phyllis Mufson. *Fabric Printing: Screen Method*. Bay Books (c/o Bookpeople, 2940 7th St, Berkeley, CA 94710), 1975, $3.95.

Resources and Supplies

Films and Filmstrips

Art Americana: Quilts and Coverlets. Slide set. American Crafts Council Research and Education Dept (44 W. 53rd St, New York, NY 10019).

Granny's Quilts. Viking Films (525 Deninson St, Markham Ontario L3R 1B8 Canada), 1974.

The Hardman Quilt: Portrait of an Age. Hans Halberstadt, Lawren Productions (PO Box 666, Mendocino, CA 95460), 1975.

Quilting Women. Appalshop (Box 743, Whitesburg, KY 41858), 1976. Wonderful film.

Patchwork in Minnesota. Filmstrip. Midwest Visuals (Box 38, Brimson, MN 55602).

Under the Covers—American Quilts. Millie Paul, Pyramid Films (Box 1048, Santa Monica, CA 90406), 1976.

Women's Work. Leslie Hill (10307 Ilona Ave, Los Angeles, CA 90064), 1973.

Note: It is not easy to track down who rents films or even what is available. For example, there is a film called "The Three Dreams of Grace McNance Snyder," about the famous quilter's life, which my film researcher could not find listed anywhere. A new book, not yet out as I write this, may solve these problems: *Craft Films, An Index of International Films on Crafts*, Neal-Schuman Publishers (37 W. 53rd St, New York, NY 10019), $19.95.

Magazines

These periodicals may be of interest to machine quilters. Write for current prices.

Canada Quilts. Mary Conroy, editor, 360 Stewart Dr, Sudbury, Ontario P3E 2R8, Canada, 5 times/yr.

Elna Magazine. Twice a year, available at Elna dealers. Patterns and ideas.

Lady's Circle Patchwork Quilts. Carter Houck, editorial director, 23 W. 26th St., New York, NY 10010, quarterly.

Needlecraft for Today. Fredrica Daughtery, editor, PO Box 10142, Des Moines, IO 50349, bimonthly.

The Needle's Eye. 1801 Whitney, Idaho Falls, IO 83401, 10 issues/yr.

Open Chain, The Newsletter for Thread-Benders. Robbie Fanning, editor/publisher, PO Box 2634, Menlo Park, CA 94025. Monthly review of needleart books.

Progressive Farmer. PO Box 2581, Birmingham, AL 35202.

Quilt. Aloyse Yorko, editor, 79 Madison Ave, New York, NY 10016, quarterly.

Quilt World. Barbara Hall Pedersen, editor, The House of White Birches, Box 337, Seabrook, NH 03874, bimonthly.

Quilter's Journal. Joyce Gross, editor, Box 270, Mill Valley, CA 94941, quarterly. Scholarly, no patterns.

Quilter's Newsletter Magazine. Bonnie Leman, editor, Box 394, Wheat Ridge, CO 80033, monthly. Patterns, how-to's, people exchange.

Quilting and Related Needlework. Ruth Briggs, editor, PO Box 403, Rancho Santa Fe, CA 92067, quarterly.

Treadleart. Janet Stocker, editor, 2458 W. Lomita Blvd, Suite 215, Lomita, CA 90717, bimonthly.

Tumbling Alley. Evelyn Brown, editor, 425 NE 6th St, Gainesville, FL 32601, bimonthly.

Note: Back issues of old magazines can often be found through Way's Magazines Unlimited, PO Box 193, Seattle, WA 98111. Send a letter telling what you want with a pre-addressed stamped envelope.

Quilt Groups

There are many local quilt groups. Ask your public librarian to help you find those in your area.

Hearthside Crafts Quilter's Club, PO Box 305, Westview Station, Binghamton, NY 13905. Publishes "The Patchword," $4/yr.

The National Quilting Association, PO Box 62, Greenbelt, MD 20770. Quarterly newsletter "Patchwork Patter," $5/yr.

North American Quilt Guild, PO Box 1195, Shepherdstown, WV 25443. Quarterly newsletter "Clearinghouse," $15/yr.

Note: Many quilters interested in fabric and fiber as an art form also belong to American Crafts Council, Embroiderers' Guild of America, and/or National Standards Council of American Embroiderers. Ask your public librarian for the addresses or see our ethnic embroidery book resource page.

Yearly Conferences

Watch the quilt magazines for dates.

Black Hills Quilters' Seminar (June), 818 St. Patrick St, Rapid City, SD 57701.

Continental Quilting Congress (Fall), PO Box 561, Vienna, VA 22180.

Kansas Quilt Symposium, c/o Helen Spencer Museum of Art, University of Kansas, Lawrence, KS.

Lincoln Symposium (Summer), PO Box 6081, Lincoln NB 58506.

National Quilting Association (Summer), Box 62, Greenhelt, MD 20770.

Patch in Time (not yearly), Mill Valley Quilt Authority, PO Box 270, Mill Valley, CA 94941.

Quilt Conference (and wholesale quilt market—December), c/o Great Expectations, 618 Town and Country Village, Houston, TX 77024.

Quilt National (Summer), PO Box 747, Athens, OH 45701.

Southern Quilt Symposium (Spring), Bets Ramsey, Box 4146, Chattanooga, TN 37405.

West Coast Quilter's Conference (Summer), DeLoris Stude, 3335 NE 53rd St, Portland, OR 97213.

Winter Fantasy (Winter), Minnesota Quilters, 1630 37th Ave NE, Minneapolis, MN 55421.

Supplies

The most complete mail-order source for machine quilters is: Treadleart, 2458 W. Lomita Blvd, Suite 215, Lomita, CA 90717. Books, pamphlets, designs, marking pens, fabric crayons, machine-embroidery thread and hoops, opaque projectors, scissors, shank converters and feet, and much more.

Thread and Machine-Embroidery Supplies

Aardvark Adventures, 1191 Bannock, Livermore, CA 94550. Also has my favorite spiral-bound graph-paper notebooks.
Folklorico, PO Box 626, Palo Alto, CA 94301.
Verna Holt's Machine Stitchery, 700 S. Jones Blvd, Las Vegas, NV 89107.
Leonida's Embroidery Studio, 301-99 Osborne St, Winnipeg, MN R3L 2R4, Canada.
LuRae's Creative Stitchery, PO Box 291, Bountiful, VT 84010.
Vi Elliston, Bernina Sewing Centre, 3625 Weston Rd, Unit 8, Weston, Ontario, M9L 1V9, Canada.

Fabric, Cotton and Blends

The Contemporary Quilt and Fabrics, 2863 N. Clark, Chicago, IL 60657. All quilt supplies.
Gutcheon Patchworks, 611 Broadway, New York, NY 10012. Yardage, kits, patterns, books.
Saddle Valley Stitchery, Box 144, Saddle River, NJ 07458.
Sew What, 152 W. 42 St., New York, NY 10036. "Batches of patches."
Helen Squire Quilt Supplies, Box 603, Woodcliff Lake, NJ 07675.

Note: Also check the ads in the quilt magazines.

Fabric, Leather and Imitation Leather

Berman Leathercraft, 147 South St, Boston, MA 02111. One pound bags of leather scraps.
Clearbrook Woolen Shop, PO Box 8, Clearbrook, VA 22624. Packets of Ultrasuede scraps.

Batting

Buffalo Batt and Felt Corp, 3307 Walden Ave, Depew, NY 14043. Super Fluff polyester. King-size bonded sold in quantity.
Fairfield Processing Corp, 88 Rose Hill Ave, Danbury, CT 06810. Extra-loft, Poly-fil, and Ultra-loft polyesters.
Sears, Roebuck, and Co. See catalog or your nearest store for cotton batting.
Stearns and Foster, PO Box 15380, Cincinnati, OH 45215. Fat Batt and Mountain Mist polyesters; Mountain Mist cotton batting.
St. Peter Woolen Mill, 101 Q W. Broadway, St. Peter, MN 56082. Wool batting.
Yours Truly, PO Box 80218, Atlanta, GA 30366. Large polyester batts—102 × 104 and 120 × 120 (260 × 265 cm and 305 × 305 cm).

Down and Comforter Kits

Frostline, Frostline Circle, Denver, CO 80241.
Holubar, PO Box 7, Boulder, CO 80306.
Recreational Equipment Inc., 1525 11th Ave, Seattle, WA 98188.

Mail-Order Art Supplies

Dick Blick, PO Box 1267, Galesburg, IL.

Templates and Stencils

Childcraft Education Corp, 20 Kilmer Rd, Edison, NJ 08817. Plastic templates, cube designs, giant grid pattern rubber stamp, and more.
Creative Publications, PO Box 10328, Palo Alto, CA 94303. Exciting supplies for teachers of math but perfect for designing quilts (pattern blocks, huge rolls of graph paper, etc.).

Roy Daniel, 10 Union St, Camden, ME 04843. Hand-made tin templates.

Developmental Learning Materials, 7440 Natchez Ave, Niles, IL 60648. Shape templates, circle maker, etc.

Distlefink Designs, Box 358, Pelham, NY 10803. Patchwork Planner (self-stick patches on a planning board).

Needleart Guild, 2729 Oakwood NE, Grand Rapids, MI 49505.

Pilot Products, PO Box 4509, Baltimore, MD 21212. Stencils, about $2.50 per name, good for free-machine quilting patterns.

Victory Tool and Die Co, Inc., 131 Colvin St, Rochester, NY 14611. Ardco metal quilt templates.

Dyes and Photo Silkscreening

Cold Type Supply, Inc., 400 N. Beach, Ft. Worth, TX 76111. Blue-print chemicals.

DYE Textile Resources, 3763 Durango Ave, Los Angeles, CA 90034. Dyes, waxes, fabrics, blue- and brown-prints.

My Shirt, 193 E. Gish Rd, San Jose, CA 95112. Photo craft materials.

Straw Into Gold, 5533 College, Oakland, CA 94618. Catalog $1 (worth ten times that in information).

Unicor Inc., PO Box 382, Champaign, IL 61820. Dry-dye on transfer paper.

Miscellaneous Supplies

C-Thru Ruler Company, 6 Britton Dr., Bloomfield, CT 06002.

Dritz/Scovill, Spartansburg, SC 29304. Heavy-duty gripper snap attacher.

The Mill Store, Box 552, Palmer, MA 01069. Low-cost notions and trims.

Hollinger Corporation, 3810 South Four-Mile Run Dr, Arlington, VA 22206. Acid-free boxes for storing quilts.

Talas, 104 Fifth Ave, New York, NY 10011. Acid-free tissue paper for storing quilts.

Artists

These are the artists whose work has been pictured in this book. All accept commissions, and teach and lecture nationally. (Please include a pre-addressed stamped envelope if you write.)

Merry Bean, 901 S. 26 Pl, Arlington, VA 22202.

dj bennett, 781 Highview Terrace, Lake Forest, IL 60045.

Sas Colby, 2808 Ellsworth, Berkeley, CA 94705.

Margaret Cusack, 124 Hoyt St, Brooklyn, NY 11217.

Lenore Davis, 655 Nelson Pl, Newport, KY 41071

Radka Donnell, 13 Acron St, Cambridge, MA 02139; and Malergasse 3, Zurich 8001, Switzerland.

Robbie and Tony Fanning, PO Box 2634, Menlo Park, CA 94025.

Elizabeth Gurrier, c/o Fannings, PO Box 2634, Menlo Park, CA 94025.

Ernest B. Haight, RFD #1, David City, NE 68632.

Caryl Rae Hancock, c/o Fannings, PO Box 2634, Menlo Park, CA 94025.

Cindy Hickok, 523 Briar Path, Houston, TX 77079.

Doris Hoover, 3505 Evergreen, Palo Alto, CA 94301.

Jude Lewis, 2880 SW Upper Dr. Lake Oswego, OR 97034.

Joan Michaels-Paque, 4455 N. Frederick Ave, Shorewood, WS 53211.

Peggy Moulton, 98 Estates Dr, Orinda, CA 94563.

Alice Newton, Box 3066, Bakerton, WV 25410.

Fay Quanstrom, 353 S. Stewart Ave., Lombard, IL 60148.

Joan Schulze, 808 Piper Ave, Sunnyvale, CA 94087.

Joy Stocksdale, 2147 Oregon St, Berkeley, CA 94705.

Nina Stull, 39512 Platero Pl, Fremont, CA 94538.

Sewing Machine Company Addresses

Bernina
    70 North Orchard Dr
    Salt Lake City, UT 84054
Brother International Corporation
    8 Corporate Pl
    Piscataway, NJ 08854
Elna
    see White Sewing Machine Company
Kenmore (Sears, Roebuck & Co)
    Sears Tower
    Chicago, IL 60607
Morse Electro Products Corporation
    101-10 Foster Ave
    Brooklyn, NY 11236
Necchi Development Corporation
    c/o Allyn Distributing Co
    1244 Broadway
    Denver, CO 80203
Nelco Sewing Machine Company, Inc.
    63 Wall St
    New York, NY 10005
New Home Sewing Machine Company
    171 Commerce Rd
    Carlstadt, NJ 07072

JC Penney Co, Inc. Pencrest
    1301 Avenue of the Americas
    New York, NY 10019
Pfaff International Corporation
    610 Winters Ave
    Paramus, NJ 07652
Riccar America Company
    3184 Pullman St
    Costa Mesa, CA 92626
The Singer Company
    Consumer Products Division
    321 First St
    Elizabeth, NJ 07207
Viking Sewing Machine Company, Inc.
    2300 Louisiana Ave North
    Minneapolis, MN 55427
Ward's (Montgomery Ward)
    PO Box 8339
    Chicago, IL 60680
White Sewing Machine Co
    11750 Berea Rd
    Cleveland, OH 44111

Index